D1559937

Russell Kirk

and the Age of Ideology

Russell Kirk

and the Age of Ideology

W. Wesley McDonald

University of Missouri Press

COLUMBIA AND LONDON

Copyright © 2004 by
The Curators of the University of Missouri
University of Missouri Press, Columbia, Missouri 65201
Printed and bound in the United States of America
All rihts reserved
5   4   3   2   1   08   07   06   05   04

Library of Congress Cataloging-in-Publication Data

McDonald, W. Wesley, 1946–
    Russell Kirk and the age of ideology / W. Wesley McDonald.
        p.   cm.
Includes bibliographical references and index.
    ISBN 0-8262-1512-2 (alk. paper)
    1. Conservatism—United States—History—20th century.
2. Kirk, Russell.   I. Title.
JC573.2.U6M37   2004
320.52'092—dc22   2003023386

♾™   This paper meets the requirements of the
American National Standard for Permanence of Paper
for Printed Library Materials, Z39.48, 1984.

Designer: Elizabeth K. Young
Typesetter: Phoenix Type, Inc.
Printer and binder: Thomson-Shore, Inc.
Typefaces: Times and WashingtonD

To my wife, **Alice J. Baumgart,** in appreciation for all the years of devoted love, and to the memory of my father, **William E. McDonald** (1918–2003)

Contents

PREFACE

ONE OF MY GOALS in writing this book is to rescue Russell Kirk from his hagiographers, who, since his death, sometimes venerate him at the expense of understanding the substance of his thought or quote him selectively to promote agendas that would have been foreign to his thinking and nature. Much of what today passes for "conservatism" would not have pleased my subject. Always suspicious of proponents of global military adventures, expansive government, and social innovation, he would have cast a skeptical eye on the ambitious schemes advanced by prominent conservatives to spread democracy throughout the world, link government to private faith-based organizations under the rubric of "compassionate conservatism," and cleanse ourselves of customs and symbols to avoid offending some perceived "victim" group. On the basis of my personal knowledge of him gleaned through the years as his former research assistant and later friend, I do not believe that he would have wanted to become an empty icon for a political movement. I hope that my examination of his social and political thought will correct misperceptions about Kirk's legacy and lead to an appreciation of his teachings by those who eschew partisan politics. Insofar as my book accomplishes these ends, it will serve as a tribute to the memory of an esteemed teacher.

Russell Kirk first entered my life when I was a freshman at Towson State College (now Towson University) in Baltimore, Maryland. I had developed a campus reputation as one of Senator Barry Goldwater's most outspoken supporters during his 1964 campaign for the presidency. Such enthusiasm was hardly appreciated or admired. On this heavily Democratic campus, to declare yourself publicly to be a Republican, much less a supporter of the "extremist" Barry Goldwater, was to invite derision, contempt, and ridicule from most of your classmates and from nearly all the faculty. A tiny band of us, impervious to such censure and blithely unaware that some professors might reward our enthusiasm with less than desirable grades, soldiered on, in the mistaken belief that our candidate was electable. Such are the follies of youth.

Conservatism in those days meant to me opposition to atheistic communism, socialism, anything "un-American," and most things connected with the presidency of Franklin Roosevelt. I knew nothing of Edmund Burke, John Adams, John C. Calhoun, or about any of those titanic figures who had articulated and sustained through the generations a tradition of conservative ideas. My introduction to Kirk and the conservative intellectual tradition came when a fellow student and Goldwaterite, P. Michael Ratliff (now vice-president of the Intercollegiate Studies Institute), gave me his tattered copy of *The Conservative Mind,* with the recommendation that I read it. Neither of us could have imagined then how that single act would dramatically shape my life.

During my college years, I devoured nearly everything Kirk wrote. Mike Ratliff and I persuaded the college in 1966 to invite Kirk as guest speaker. Unfortunately, I had not seen a picture of him. But, since his books and essays were written in a forceful, manly style, I imagined Kirk was a dynamic, charismatic figure; the sort of a man who fills a room with his personality as soon as he enters. Imagine my shock when the man who appeared was short and rotund and dressed in an unfashionable dark three-piece suit. Instead of the brilliant conversationalist whom I had awaited, the speaker was painfully shy and often stammered.

My college senior thesis was nevertheless written partly about this taciturn figure. The following year, while a graduate student at Bowling Green State University, I begin a master's thesis on Kirk's political thought. During this time I took the liberty of contacting Kirk to ask him some routine questions about his work—the usual sort of request I assumed that he must have often received from other students and readers. What books would he recommend? Who had influenced his thought most profoundly? Could he sum up his major ideas in a few paragraphs? I never really expected that someone of his stature would answer a letter from a mere graduate student. At most, I thought, he might forward a copy of his bibliography, along with a few polite platitudes. Instead, I received a letter graciously inviting me to visit his home, Piety Hill, in Mecosta, Michigan. A fellow graduate student and I drove up from Bowling Green, Ohio, a few weeks later. When we arrived at his home, Kirk was engaged in one of his favorite pastimes—planting trees. He barely took notice of our arrival. This apparently indifferent reception took me aback. I had been accustomed to having hosts notice my arrival. I had not yet learned that at Piety Hill Kirk's numerous guests were expected to look after themselves, until everyone gathered for the evening repast.

That first evening we all took dinner in the dining room of the Old House built by his grandfather (destroyed by fire in 1975). At the head of the dining table sat Kirk and at the other end his wife, Annette, who was then pregnant with their third daughter, Felicia. Around the table were several other guests in addition to my friend and myself. The only one of the guests whom I can still recall was a midwestern newspaper editor who later annoyed Kirk by writing an article in which he described his host as "diffident." An unhappy choice of words, but I knew what he meant.

At dinner I struggled to make intelligent conversation. My efforts elicited only an occasional "uh-huh." Kirk was, in the words of his old friend Sidney Gair, about as "communicative as a turtle." But on that first evening, I interpreted his taciturn responses as a form of rejection. He must think I'm an idiot, I began to fear. Annette, though, sensing my anguish, barked, "Russell, speak to the boy!" Only after this admonition did he answer my question about Cardinal Newman's Illative Sense.

Summer 1969 was spent at Piety Hill putting my master's thesis into shape. I slept on the second floor of Kirk's library, an old converted toy factory, when I was allowed to slumber. Kirk worked the graveyard shift then. At about midnight, he would begin his nocturnal tasks, sitting in his straight-back chair behind a sturdy wooden table. The chair looked so uncomfortable that I was convinced it had been deliberately designed to mortify the flesh. Gazing distractedly off into space, he would puff on his thick cigar while he collected his thoughts. Then he would pound furiously away on his antediluvian Remington electric typewriter, from which words would pour out steadily until about five or six in the morning. Finished, he would look up from his typewriter to ask me, "Mr. McDonald, care to go for donuts and coffee?" If I couldn't make it through the night and had retired early, he would go upstairs to fetch me from my cubbyhole. We would stroll down to the town bakery as the sun peaked over the horizon. At about eight in the morning, we would both turn in. Kirk would sleep for about four hours before rousing himself to begin the day's routines. As for me, I was soon a sleep-deprived wreck. Eventually, I adjusted to the rhythm of his life, but today still blame my mentor for my continued bouts of insomnia.

Kirk tended to be stiff and formal with people he didn't know well. Even with me, it took him several years before he stopped addressing me as "Mr. McDonald." I vividly recall the thrill I felt the first time he called me "Wes." It was a sign that I had been accepted as a friend. Much of our time together was spent in silence. He didn't invite idle conversations, but told stories and showed his visitors some of the strange haunts of Mecosta County. Those who peppered him with endless questions about his work annoyed him. Usually, when I would ask him a question, he would reply by pointing to a book or essay from which I was expected to root out the answer. Kirk avoided emotionally charged debates. It was obvious that he was more comfortable with the written word than with face-to-face confrontations.

Each summer for the next several years, I would spend at least a few weeks in Mecosta. Then in 1977, Kirk invited me to be his assistant. "You'd earn a tidy sum; and could add an item of experience to your curriculum vitae," he wrote. "You would get lodging, food and two dollars an hour for as long as you might like to labor daily." How could I refuse such a generous offer? That summer I worked on his inchoate *Decadence and Renewal in the Higher Learning* manuscript and an edition of *The University Bookman,* a quarterly review of books he edited, as well as sundry other tasks.

My least favorite assignment was planting trees. Kirk had a peculiar obsession with planting saplings all over Piety Hill. His habit of randomly sticking pathetic-looking twigs into the ground, with the expectation they would eventually become trees, had little to do with the art of landscaping. Rather, it was a personal reforestation project in which he was trying to undo some of the damage done by his ancestors who had logged out the area. He lavishly praised my "green thumb," but I knew such praise was insincere. It was my conscript labor that he wanted. Soon, I learned to guess when the urge to plant twigs might overtake him. On those occasions, I would flee Piety Hill and return only after I felt that his impulse had passed.

The last time I officially served as his assistant was in 1980, when the Marguerite Eyer Wilbur Foundation awarded me a nine-month fellowship to complete my doctoral dissertation on Kirk's political thought. While performing my duties as his research assistant, I used his library to begin my work on a study of his social and political thought.

Since Kirk was often away on lecture tours, we assistants were left largely to our own devices. The highlight of our day came in the morning, when we would pick up the mail at the Mecosta Post Office and bring it back to the Kirk kitchen. At the kitchen table, we would read both our personal mail and the newspapers, and engage in lively discussions about current events. Then I would walk over to the library, where I would sort out Kirk's mail and start on my own work. If Kirk was home and had guests, we would all gather in the evening in his large dining room for the main meal. Otherwise, my roommate and I would practice our culinary skills on each other. Finding ourselves wanting in that department, we persuaded the eldest of the Kirk daughters, Monica, to do our cooking. Kirk disapproved of this arrangement when he discovered that Monica was spending more time secretly watching forbidden soap operas on my television set than cooking.

That summer I helped compile the selections for Kirk's forthcoming *Viking Portable Conservative Reader,* an anthology of the selected writings of great conservative thinkers. Photocopy machines being a rarity then, I would truck large stacks of books to Central Michigan University in Mt. Pleasant, twenty miles away, photocopy texts, and bring them back to the Kirk library, where I would do cutting and pasting. I then wrote a brief synopsis for each selection to help Kirk in composing his introductory essays for the entries. Occasionally, I would recommend items for inclusion in the anthology.

During the time spent at their home, Russell and Annette Kirk became a second family. Their many acts of kindness and generosity are beyond my ability to repay. More than anyone else, aside from my parents, this couple was responsible for what modest accomplishments I have achieved as a scholar since knowing them.

I am also indebted to many other people who have given of their time and labor in helping me to complete this project. First and foremost, I must mention Dr. Claes Ryn, the Catholic University of America, who originally encouraged me to pursue my interest in Russell Kirk's work. Without Professor Ryn's insights and perceptive criticisms, this book would have not been written. His gentle nagging over the years to "finish the book" reminded me that despite other pressing demands on my time, I had an unfinished manuscript lying on my desk.

My colleague, Dr. Paul Gottfried, read many of the chapter drafts and made numerous suggestions for revisions. My arguments were honed and sharpened by the long, agitated conversations we held about Kirk and the conservative intellectual movement. Like Claes Ryn, Gottfried introduced me to ideas that shed light on Kirk's thought from a perspective that had been previously unavailable to me.

The late Dr. Warren Fleischauer, a longtime friend of Kirk, was kind enough to read early draft versions of this book when it was still barely readable. Others who made useful suggestions were Admiral P. Michael Ratliff (USN, ret.), currently with the Intercollegiate Studies Institute, and Dr. Bruce Frohnen, Ave Maria School of Law.

Appreciation is likewise due to the Marguerite Eyer Wilbur Foundation and the H. B. Earhart Foundation for the generous grants they bestowed upon me to help sustain my research. I am equally grateful to Elizabethtown College for research grants and an extended sabbatical leave (2001–2002) to complete this project, and for providing me with library resources. Thanks are due to Dr. Christopher Woltermann, who proofread my manuscript and provided detailed suggestions for making it better. James Person, a biographer of Kirk, read the first two chapters of the manuscript and corrected factual errors. I am also grateful to the three University of Missouri Press anonymous reviewers, who labored assiduously over my text and whose comments improved the final product. I especially thank Ms. Beverly Jarrett, director and editor-in-chief of the University of Missouri Press, for skillfully shepherding this book to publication.

To my wife, Dr. Alice Baumgart, I owe many debts. She was a diligent proofreader and my best critic, as I applied myself to what must have seemed a Sisyphean chore. With the love and patience of a devoted wife, she kept asking me until I went back to work, "When are you going to finish the damn book?" Nor can I forget my faithful parents, the late William E. and Marie C. McDonald, who never lost hope that I would make something of myself—and this study.

Of course, I alone am responsible for all errors, misstatements, and sins of omission.

Russell Kirk

and the Age of Ideology

Introduction

The publication of *The Conservative Mind* in 1953 had a dramatic three-fold impact on the tenor and direction of a nascent conservative intellectual movement in America. First, this 450-page history of conservative ideas from Edmund Burke to George Santayana reinvigorated a movement adrift and barely conscious of its own history. As historian George Nash recalls, "no articulate, coordinated, self-consciously conservative intellectual force existed in the United States. There were, at most, scattered voices of protest, profoundly pessimistic about the future of their country." Second, its articulation of a viable intellectual conservative tradition in the English-speaking world fortified and legitimized a body of ideas that had been dismissed by many respected intellectuals of the day as the bleatings of bourgeois Babbitts. "In the teeth of Liberal assertions that conservatives are superannuated and inarticulate," M. Stanton Evans, the noted conservative editor and columnist, exclaims, "Kirk hurled a monumental defense of the conservative philosophy."[1] The ideas then fashionable in intellectual circles were of a liberal or socialist nature. Last, *The Conservative Mind* would establish its young author, Russell Kirk, then an assistant professor of the history of civilization at Michigan State College, as a major intellectual force in American politics and letters.

Still only thirty-five and at the height of his intellectual and literary powers, Kirk turned out five more books in just four years: *St. Andrews* (1954), a history of the Scottish university town where he lived between 1948 and 1953; *A Program for Conservatives* (1954); *Academic Freedom: An Essay in Definition* (1955); *Beyond the Dreams of Avarice* (1956); *The American Cause* (1957); and *The Intelligent Woman's Guide to Conservatism* (1957). *Time* and the *New York Times Book Review* reviewed his books favorably, the latter proclaiming that *The Conservative Mind* "merits the responsible attention of all informed persons

---

1. George H. Nash, *The Conservative Intellectual Movement in America: Since 1945*, xv; M. Stanton Evans, *Revolt on the Campus*, 62.

who are not rattled by unpopular beliefs." In a cover story, *Time* listed him as one of America's leading intellectuals. *Newsweek* took note of his achievements and hailed the prolific young scholar as "one of the foremost intellectual spokesmen for the conservative position."[2]

His literary output during the approximately four decades of his most active professional writing was truly staggering: twenty-four nonfiction works; three novels; three books of collected short stories; approximately two thousand articles, essays, and reviews; 2,687 short articles for his nationally syndicated newspaper column, "To the Point," published between April 30, 1962, and August 3, 1975, as well as his monthly *National Review* column, "From the Academy" (November 1955–April 1981), in which Kirk took aim at the decay of American education.[3] Russell Kirk has written more, it would be fair to say, than the ordinary American has read.

During the last years of his life, despite his declining health, his Herculean literary labors continued unabated. He worked on several books simultaneously, some of which were published posthumously: *The Politics of Prudence* (1993); his long anticipated memoirs, *The Sword of the Imagination: Memoirs of a Half-Century of Literary Conflict* (1995); and *Redeeming the Time* (1996). Only his death prevented him from writing a book of children's tales ("long in contemplation"), three more volumes of his essays, and completing more volumes, in addition to the thirty volumes he had already edited, for the Library of Conservative Thought.[4]

Although Kirk never regained the celebrity status he enjoyed as a leading intellectual figure of the 1950s, his works continued to influence American intellectual discourse. Twenty-five years after the publication of *The Conservative Mind,* many conservatives, such as Donald Atwell Zoll, himself a significant voice in the postwar resurgence of conservative ideas, considered Kirk to be "a premier figure in the twen-

2. Gordon Keith Chambers, "Goodwill Is Not Enough," *New York Times Book Review,* May 7, 1953, 29; *Time,* August 13, 1955, 88, 90–92; *Time,* March 19, 1956, 70; "America and the Intellectual: The Reconciliation," *Time,* June 11, 1956, 65–70; *Newsweek,* March 28, 1955, 60.

3. See Charles Calvin Brown, *Russell Kirk: A Bibliography.* I have, of course, included the works that Kirk published since 1981.

4. Kirk, *The Sword of Imagination: Memoirs of a Half-Century of Literary Conflict,* 475.

tieth century revival of aesthetic conservatism." Self-identified conservative political leaders expressed gratitude to him. Barry Goldwater, the 1964 Republican candidate for the presidency, declared that in addition to Friedrich A. von Hayek's *The Road to Serfdom,* "Russell Kirk's *The Conservative Mind,* published the year I entered the Senate, was also important to me. Kirk gave the conservative viewpoint an intellectual foundation and respectability it had not attained in modern society. He assailed the planning mentality of the times," which he "rightly said undermined the role of family and the community." Another legendary figure of the conservative movement, President Ronald Reagan, saluted Kirk as one of the "intellectual leaders" who, by having "shaped so much our thoughts," helped to make the conservative political victories in the 1980 election possible.[5]

The Young Kirk Faces His Critics

Kirk's rise to preeminence in American conservative letters and political thought in the 1950s provoked a noticeable stir within the American intellectual establishment. His work was widely discussed and critically evaluated in scholarly books and prominent journals and newspapers. Even the harshest assailants of the "New Conservatism" grudgingly recognized him as an intellectual figure worthy of serious attention. However, Kirk's works puzzled and alarmed some of his critics. They did not know what to make of a conservative who did not fit neatly into their preconceived notions. Kirk was often as harsh in his criticism of business as he was of government or labor. He was as troubled by the growth of the military establishment and the prospect of environmental destruction as any liberal activist. Although he relentlessly attacked liberal shibboleths, he exhibited no interest in developing alternative

5. Donald Atwell Zoll, "The Social Thought of Russell Kirk," 113; Barry Goldwater with Jack Casserly, *Goldwater,* 110; Ronald Reagan, "Fellow Conservatives: Our Moment Has Arrived," *Human Events,* April 4, 1981, 7. This is a transcript of a speech delivered by President Reagan to the Conservative Political Action Conference held at the Mayflower Hotel in Washington, D.C., on March 20, 1981; reprinted in *New Guard* 21 (Spring 1981): 2. Vice President George Bush began his speech at the same event with a quotation from Russell Kirk. See Bush, "This President Not to Be Deterred," *New Guard* 21 (Spring 1981): 5. The newly elected administration, which was the first in American history to consider itself conservative, clearly acknowledged its indebtedness to one of the chief exponents of the conservative position.

government programs. Instead, his works were mostly about long-dead and frequently forgotten political thinkers and literary figures that his critics viewed as irrelevant to contemporary concerns. The often-intemperate attacks on his work would affect his reputation for the remainder of his life.[6]

A summary of the views of some of his adversaries serves a twofold purpose. First, these critical responses to his work yield useful information about his reputation in American politics and letters. Their excited and often extravagant remarks suggest the seriousness with which his critics regarded Kirk's challenges to the prevailing ideological currents. They were, in effect, acknowledging his importance as a formidable voice on the Right. Second, the arguments of his critics remind us that the intellectual atmosphere of the 1950s, against which he was struggling to find recognition, was characterized by intolerance toward admitting conservative ideas into the realm of intellectual respectability.[7]

By the mid-1950s, Kirk's growing body of publications stirred historian Harvey Wheeler to write the earliest extensive serious criticism

---

6. Many histories of the American conservative movement during the 1950s and 1960s are available. Readers wanting a more complete understanding of the intellectual debates occurring during those decades should consult the following books: Patrick Allitt, *Catholic Intellectuals and Conservative Politics in America* and *Catholic Converts: British and American Intellectuals Turn to Rome;* Paul Gottfried, *The Conservative Intellectual Movement;* and Nash, *The Conservative Intellectual Movement in America.*

7. Kirk had supporters both inside and outside academe who frequently rose to his defense. The late Francis Wilson, for example, hailed Kirk's *A Program for Conservatives* as "a brilliant contribution to the defense of conservatives and to the rejection of liberalism." Francis G. Wilson, "Past in Present," review of *A Program for Conservatives,* by Russell Kirk, *The Saturday Review,* November 6, 1951, 21. Historian Samuel Flagg Bemis praised Kirk as a "gifted author" and added that "never has an historian of politics done a better job analyzing a clear-cut body of political thought that lay behind" John Randolph of Roanoke. Samuel Flagg Bemis, "Precursor of Secession," review of *Randolph of Roanoke: A Study in Conservative Thought,* by Russell Kirk, *York Review,* December 1951, 281. *The Conservative Mind* "is carefully wrought and honestly made," proclaimed August Heckscher, the chief editorial writer for the *Herald Tribune.* "It embodies a point of view which deserves a hearing." August Heckscher, review of *The Conservative Mind,* by Russell Kirk, *New York Herald Tribune Book Review,* August 2, 1953, 4. Furthermore, Kirk was delighted with the critical success of *The Conservative Mind.* He wrote to his old friend, T. S. Eliot, that forty-seven of the first fifty reviews were favorable. Kirk to Eliot, August 6, 1953, Kirk Papers, cited in Nash, *The Conservative Intellectual Movement,* 66.

of Kirk's political thought. Wheeler professed little sympathy for either Kirk's political principles or "the conservative tradition." Kirk's kind of "conservatism" and his sudden popularity within conservative circles clearly puzzled Wheeler. Conservatives were supposed to defend laissez-faire capitalism. Instead, Kirk broke the rule by "seriously offering us the political theory of the Waverley Novels," which was sharply at variance with the pro-capitalist bias of most modern American conservatives. In spite of the apparent incongruence between Kirk's position and the allegedly dominant themes of contemporary conservatism, Wheeler saw Kirk as a respectable alternative to liberal ideas. According to Wheeler, Kirk had helped to "mobilize adherents against the key elements of old liberalism" and to provide a "persuasive voice" to the anti-Communists. Additionally, Wheeler noted approvingly, Kirk bemoaned the social and cultural transition from the traditional community to the depersonalized Suburbia, and provided intellectual ballast against the forces of revolutionary innovation.[8]

A far less charitable critic of Kirk was Harvard historian Arthur Schlesinger, Jr., who had close ties to the Democratic party and later to the Kennedy family. In his essay "The Politics of Nostalgia" (1956), Schlesinger accused Kirk of being both an enthusiast for the red-baiting tactics of Senator Joseph McCarthy and, contrary to Wheeler, "a roaring Manchester liberal of the Herbert Hoover school." At the same time, Schlesinger dismissed Kirk and the "New Conservatives" as representatives of "the politics of nostalgia." They espoused "the wrong doctrine in the wrong country in the wrong century directed against the wrong enemies." Despite these tirades, Schlesinger admitted that Kirk was clearly one of the central figures in the modern conservative revival.[9]

William Newman's *The Futilitarian Society* (1961) was perhaps the sharpest and most impassioned attack that Kirk endured from liberal antagonists during this period. In this polemical work, which devotes an entire chapter to Kirk, Newman set out to write a comprehensive study of the major contemporary "conservative" thinkers, including Peter Viereck, Walter Lippmann, and Clinton Rossiter. He castigated

8. Harvey Wheeler, "Russell Kirk and the New Conservatism," *Shenandoah* 7 (November 2, 1956): 20, 31–34.

9. Arthur M. Schlesinger, Jr., *The Politics of Hope* (Boston: Houghton Mifflin, 1963), 76–80. See footnote 13 for a discussion of Kirk's attitude on Senator McCarthy's anti-Communist crusade.

conservatives as a group as "futilitarian" because they are "dead set against innovation." Change, being inherently good in Newman's mind, apparently needed no further justification. Further, because conservatives "will not allow the experimentation, change, discovery, and adventure that are necessary to the solution of [society's] problems," they fear freedom. In fact, conservative appeals to values such as tradition, prescription, authority, and prejudice serve only to limit and restrict the freedom of the individual. Conservatives "want to destroy possibilities, because [they] cannot face the costs of freedom." The only legitimate limits on man, asserted Newman, a radical social libertarian, are the ones he "creates for himself." Because of Kirk's allegedly dogmatic political Calvinism and brutally anti-democratic bias, he has given conservatism "a bad temper." Newman's bizarre description of Kirk as "a sort of Karl Marx of conservatism" who had converted conservatism into a "full-blown ideology" reveals the extent to which he was struck by Kirk's reputation within conservative circles. Kirk is, he concluded, "the most important figure in American conservatism since 1945 and probably during the twentieth century."[10]

In the early 1960s, the late Clinton Rossiter, a professor of history at Cornell University, and Peter Viereck, a poet and professor of history at Mount Holyoke College, both wrote major historical studies of the American conservative tradition.[11] Unlike Wheeler, Schlesinger, and Newman, however, they were more sympathetic to the conservative tradition and its role in American politics. But, because they warmly endorsed much of the liberal political agenda of their era while condemning conservative opposition to it, conventional conservative thinkers kept their distance from these "vital center" conservatives. While insisting they were conservatives, Viereck and Rossiter went after the apparent commercial mentality of the Barry Goldwater/*National Review*

10. William J. Newman, *The Futilitarian Society,* 409–12, 29, 138.
11. A trenchant criticism of totalitarianism, Peter Viereck's *Conservatism Revisited: The Revolt against Revolt* (1949) was the first book after 1945 to use the word "conservative" in its title. "[M]ore than any other [book] of the early postwar era," observes Nash, it "created the new conservatism as a self-conscious force.... As least as much as any of his contemporaries, Peter Viereck popularized the term 'conservative' and gave the nascent movement its label." Nash, *The Conservative Intellectual Movement,* 60. Published nearly a decade later, Clinton Rossiter's *Conservatism in America: The Thankless Persuasion* (1955) examined the influence of conservative ideas on the American political tradition.

conservatives. In practical politics, Rossiter and Viereck supported the Eastern pro–New Deal internationalist wing of the Republican party and the Adlai Stevenson wing of the Democratic party.[12] Both were, therefore, critical as well as admiring of Kirk.

Viereck, who may have chafed at Kirk's growing prominence as a voice of conservatism, scolded him as a "bankrupt" thinker because he was "morally evasive" on McCarthyism and had succumbed to the "conservatism of nostalgia," which Viereck defined as "the confusion of concrete living roots with abstract yearning for roots." But among "rightists," Viereck admitted that Kirk was "intellectually and ethically the most respectable."[13] Rossiter's attitude toward Kirk's traditionalism largely paralleled that of Viereck. After describing Kirk as one who has the "sound of a man born one hundred and fifty years too late and in the wrong country," Rossiter conceded that he "need have no fear of being barred from a high place in the histories yet to be written of the intellectual ferments of postwar America. If his is not a doctrine to be followed, it is certainly one to be understood and, if only for its eloquent obstinacy, respected."[14]

IN SEARCH OF THE REAL KIRK

Although often the subject of critical assessment from both the Left and the Right, a more thorough examination of Kirk's position, taking into consideration the totality of his work, may be needed. Too much

12. Viereck, *Conservatism Revisited,* 145–51; Rossiter, *Conservatism in America,* ix.

13. Viereck, *Conservatism Revisited,* 149–50. See also Claes G. Ryn, "Peter Viereck: Unadjusted Man of Ideas," *Political Science Reviewer* 7 (Fall 1977): 357–60 for a discussion of Viereck's "complex relationship" to Kirk. This would not be the only time in Kirk's career that he would be accused of sympathizing with the anti-Communist "witch-hunting" activities of Senator McCarthy. Yet, the charge lacks substance. Kirk was out of the country during much of the time that McCarthy was busy ferreting out alleged Communists in the American government. Moreover, when he heard of fellow conservative William Buckley's intention to write a book defending McCarthy, he described the proposed book as an example of "defending conservatism at its weakest link." Kirk to Ross Hoffman, November 24, 1952. While "Kirk's position in the McCarthy affair cannot be characterized in a single phrase," Nash pointed out, "Kirk was certainly no admirer of the senator." But he did believe "that the McCarthy 'menace' had been exaggerated." Nash, *The Conservative Intellectual Movement,* 115–16.

14. Rossiter, *Conservatism in America,* 222.

attention has been given to his prescriptions on topical political issues rather than to those principles in his thought that go beyond practical politics. Too often, the appraisals of Kirk as a political and social thinker have been superficial. No prior analysis of his thought, for instance, has dealt extensively with the ethical and philosophical aspects of his work. My aim in this book is to remedy these deficiencies by offering a critical evaluation of his social and moral thought in particular.

More specifically, I intend to explore Kirk's answer to those doctrines associated with the Right that rest on generally utilitarian assumptions. Before the publication of *The Conservative Mind,* conservatism was usually synonymous with "laissez-faire liberalism." Many opponents of what was perceived to be the ineluctable slide of New Deal politics toward collectivism sought remedies in various doctrines of atomistic individualism largely descended from nineteenth-century laissez-faire liberalism. The principles of private property, free market, limited government, self-reliance, and individualism were advocated by Ludwig von Mises, Frank Knight, Friedrich von Hayek, and Henry Hazlitt and, in later years, by Murray Rothbard, Milton Friedman, and others. Today, they are referred to as "libertarians" to avoid confusion with modern liberals who advocate governmental planning to deal with societal problems. The libertarians seek the removal of all social and governmental restraints upon the autonomous individual. In Kirk's eyes, however, they unduly favor commercial values at the expense of the norms of civilization. Kirk argued that sound defenses against the growth of state power cannot be grounded upon Benthamite notions of "utility," but must be based on a conservative individualism that recognizes the social nature of man and the moral prerequisites of true liberty. Many libertarians, in reply, inspired by Benthamite and Spencerian notions of individualism, saw the power of the state and the strictures of society as generally inimical to a creative and productive world of sovereign individuals.

By the early 1960s, Kirk felt that the influence of the libertarians on practical conservative politicians and businessmen had largely waned, and he considered himself primarily responsible for this happy result: "In general, the student conservatives and their clubs [have] grown more sensible, and turn toward more genuine political theory. Take, for example, the Intercollegiate Society of Individualists [now Intercollegiate Studies Institute]. They began, a decade ago, by uttering the individualist and old liberal slogans; but they have learned and reformed. Burke is now their mentor, and your servant is their chief living authority."[15]

I intend to examine the influence exerted by Kirk in drawing American conservatism away from libertarianism toward a more traditional form of conservatism. While it is apparent that libertarians and traditional conservatives are united to some extent in their opposition to the collectivist dogmas of the Left, the ongoing disputes between these rival groups are rooted in fundamental differences over the nature of a responsible conservatism. Because he thought they failed to acknowledge the existence of ethical norms above subjective interests, Kirk believed that the libertarians ultimately lacked any principle except the judgment of the marketplace for deciding among competing claims of the Good. Kirk, for his part, affirmed the existence of an ethical universal beyond the economic calculus of private advantage, a moral standard that exists "beyond the dreams of avarice." Moreover, he regarded the development of the life of the imagination as an indispensable guide to this principle. The imagination constitutes a uniquely human faculty that enables one to apprehend intuitively the source of an enduring good and happiness. Supported by the moral imagination, the individual possesses the ability to check the impulses of the moment with reference to his ultimate moral purpose. Man's higher self, of which the moral imagination is a part, refers to that aspect of his soul that operates under the governance of universally valid norms.

While Kirk cautioned against the excessive growth of centralized governmental authority, he stressed that government and society can serve a civilizing function. In contrast to atomistic individualism, a true conservatism recognizes man's spiritual and social nature. It defends and fosters a community of spirit in which generation links with generation. According to Kirk, this link is achieved through obedience to what T. S. Eliot called "the permanent things"—those enduring moral norms which stride beyond the particularities of time and place and which, because they form the basis of genuine civilized existence, can be neglected only at great peril. "The permanent things," reflected in religious dogmas, traditions, humane letters, social habit and custom,

15. Kirk to Jerry Pournelle, April 20, 1963, Russell Kirk Papers. See also W. Wesley McDonald, "The Political Thought of Russell Kirk: A Study in Contemporary Conservatism," 119.

and prescriptive institutions, create the sources of true community, which is also the final end of politics. In this understanding of the moral foundations of traditional conservatism, Kirk freely admitted his indebtedness to Edmund Burke and to those thinkers presented in *The Conservative Mind* as constituting a truly compelling conservative tradition.

What is popularly called "conservatism," many believe, led to the political victories of Ronald Reagan in the 1980s. It also made possible the historic Republican takeover of Congress in 1994, and appeared to be temporarily victorious in American political, cultural, and moral life. But was this "resurgence of conservatism" what Kirk propounded, or was its central inspiration more closely attuned to the views of the libertarians or of the welfare state–oriented Neoconservatives? Did any or all of these positions define the orientation of what would come to be known as the conservative revival? To what extent did Kirk's ideas play a formative role in this process? Such forbiddingly complicated questions may not be answerable. The various strands of the social and cultural forces that came together in the postwar conservative revival may need more time to be fully untangled and understood.[16] My own sights are aimed at a more modest goal—the examination of that body of ideas which Kirk produced as a conservative thinker. If the resurgence of conservatism in politics and culture in recent decades has been in some sense inspired by Kirk's ideas, then we should know the tradition to which these ideas are related and why they may have lost their appeal to a later generation of conservatives.

One characteristic of Kirk's style and approach is the tendency to express his principles through the words and ideas of those figures he most admired within the British and American conservative tradition. He is clearly guided by these minds, but, as I intend to demonstrate, he applies this tradition of ideas in an innovative way as a response to contemporary ideological challenges. Therefore, I often quote from or otherwise refer to those conservative thinkers to whom Kirk is either indebted for his philosophical insights or whose principles parallel and support his. The ideas championed by Edmund Burke, Irving Babbitt, and Paul Elmer More will loom especially large in these pages. My co-

---

16. One impressive attempt to analyze and examine the various contending strands of thought that make up the postwar conservative movement can be found in Gottfried's *The Conservative Movement.*

pious references to Babbitt are intended to illustrate the magnitude of his influence on both the style and substance of Kirk's moral and social thought. While his intellectual indebtedness to Burke has been noted, the arguably even greater formative influence on Kirk of Babbitt has remained underappreciated. Kirk expressly acknowledged the indispensability of Babbitt's thought for his own development at a 1983 conference held at the Catholic University of America in Washington, D.C.: Babbitt "has influenced me more strongly than has any other writer of the twentieth century. It was through Babbitt that I came to know Edmund Burke, and Babbitt, as much as Burke, animates my book, *The Conservative Mind*."[17] By his admission, Kirk is clearly as much a Babbittian as he is a Burkean. In addition, frequent references will be made to some of the contemporary disciples of Burke, Babbitt, and More whose work has done much to make their thought relevant to later generations. Unless otherwise noted, these references are intended to elucidate those principles defended by Kirk as a disciple of Babbitt.

Some readers may complain that too little attention has been given in these pages to the shaping role of the Catholic political tradition in the evolution of Kirk's thought. Indeed, I have avoided portraying Kirk as a primarily Catholic thinker. Although he did convert to Catholicism in his mid-forties, by then he had written most of his pivotal works on conservatism and the moral imagination. The major influences before and after his conversion were not St. Thomas Aquinas, Jacques Maritain, Etienne Gilson, or John Courtney Murray, but such non-Catholics as Burke, John Randolph of Roanoke, John Adams, John C. Calhoun, More, and Babbitt. This is not to deny that he profited intellectually from Catholic thinkers, particularly Orestes Brownson, John Henry Newman, Christopher Dawson, Flannery O'Connor, and the theologian Martin D'Arcy. Kirk studied and admired all of these figures. He also famously defended the civilizing role of the Catholic Church, before becoming a Catholic convert in 1964, as a bulwark against the socially disruptive forces of innovation and militant secularism. Even so, his social and political thought does not depend upon specifically Catholic dogmas or upon an expressly Catholic manner of thinking. It is possible, in my judgment, to present Kirk's contributions as a conservative thinker

17. Kirk, "The Enduring Influence of Irving Babbitt," in *Irving Babbitt in Our Time,* 20.

without having to consider their hypothetical Catholic aspect. Other interpreters may feel differently and are entitled to read the sources as they see fit.

It is in the nature of Kirk's conservatism that all issues are connected. His ideas of order, tradition, social norms, community, and education are inseparable. Each idea is interrelated with every other and therefore cannot be understood in isolation. A certain amount of repetition will inevitably result as I deal with different aspects of the same issue. For example, the role of history as a source of ethical wisdom is discussed with reference to the concept of the moral imagination but also comes into play when the idea of tradition is analyzed. Although chapter 2 deals exclusively with Kirk's notion of the imagination as essential to the ethical life, questions of imagination come up again in the chapter on Kirk's educational theory (chapter 7), which stresses the role of the imagination in schooling. Ethical dualism, moreover, forms a unifying concept in this study.

Some brief preliminary definitions of the terms frequently used in this book are necessary. All of these terms will be of course defined more explicitly in the course of my analysis and explication of Kirk's political thought. My only purpose here is to avoid some initial confusion by noting a few of the distinctions that I intend to make between various competing philosophical orientations. The term "naturalism" will be used frequently throughout and signifies broadly any philosophical view of the world that denies the existence of permanent ethical truths, considers man as a part of nature of which nothing besides or outside exists, and attempts to account for man's behavior wholly in terms of external phenomenal forces explainable by science.[18] Marxism, Social Darwinism, positivism, Hobbesianism, Freudianism, Rousseauistic romanticism, and utilitarianism are among the schools of thought to which this definition would apply. "Utilitarianism" refers to that tradition of early-nineteenth-century liberalism commencing with Jeremy Bentham, James Mill, and John Stuart Mill. Characteristics of utilitarian thought are the doctrines of atomistic individualism and a hedonistic criterion for moral judgment. Libertarianism in its modern form owes much of its philosophical development to the earlier position.

---

18. Folke Leander, *The Inner Check,* 4–5; Eliseo Vivas, *The Moral Life and the Ethical Life,* 15.

The basic tenets of this persuasion already have been hinted at. Lastly, when the term "conservative" is used without any further qualifications, I mean to refer to that tradition of conservative ideas originating with Edmund Burke and of which Kirk proclaims himself to be an exponent.

The reader should know that my objectives do not include writing a full-fledged biography of Kirk or a comprehensive study of the American conservative movement. Biographical information will be provided for the purpose of explaining the development of Kirk's positions and for clarifying certain ideas. Readers interested in the particulars of Kirk's life are advised to consult his posthumously published memoirs and James E. Person's meticulously researched biography.[19] Since many histories of the American postwar conservative movement have been published during the last decade, not all brands of contemporary conservatism will be examined here. My analysis will be devoted primarily either to that tradition to which Kirk is attached or to those alleged expressions of conservative thought that have been antithetical to his position.

19. Kirk, *The Sword of Imagination;* James E. Person, Jr., *Russell Kirk: A Critical Biography of a Conservative Mind.*

1 Kirk and the Rebirth of American Conservatism

Michigan Roots and the Early Years

Passing tourists do not ordinarily take much notice of the tiny village of Mecosta, Michigan (approximate population: 450). Located about two hundred miles northwest of Detroit and sixty-five miles northeast of Grand Rapids, Kirk's ancestral home can be found on the map, Kirk suggested, by drawing "a line westward across the southern peninsula of Michigan, roughly from Saginaw Bay to Muskegon."[1] A flat, glaciated land deforested a century ago by the logging industry, devoid of much natural beauty and noted for its long, dreary winters and dry, mosquito-infested summers, the central portion of Michigan's lower peninsula until recently possessed little apparent special charm. Although economically depressed throughout much of the twentieth century, the region began an economic recovery during the 1980s that is presently sustained by a growing recreational interest in the area's freshwater lakes.

Similar to scores of other similar villages dotting this sparsely populated region, Mecosta (which means "Little Cub Bear" after the Potawatomi chief who ceded Indian lands to the whites) is distinguished only by its ordinariness. On its broad main street stand the township office, library, bookshop, borough office, a restaurant, a real estate office, a hardware store, a service station, two bars, and several empty buildings.

Before the turn of the century, Mecosta was a rough lumbering town supporting about two thousand inhabitants, but when the timber gave out in 1900, its year-round population dwindled to only about two hundred. Farming could offer only a subsistence living. With intensive labor and the liberal use of fertilizer and lime, some root crops and garden

1. Russell Kirk, *The Surly Sullen Bell*, 218.

vegetables can be grown. The soil, acidic and nutrient-deficient, is considered to be poorly suited for agriculture.[2] Mecosta's main industry today is tourism. During the summer months, campers and cottagers are drawn to the area's lakes. But seasonal tourism is hardly sufficient to support the rising generation. The more enterprising young natives seek their fortunes elsewhere. In this unlikely setting, which he called the "stump country," Kirk, abjuring the lure of New York literary circles, lived to write, marry, and raise four daughters.

Born in 1918 near the railway station in Plymouth, a small suburb of Detroit, where he was reared and schooled, Kirk spent his boyhood summers in Mecosta among the clannish Pierces, to whom he was related on his maternal side.[3] Living amidst the deprivations of severe rural poverty in upstate Michigan during the Great Depression could have been an intellectual and spiritual misfortune. Yet, here, despite the region's backwardness, Kirk found his spiritual home and the central focus of his work, his roots—a community where he felt spiritually linked with his ancestors who had originally settled the area. Life in this grim, inhospitable land further instructed him in the "vanity of human wishes" and the dark realities of human nature. This bleak environment, remote and harsh, permitted him to witness human nature in sharp relief. The human oddities and local legends he found there would become grist for Kirk's literary mill.

Amos Johnson, his great-grandfather who settled in Mecosta in 1879, built a square bracket house on the north end of the village, later to be known as "Piety Hill." The house sheltered one family under various names (Gilbert, Johnson, Pierce, Jewell, and Kirk) until it was destroyed by fire on Ash Wednesday in 1975. Kirk's father, Russell Andrew Kirk, who died in 1981, was a locomotive engineer with only a primary school education. Descended from Scottish farmers, he was "a man of considerable physical strength."[4] Father and son shared an uneasiness to-

2. Richard A. Santer, *Michigan: Heart of the Great Lakes,* 137; William Frederick Dunbar, *Michigan: A History of the Wolverine State,* 469.

3. Russell Kirk, *The Confessions of a Bohemian Tory: Episodes and Reflections of a Vagrant Career,* 5. See Kirk, *The Sword of Imagination* for his posthumously published memoirs.

4. *Mecosta Area History Book: 1879–1979,* 82–83; Kirk, *Confessions of a Bohemian Tory.* Or a locomotive fireman, see Russell Kirk, *Decadence and Renewal in the Higher Learning: An Episodic History of American University and College since 1953,* xviii.

ward the effects of rapid technological change upon the social fabric as well as the physical landscape of rural Michigan. His father had, he wrote, an "enduring dissatisfaction with the age of the machine," which swept away "the old rural tranquility of brick farmhouses and horses and apple orchards and maple groves" that the elder Kirk knew in his youth.

The two greatest influences on the development of young Kirk were his mother, Marjorie Rachael (Pierce) Kirk, and her father, Frank Pierce. His mother was "a tiny, tender, romantic woman endowed with forti- tude." A childhood illness drew mother and son together into a warm and mutually affectionate relationship. At the age of three, Kirk, stricken with acute nephritis, was thought to be dying. Until the age of seven, he was nearly an invalid. During those years, while bedridden, bloated, denied water, and unable to participate in the usual boys' physical sports, he marveled as his mother read him "Lewis Carroll and Stevenson and Scott and Grimm and the adventures of the noble company of the Table Round." These classic tales of adventure and fantasy stirred his imag- ination and nurtured an enduring love of literature. The strong bond of affection between mother and son lasted until her death, after an extended illness, in early 1943.[5]

The love of literature, instilled in him by his mother, was encour- aged further by his grandfather. Born in a log cabin in southwestern Michigan, Frank Pierce was a small-town banker. A few months of music study at Valparaiso University constituted his formal education beyond high school. Even so, he was, according to his grandson, "a wise man, much read in books and life" who "did more to form" his "mind and character than did anyone else except Russell's mother." Frank Pierce read voraciously even though learning was then not highly regarded in Mecosta society. Volumes of Samuel Johnson, Edmund Burke, Macaulay, Victor Hugo, Charles Dickens, and Mark Twain lined the grandfather's bookshelves. The works of history introduced the young boy to historical consciousness, while the works of great litera- ture fired his imagination. Long walks, during which they discussed "the idea of progress, the character of Richard III, the nature of immortal- ity, the significance of dreams, the style of Poe," solidified the bond

5. Kirk, *Confessions of a Bohemian Tory,* 5–6; Russell Kirk, "Small Books for Small Children," 4–5.

between Kirk and his grandfather. Frank Pierce died in 1930 just as the Depression was beginning to ruin many banks.[6]

Kirk graduated from high school in 1936 at the height of the Depression when jobs were scarce. His high school principal suggested that he apply for a scholarship to Michigan State College of Agriculture and Applied Science (now Michigan State University). Kirk's admittance as a scholarship student in 1936 commenced a connection with that academic institution that would last, except for the years when he was in the military or on a leave of absence for study at St. Andrews University, until his resignation from the faculty in 1953. In spite of this long association with the college, he was never fond of it. He eventually came to believe that "the cow college" qualified as a thoroughly decadent institution of higher learning. As a freshman, he recalled later, he was hostile to what he perceived to be the principal aim of a state educational system: the imposition of "a uniform character upon the rising generation, rendering young people obedient to the state from habit and prejudice, even when the state has dissolved the ancient loyalties that bound man to man." In addition to this aim, there "were mingled the utilitarian object of imparting technical skills and an impulse toward worldly advancement." The higher ends of education were barely tolerated as the college devoted itself to inculcating "conformity to present state policy" and developing technical skills. Kirk came to detest Dr. John Hannah, the president of Michigan State from 1941 to 1969. President Hannah epitomized for Kirk all the worst characteristics to be found in a college administrator—"materialistic, self-seeking, woefully deficient in imagination, confounding quantity with quality"—and, moreover, everything that was wrong with American higher education.[7]

Yet, despite the many deficiencies of Michigan State as an institution of higher learning, Kirk admitted that his time at East Lansing was "passed pleasantly enough." At least, his stay at the college permitted him the time to read prodigiously—"old books of travel, forgotten cor-

6. Kirk, *Confessions of a Bohemian Tory,* 11–12; Kirk, *Decadence and Renewal in the Higher Learning,* xviii; Kirk, *The Sword of Imagination,* 7–8.

7. Kirk, *Confessions of a Bohemian Tory,* 16; Kirk, *Decadence and Renewal in the Higher Learning,* 6. At the rear of Kirk's home stands an empty chicken house. Nailed to its door is one of Kirk's little jokes, a sign that reads: "The John Hannah Memorial Chicken House—so-called because it is chickenless." Hannah's only advanced academic degree was an honorary doctorate in poultry science.

ners of belles-lettres, African history, Samuel Johnson's essays" and much more.[8] He acquired knowledge in many areas not touched upon in his formal studies. He wrote as well a few essays for serious journals. Further, amidst this general academic desert, there were a few men of ability on the college faculty. The young scholar would learn much from one of them—John Abbott Clark, a professor of English, columnist for the *Chicago Tribune,* and disciple of Irving Babbitt, who taught courses in the history of criticism and in critical writing. One book, published during his undergraduate years, was Donald Davidson's neglected *The Attack on Leviathan.* Kirk recalled that the Southern Agrarian's "eloquent denunciation of political and cultural centralism . . . strongly impressed" him. The book "made coherent the misgivings" he "felt concerning the political notions popular in the 1930s."[9]

Only a few miles away from his birthplace, Kirk would spend his summer vacations from college working as a tour guide at Greenfield Village, located adjacent to the Henry Ford Museum in Dearborn, Michigan. Greenfield Village was Ford's creation. In the 1920s the automobile manufacturer had begun purchasing historically significant buildings along with their contents, such as the Wright Brothers Bicycle Shop, Thomas Edison's Menlo Park laboratory, the birthplace of Noah Webster, and Ford's own backyard machine shop. He then had them shipped to Greenfield Village to be painstakingly reassembled and renovated to assure complete authenticity. These transported and reproduced buildings were placed around a town square to give the entire vast collection the appearance of an actual nineteenth-century American town.

One June morning in 1938, a chance meeting, seemingly pregnant with symbolism, took place between the young tour guide, the future champion of community and continuity, and Henry Ford, the inventor of a machine that arguably contributed more than any other single mechanical contrivance of the twentieth century toward obliterating much of what Kirk valued. The tide of automobiles spewing out of the factories of Detroit was rapidly and relentlessly revolutionizing all aspects of American society. The automobile, denounced later by Kirk as "the

8. Kirk, *Confessions of a Bohemian Tory,* 17. The immense knowledge of African politics and culture that he acquired at this time would later serve as the backdrop for his baroque novel, *The Creature of Twilight.*

9. Kirk, *Decadence and Renewal in the Higher Learning,* 6; Kirk, *The Sword of Imagination,* 176; Kirk, *The Politics of Prudence,* 99.

mechanical Jacobin," changed forever the traditional ties binding persons to family and community. The car not only altered traditional patterns of social existence but also transformed the physical landscape itself. Ford appeared to the young Kirk to be uneasily aware of the destructive consequences that his invention had wrought upon the individual and society. His machine had "swept away nearly every vestige of the rural society of Wayne County in which he had his own roots, and now," Kirk said, describing the old inventor's mood twenty years later, Ford "wandered restlessly amid the evidences of his own irrevocable revolution, trying to save within the high brick walls of his museum in Dearborn some scraps of the old simplicities." Troubled by the thought that his work had done much to undo the old values and community that he cherished, Ford, Kirk believed, came to suffer "doubt in his heart." The elderly inventor had come to realize that there were values higher in life than production-consumption and economic efficiency. Kirk supposed that he understood the nature of Ford's despair and doubt. "When men or nations sweep away their past in the process of aggrandizement," concluded Kirk, "presently the dream of avarice gives way to a forlorn longing after things beyond recall."[10]

After graduation, Kirk received a graduate fellowship from Duke University. At Duke, Kirk made his first contact with the American South that had already captured his imagination in books. "Here was a conservative society struck a fearful blow eighty years before," he remembered, "and still dazed: decrepit though it was, I liked it better than the life of certain northern cities I knew." He sought to immerse himself in "Southern history and Southern literature." "Providence seemed to lend Kirk a hand" in this endeavor, for at Duke in 1940–1941 were two leading professors in those fields, both of them much published and nationally known: Charles Sydnor in history, Jay Hubbell (the founder of the quarterly *American Literature*) in the latter discipline. Without consulting them, though, he chose to write his master's thesis on the politics of John Randolph of Roanoke, declaring the fiery Virginia planter-statesman to be "the most interesting man in American history, and most neglected." A decade later Kirk's thesis would be published, and it would endure

10. Kirk, *The Politics of Prudence,* 42–49; Kirk, *Confessions of a Bohemian Tory,* 19–20; Kirk, *A Program for Conservatives,* 215–16; Kirk, *The Sword of Imagination,* 42–49.

as one of his most important contributions to contemporary conservative literature. While researching Randolph's politics, Kirk discovered a far more powerful conservative mind. "The eccentric genius of the planter-orator helped to form my mind and style," he remembered, "and about the same time, I began to apprehend a greater thinker and statesman, who remained thereafter my guide in much: Edmund Burke." Although his mentors at Duke University fully expected him to return to do his doctoral work, he never saw them again.[11]

Upon completing his studies at Duke in 1941, Kirk returned to his job as a tour guide at Greenfield Village. But when the village closed for the duration of World War II, he went to work as a file clerk at the sprawling Rouge plant of the Ford Motor Company. Life at the Ford plant was dreary. "In a lodging-house in Dearborn I sank rapidly into an apathy which the modern industrial system induces," Kirk recalled, "sleeping long, ignoring the future, reading nothing but Charles Lamb in the course of six months, and filled with a sense of the disjointedness of the time." From this clearly unhappy existence, the U.S. Army "rescued" him. Three of his four years in the military would be spent stationed in the Great Salt Lake Desert. In that lifeless, barren desert, with the leisure to reflect upon the first principles that governed his life, he "commenced, very languidly, to move from" his "Stoicism toward something more." He came "some way toward an apprehension of Divine nature" and "a proper understanding of my own nature." Rejecting his youthful infatuation with the doctrines of narrow reason and skepticism, he began, he recalled, "to perceive that pure reason has its frontiers, and that to deny realms beyond them is puerility." He learned as well that all mankind is a "part of some grand and mysterious scheme, which works upon us through Providence." In the remote desert, Kirk apprehended the fundamental principles that were to guide his thinking throughout his life. "Mine was not an Enlightened mind, I now was aware," but "a Gothic mind, medieval in its temper and structure. I did not love cold harmony and perfect regularity of organization; what I sought was variety, mystery, tradition, the venerable, the awful."[12]

11. Kirk, *The Sword of Imagination,* 51; Kirk, *Confessions of a Bohemian Tory,* 18–19, 53.
12. Kirk, *Confessions of a Bohemian Tory,* 20–23.

Following his discharge from the military, Kirk was offered a post as an instructor in the history of civilization at Michigan State. After a few uneventful and unhappy years on the college's teaching staff, he took a leave of absence to write a history of the principal conservative thinkers of England and America. To research the book, he traveled to the medieval university of St. Andrews, in Scotland just north of Edinburgh. "In Scotland and England I found, as Hawthorne had found a hundred years before, the metaphysical principle of continuity given visible reality," he wrote. He further averred that "British society and the face of Britain were for me the expression (as they had been the inspiration) of Burke's principles of social immortality and of social reform: the past ever blending with the present, so that the fabric continually renews itself, like some great oak, being never either wholly old or wholly young."[13] The dissertation he wrote while at St. Andrews, entitled "The Conservatives' Rout" (because conservative ideas had lost ground to modern radical ideologies) earned him the Doctorate of Humane Letters degree. He remains today the only American recipient of this degree from that ancient Scottish institution of higher learning. His dissertation would be published as *The Conservative Mind.*

THE CONSERVATIVE MIND AND THE STATE OF CONSERVATISM AT MID-CENTURY

Although only thirty-five in 1953 when his critically acclaimed history of conservative ideas from Edmund Burke to George Santayana was published, Kirk had compiled an impressive record of literary accomplishments. In addition to numerous scholarly essays, he had published several short stories and one other book, *Randolph of Roanoke: A Study in Conservative Thought. The Conservative Mind,* however, was destined to launch Kirk's career in a totally different direction, transforming him from an unknown instructor of history at Michigan State College to one of the leading intellectual figures in the American political tradition. Later, the book would play a crucial role in the postwar revival of conservative ideas and reawaken interest in thinkers as varied as John Randolph of Roanoke, James Fenimore Cooper, William Malleck, Nathaniel Hawthorne, and others. "The impact of *The Conservative Mind* when it first appeared in 1953 is hard to imagine now," the late

13. Ibid., 27.

Henry Regnery, Kirk's publisher, remembered in his memoirs twenty-six years later. "After the long domination of liberalism, with its adulation of the 'common man,' its faith in mechanistic political solutions to all human problems, and its rejection of the tragic and heroic aspects of life, such phrases as 'the unbought grace of life' and the 'eternal chain of right and duty which links great and obscure, living and dead,' and a view of politics as 'the art of apprehending and applying the Justice which is above nature' came like rain after a long drought."[14] *The Conservative Mind* challenged the most cherished beliefs of the intellectual elite for whom conservative ideas had been relegated long ago to the intellectual dustbin of history. The bulk of respectable scholarly opinion was thoroughly convinced that conservatism was either intellectually exhausted or a European aristocratic ideology fundamentally ill-suited for transplantation in the liberal soil of American politics. Some critics felt that the persistence of conservative notions in an enlightened liberal age could be explained only as evidence of psychological maladjustment. More than just a rarity in American politics, conservative minds were thought to have become an extinct species.

A few noteworthy representative examples taken from books and articles that were especially influential during the first half of the twentieth-century furnish ample evidence of this intolerant mind-set. In a popular history of American intellectual thought, *Main Currents of American Thought* (1927), that exerted considerable influence on scholarly perceptions of the American political tradition, Vernon Parrington advanced the view that America's only legitimate tradition in politics was liberalism. Conservatism to his mind constituted merely an aberration, a

14. Henry Regnery, *Memoirs of a Dissident Publisher,* 155. In chap. 8, "Russell Kirk: Conservatism Becomes a Movement," Regnery, Kirk's publisher, recounted the genesis of the publication of *The Conservative Mind* from the point when Kirk was first introduced to Regnery by Sidney Gair, a mutual friend, and the period through the 1950s when Kirk published six books with the Regnery Publishing Company. The correspondence between Regnery and Kirk is presently deposited at the Clarke Historical Library at Central Michigan University, Mount Pleasant, Michigan, and the Russell Kirk Center for Cultural Renewal, Mecosta, Michigan. These letters contain not only a fascinating account of the struggling birth pangs of the nascent conservative movement in the 1950s but also offer a vivid portrait of a rare friendship and mutual respect between publisher and writer. Before Regnery met Kirk, Gair had described him to Regnery as "about as communicative as a turtle, but when he gets behind a typewriter, the results are most impressive." Regnery, *Memoirs,* 147.

temporary deviation from America's progress toward expanded liberties and ever-greater equality and democratization. Parrington treated conservative thought as if it played no vital, essential role in the development of American political ideas. Consistent with this approach, Louis Hartz, in his widely regarded *The Liberal Tradition in America* (1955), argued that America never actually possessed a real conservative tradition. A conservative reaction occurs only when a nation's existing feudal institutions are threatened by class upheaval. But America had possessed neither feudal institutions nor an aristocratic ruling class. Having been a thoroughly middle-class society of farmers and shopkeepers ("petit-bourgeois") nearly since the first settlers came to its shores, America, unlike the class-ridden societies of Europe, never had to develop a conservative tradition to defend the ancién regime from revolutionary radicalism. Lockean liberalism, he concluded, had triumphed in all aspects of American political life.[15]

Lionel Trilling, although less sanguine than either Parrington or Hartz about the apparent absence of a viable conservative intellectual tradition, was just as emphatic. "In the United States at this time liberalism is not only the dominant but the sole intellectual tradition," he famously declared in 1943. "For it is the plain fact that nowadays there are no conservative or reactionary ideas in general circulation." Trilling, though, did admit that impulses "to conservatism or to reaction" exist. "Such impulses are certainly very strong, perhaps even stronger than most of us know." But these impulses, in Trilling's mind, did not constitute an intellectual tradition. Conservatism, by its very nature, is devoid of ideas—it exists merely as a psychological tendency in some people. The "conservative impulse and the reactionary impulse do not, with some isolated and some ecclesiastical exceptions, express themselves in ideas but only in action or in irritable mental gestures which seek to resemble ideas." This absence of a conservative tradition in American political thought, however, did not especially cheer Trilling. It is dangerous for us to suppose that the intellectual condition of conservative and reactionary thought, he added, is "a fortunate thing." In the modern situation "it is just when a movement despairs of having ideas that it turns to force, which it masks in ideology. What is more, it is not conducive to the real strength of liberalism that it should occupy the intellectual

15. See Louis Hartz, *The Liberal Tradition in America,* chap. 1.

field alone." An intelligent adversary, he concluded, "would force liberals to examine their position for its weaknesses and complacencies."[16]

In his revised edition of *Conservatism in America* Clinton Rossiter, who described his own philosophical position as "in principle well removed from Dr. Peale in the direction of Dr. Niebuhr and well removed from Russell Kirk in the direction of Walter Lippmann," agreed that America's political tradition is liberalism. On the one hand, to reject it would be "to move outside the mainstream of American life." Conservatism, on the other hand, he called the "thankless persuasion," because it was committed to the delicate, ever precarious task of preserving while allowing for reform necessary to the continued viability of society. This middling position is difficult to occupy, in Rossiter's opinion, "because there are no sure theoretical landmarks that help men to find 'a point' located flexibly somewhere between underadjustment and overadjustment to the imperatives of the new America." Rossiter could find little merit in the efforts of some conservatives, especially those like Kirk, to recover the ideas that have sustained conservatives in bygone generations. The solution to America's problems, he felt, was not to embrace the principles of Burke, Coleridge, and John Adams. "This, it seems to me, is especially bad and useless advice—bad because it asks the conservative to commit political suicide, useless because what it asks is in reality inconceivable," Rossiter wrote. "America is different, both in history and present state, and the full Conservative tradition simply will not flourish on this soil."[17]

Two other tactics were employed to disparage conservatism as a creditable alternative to liberalism. One group of critics held that conservative expressions were mere symptoms of probable mental maladjustments; other critics defined conservatism as an ideology of the privileged and wealthy business classes.

As a result of a combination of psychological and political-opinion tests, surveying those who identified themselves as conservatives, Herbert McClosky concluded in an article on conservatism and personality

16. Lionel Trilling, *The Liberal Imagination: Essays on Literature and Society,* vii–viii. See also pp. 254–55 for Trilling's discussion of the paucity of conservative ideas in American fiction and the deleterious effect of that fact on the general quality of intellectual life in America.

17. Rossiter, *Conservatism in America,* viii–ix, 262, 251, 261.

that conservatives, as a group, possessed a wide variety of abnormal and irrational personality traits. The conservative is, he wrote, "psychologically timid, distrustful of differences, and of whatever he cannot understand. He fears change, dreads disorder, and is intolerant of nonconformity. The tendency of the prototypic conservative to derogate reason and intellectuality, and to eschew theory, seems in some measure to be an outgrowth of these and related elements in his personality." Hostility, suspicion, and the exhibiting of compulsive-obsessive traits are, he concluded, the principal components of the conservative personality.[18] The conservatives' extreme emphasis on duty and order and their fetish for community, McClosky felt, was a direct consequence of their personality attributes. The implication of McClosky's seemingly scientifically objective research was that conservatives are really very unpleasant characters. Their case need not be examined because the mentally healthy individual would not be inclined to espouse any of their beliefs.

In another effort to pigeonhole the American Right, a number of liberal critics described conservatism as a class-based ideology reflecting the interests only of the rich and wellborn. "To write about conservative politics in America," wrote Gordon Harrison in 1954, "is to chronicle the political performance of American business." The "conservative function in politics has been performed by the party chiefly representing the business point of view. More than ever is that true today. There is no indication that it will be less true in the future." If one wants to understand political conservatism, he concluded, then one "must look primarily to the attitudes of business." Arguing in the same vein, Ludwig Freund held that the "underlying common feature of conservatism, which seems to bridge all national and other differences of its varied expressions is one criterion, and one alone: the defense of a long-established order and of the privileges of the ruling class therein, or, if this order is gone, the desire for either the total restoration, or the restoration of essential parts, of that order as well as the special class structure

18. Herbert McClosky, "Conservatism and Personality," 40–43. One indicator of the influence and durability of McClosky's assessment and description of the personality of the conservative is that, a decade later, Allen Guttman, in his study of American conservatism, could uncritically cite these findings. See Allen Guttman, *The Conservative Tradition in America,* 162.

which characterized it. This means that in the Western world, conservatism has always involved a defense of the position of the 'rich and well-born'—that is, of those who are one or the other or both."[19]

During the year *The Conservative Mind* was published, a "Vital Center" liberal, Arthur M. Schlesinger, Jr., offered some gratuitous advice to "the New Conservatives" who were beginning to become a visible force in American culture and politics. He concurred with Hartz's soon-to-be fashionable interpretation of the American political tradition (Hartz's book was published two years later). Given America's nonfeudal political tradition, a conservatism expressed in terms of aristocratic responsibility would be a "hothouse growth" here. Instead, he suggested, a distinctly American conservatism should be based upon "the actual circumstances of American society" and "the concrete life of the American people." American conservatism should adopt a business mentality, he counseled, and become a philosophy of plutocracy. The business community "must be the central fact in American conservatism. The dominant concrete condition which an authentic American conservatism must interpret is the politics and ideas of the American business community." He challenged conservatives such as Kirk and Peter Viereck to "stop pretending that the business community does not exist, or that it is bad form to talk about it," and to "recognize that conservatism is a meaningless conception in American political life except as a label for the ideas of politics of American business."[20]

Such "advice" smacked of intellectual dishonesty—a disingenuous, and perhaps cynical as well, attempt to preserve liberal advantage by intellectually disemboweling conservatism. If conservatives had adopted Schlesinger's recommendation, they would have marched off compliantly en masse into political obscurity. As he surely knew, his prescriptions would have enfeebled conservatism as a political and intellectual movement. Schlesinger was asking conservatives in effect to revert to the widely discredited atomistic individualism of Jeremy Bentham, Herbert Spencer, and the Manchester school of economics. These doctrines

19. Gordon Harrison, *Road to the Right: The Tradition and Hope of American Conservatism,* vii; Ludwig Freund, "The New American Conservatism and European Conservatism," 11.

20. Arthur M. Schlesinger, Jr., "The New Conservatism in America: A Liberal Comment," 65, 69–70 (Schlesinger's emphasis).

failed because they lacked warmth, a recognition of values that transcend narrow economic self-interest, and a sense of community in which the person finds self-identity and purpose. Schlesinger no doubt appreciated these facts.

The tendency of liberal critics to equate conservatism with a business-oriented ideology was patently self-serving. By describing conservatism as merely a free-market ideology and identifying it with the economic interests of the American business community, they could facilely dismiss this straw man as a shallow and unappealing alternative to liberalism. Such a narrowly focused doctrine would amount to little more than an impotent disgruntled protest to the prevailing liberal dogmas. An ideology of privilege for the wealthy would present little threat to the dominant classes. Schlesinger began his article by chiding conservatives for possessing a weak intellectual tradition and for having never "dared to articulate a broader social philosophy." Apparently, Schlesinger hoped that they would remain intellectually moribund and politically ineffective.[21]

In summary, conservatism's liberal adversaries attempted to discredit its intellectual substance and diminish its strength as a potent political force by: (1) arguing that it was politically incompatible with American traditions; (2) declaring it a product of the politics of irrationality; (3) describing the object of an "intelligent conservatism" to be to conserve liberal gains; and, lastly, (4) defining it as an ideology devised solely to defend the economic interests of the business community.[22]

One factor did give, though, some credence to the charge that conservatism was basically about laissez-faire economics. Preceding the publication of *The Conservative Mind,* the voices on the intellectual

21. Ibid., 61. Schlesinger's "conservatism" would be realized under the label "neoconservatism" three decades later. Whether the neoconservatives present a viable alternative to liberalism is a question that will be addressed in chapter 8.

22. Despite the recent electoral successes of conservative candidates and the emergence of a vibrant conservative intellectual movement since the publication of *The Conservative Mind,* some liberals today still doubt whether conservatives have a mind. See, for example, Alan Wolfe, "The Revolution That Never Was," 34–42. "[D]espite decades of trying, and a golden opportunity handed to them by liberal failure," Wolfe complains, "conservatives in America have been unable to come up with any sustained and significant ideas capable of giving substance to their complaints against the contemporary world."

Right in America had been dominated by those of the libertarian persuasion. The older themes of tradition, localism, prescriptive rights, and limited government espoused by Edmund Burke, John Adams, John C. Calhoun, and Orestes Brownson had been virtually extinguished in America since Irving Babbitt and Paul Elmer More had ceased their work. The libertarians believed, by contrast, that the predominant threat to freedom in the West came from the advances of such collectivist ideologies as communism and socialism (both then gaining ground in postwar Europe), and in America from the New Deal liberalism of the Franklin Roosevelt administration. Everywhere libertarians saw evidence of the individual progressively surrendering his rights and freedoms to the leviathan state. In response, they revived the principles of the old liberalism of Adam Smith, Jeremy Bentham, Herbert Spencer, and the Manchester school. Against the onslaught of collectivist ideas, libertarians countered with a defense of the free market system, private property, limited government, and individual self-reliance. During the 1940s and 1950s two libertarian theorists were especially influential: Friedrich A. Hayek (1899–1992) and Ludwig von Mises (1881–1973). The first widely discussed challenge to liberal and socialist economic programs came from Hayek's book, *The Road to Serfdom,* published in 1944. An Austrian economist who emigrated to Great Britain in the 1930s, Hayek argued that all economic planning must inevitably lead to dictatorship. By their very nature, comprehensive governmental controls on economic activity are inherently totalitarian because they are necessarily destructive of liberty, capricious and arbitrary. Against this socialist "road to serfdom," Hayek appealed to the principles of individualism and classical liberalism.[23]

Another Austrian, Ludwig von Mises, who had immigrated to the United States in the 1940s, also became a powerful voice for laissez-faire economics. He was even more "totally devoted to pure laissez-faire than his pupil Hayek," George Nash points out. Hayek had "dissociated himself from pure 'laissez-faire'" and "argued the need for vigorous government action to establish the 'rule of law' and maintain the 'design' of a free market." According to Mises, the chief threat to civilization was "the ideology of etatism," which he defined as "the trend toward government control of business." Fundamental to Mises's posi-

---

23. Nash, *The Conservative Intellectual Movement,* 3–4.

tion was his belief that governmental centralized planning and individual liberty are incompatible. Socialism, then, would always mean the destruction of individual liberty. The result of socialist planning, he predicted, would be the creation of a great governmental apparatus of control and coercion in which the individual is subordinated to the will of the socialist state.[24]

Both Hayek and Mises had a considerable impact upon the development and growing acceptance of free market ideas during the decades after World War II. The American publication of Hayek's *The Road to Serfdom* in 1954 was hailed by H. Stuart Hughes as "a major event in the intellectual history of the United States." When Mises's most enduring work, *Human Action,* appeared in 1949, Henry Hazlitt predicted that if "any single book can turn the ideological tide that has been running in recent years so heavily toward statism, socialism, and totalitarianism," it would be this book.[25] Many other articles and books defending libertarian principles emerged from such writers as Henry Hazlitt, John Chamberlain, and Frank Chodorov, a disciple of Albert Jay Nock. During the 1940s and 1950s, libertarian voices were nearly the sole ones heard on the intellectual Right.

Nevertheless, many American conservative intellectuals were growing discontented with the libertarian direction of postwar conservatism. They were troubled by the prospect that economic doctrines alone might eventually be considered as the total answer to all of America's problems. The obsession with economic issues neglected the more important and fundamental crises confronting Western civilization: the abandonment of old moral values, the decline of community, the decay of religion, and the breakup of old patterns of life. These issues were seen as prior in importance to the economic issues addressed by the libertarians. The publication of three books in close succession, Richard Weaver's *Ideas Have Consequences* (1948), Peter Viereck's *Conservatism Revisited* (1949), and Kirk's *The Conservative Mind* (1953),

24. Ibid., 7, 26–27; Ludwig von Mises, *Omnipotent Government: The Rise of the Total State and Total War* (New Haven, Conn.: Yale University Press, 1944), 6, quoted in Nash, *The Conservative Intellectual Movement,* 8.

25. H. Stuart Hughes, "Capitalism and History," *Commentary* 17 (April 1954): 407, quoted in Nash, *The Conservative Intellectual Movement,* 29; Henry Hazlitt, "The Case for Capitalism," *Newsweek,* September 19 1949, 70, quoted in Nash, *The Conservative Intellectual Movement,* 9.

marked the beginning of the shift in the emphasis of American conservatism away from the atomistic individualism of the libertarians toward a deeper appreciation of man's social nature.

The moral cancer gnawing away at the foundations of Western civilization had its origins, according to Weaver's *Ideas Have Consequences,* in a medieval debate among scholastic thinkers over the issue of the existence of universals. The "defeat of logical realism in the great medieval debate," he argued, "was the crucial event in the history of Western culture; from this flowed those acts which issue now in modern decadence." The error originated with William of Occam (1285–1349) "who propounded the fateful doctrine of nominalism, which denies that universals have a real existence." The consequence was to be a revolution in morality. Moral judgment would eventually come to be based not upon transcendent values, but one's personal preferences. That which maximizes pleasure is good, while that which causes pain is bad. Weaver concluded that nominalism meant the virtual denial of truth, of principle claiming to have transcendent validity. "With the denial of objective truth, there is no escape from the relativism of 'man the measure of all things.'"[26]

The following year, Peter Viereck, a professor of history at Mount Holyoke College and a widely admired poet, strove to define the new conservatism in the postwar era in *Conservatism Revisited.* What he emphatically opposed was a conservatism that amounted to no more than a defense of laissez-faire capitalism. According to Viereck, conservatism does not entail a "fetish of laissez-faire economics." Rather, the history of conservatism had been one of putting "social justice before laissez-faire." Central to conservatism, he argued, "is a humanist reverence for the dignity of the individual soul" which is "incompatible with fascist or Stalinist collectivism; incompatible with a purely mechanistic view of man; incompatible with a purely economic view of history." Transcendent moral values must have precedence over merely economic values. Even sophisticated defenses of the free market system would never be sufficient, in Viereck's view, to offset the appeal of Marxist ideology. "In place of the economic capitalist philosophy of Adam Smith and the economic socialist philosophy of Marx," Viereck predicted, "the world through trial and error will come to see *the eco-*

26. Richard M. Weaver, *Ideas Have Consequences,* 3–4.

nomic necessity of an antieconomic philosophy, the material necessity of antimaterialism." As Claes Ryn points out, summarizing Viereck's position, Viereck saw in "the preference for laissez-faire economics a bias unduly favoring commercial and utilitarian values." His new conservatism, by contrast, was "closer to the great Western cultural traditions" and supported "ethical and other restraints on the forces of the market."[27]

In the same vein as Weaver's and Viereck's books was Kirk's *The Conservative Mind.* Its publication, however, would be an event of quite another order. As George Nash notes, the appearance of *The Conservative Mind* "dramatically catalyzed the emergence of the conservative intellectual movement."[28] While Weaver's and Viereck's books are still read, *The Conservative Mind* would have a far greater impact upon the resurgent conservative movement. Kirk's purposes in this book were far more ambitious than those of either Weaver or Viereck. First, Kirk was writing a history of conservative ideas, the first such history attempted by anyone. But his intent was more than historical; it was didactic and polemical. The rationalism of the philosophes, the romantic idealism of the Rousseauists, Benthamism, positivism, Marxism, Social Darwinism, pragmatism, and socialism were among the ideologies Kirk condemned as inimical to the social order of the post-1789 world. From them sprang the belief in the perfectibility of man, the enthusiasm for social and economic leveling, the impulse for innovation coinciding with a concomitant contempt of tradition, the denial of the power of Providence in history, and the rejection of "the permanent things," defined as those enduring moral values which make civilized social existence possible. Against the proponents of radical innovation, Kirk enthusiastically defended tradition, old values, and prescriptive establishments.

Second, his study of conservative thinkers was, as he pointed out, "a prolonged essay in definition."[29] What Kirk discovered was a tradition battered and often routed by its adversaries but still vibrant, stemming from Edmund Burke, the founder of "true" conservatism, and extending down through the generations, linking writers, poets, and statesmen. Among those belonging to this tradition in Britain were such men

27. Viereck, *Conservatism Revisited,* 39–40, 33, and 44 (Viereck's emphasis); Ryn, "Peter Viereck," 325.
28. Nash, *The Conservative Intellectual Movement,* 61.
29. Kirk, *The Conservative Mind,* 3.

as Samuel Taylor Coleridge, Benjamin Disraeli, Cardinal John Henry Newman, James Fitzjames Stephen, W. E. H. Lecky, and T. S. Eliot, and in America, the Adams family, John Randolph, John Calhoun, Orestes Brownson, Irving Babbitt, and Paul Elmer More. From a body of intimately related and mutually supportive ideas common to these men of conservative instincts, Kirk was able to distill the essence of the conservative position. As a consequence of discovering this tradition and articulating and applying its principles to modern challenges, he fortified and strengthened the conservative position by rendering traditional conservative ideas once more intellectually creditable. Conservatism could no longer be airily dismissed as merely the momentary, aberrant, disgruntled dissent of the privileged few against the prevailing liberal orthodoxies. Rather, he demonstrated in a compelling fashion both that conservatism is an integral part of the Western political tradition and that the American political tradition is Burkean. In an age of liberal complacency, Kirk issued a challenge that could not be easily ignored. Others, closely associated with the resurgence of conservative ideas in America, quickly grasped the significance of this assault on liberal dogmas. In his review of *The Conservative Mind,* Gordon Keith Chalmers described Kirk as being "as relentless as his enemies, Karl Marx and Harold Laski, considerably more temperate and scholarly, and in passages of this very readable book, brilliant and even eloquent." Soon thereafter, Robert Nisbet hailed the book for having broken "the cake of intellectual opposition" to conservatism. Jeffrey Hart later proclaimed that Kirk had "devulgarized" conservatism.[30]

Through his recovery of an intellectually formidable conservative tradition, Kirk buried whatever substance there was in John Stuart Mill's jibe that conservatives were "the stupid party." But Kirk's achievement was not limited to this accomplishment. His definition of conservatism, with his powerful argument that Burkean conservatism embodied the principles of true conservatism, had the effect of pulling the conservative movement away from its flirtation with the atomistic individualism and utilitarian moral principles of the libertarians toward an apprehension of both man's social nature and the transcendent moral

30. Gordon Keith Chalmers, review of *The Conservative Mind,* 7; Robert Nisbet to Kirk, September 10, 1953; Nash, *The Conservative Intellectual Movement,* 67.

values that form the basis of civilized social existence. These issues will be developed more fully in chapters 2, 3, and 6.

THE IDEA OF CONSERVATISM

Conservatism in its modern sense, wrote Kirk, "did not manifest itself until 1790" with the publication of Burke's *Reflections on the Revolution in France.* Historically, then, modern conservatism was born in a reaction to the excesses of the French Jacobins who sought to overthrow the old moral, political, and social order of Europe. To Burke belongs the credit for founding modern conservatism, explained Kirk, because he "defined in the public consciousness, for the first time, the opposing poles of conservation and innovation." While Kirk attributed to Burke the first expression of the principles of conservatism, the word "conservative" is not in any of Burke's works. As Kirk noted, Burke's French disciples coined this neologism. After the French Revolution, F. A. R. de Chateaubriand (1768–1848) entitled his journal, founded to defend the cause of clerical and political restoration in France, *Le Conservateur.* Soon afterward, others who fought against the ideas of the Revolution took up the name. John Wilson Croker, George Canning, and Robert Peel clapped it onto the Tory party "that no longer was Tory or Whig, once the followers of Pitt and Portland joined forces." The first British use of the term, however, is a matter of some scholarly disagreement. Most historians have credited its first use to John Wilson Croker, the Tory parliamentarian and wit. Yet Myron F. Brightfield, in his biography of Croker, contended that the "first public suggestion of the substitution of 'Conservative' for 'Tory' came in an article published in the *Quarterly Review* in 1830." Croker, added Brightfield, "according to the best available evidence," had "nothing to do with this piece." The passage in question comes near the end of the article in which the anonymous author, following a lengthy discussion of a variety of current domestic British political issues, offered the suggestion that the Tory party should be renamed the Conservative party.[31] So, it re-

31. Noel O'Sullivan, *Conservatism,* 9–10; Kirk, *The Conservative Mind,* 5–6; Myron F. Brightfield, *John Wilson Croker,* 403n19; "Internal Policy," *Quarterly Review* 47 (January 1830): 276. E. J. Payne, in his introductory essay to the *Select Works of Burke,* attributes this article to Croker. See Payne, ed., *Select Works of Burke* (Oxford: Clarendon Press, 1904), vol. 1, xii.

mains unclear whether Croker or some unknown author should be given credit for the first use of the word "conservative" in its modern political sense.

If the precise origin of the term "conservative" is still a matter of some debate, the disagreements over the definition of conservatism remain even more rancorous and inconclusive. Conservatism resists facile definitions because one of its characteristics is that its proponents do not presume to have predefined solutions to all political and social questions. As Keith Feiling once wrote, conservatism "is not so much a fixed programme as a continuing spirit." Many hostile critics of conservatism frequently reproached conservatives for failing to design a sharply defined program with precise policies for social improvement. However, the absence of ready-made policy conservative recommendations for all the problems to which the flesh is heir never troubled Kirk. It is the ideologues, he observed, not the conservatives, who are always prepared with ready-made answers. "Strictly speaking, conservatism is not a political system, but rather a way of looking at the civil social order," he held. "The conservative of Peru . . . will differ greatly from those of Australia, for though they may share a preference for things established, the institutions and customs which they desire to preserve are not identical." What the conservatives "have in common is a similar view of human nature, of the ends of society, and of the most nearly satisfactory *methods* for seeking the common good."[32]

A central theme in Kirk's work was to differentiate conceptually between conservatism and ideology. Conservatism is not an ideology, he strongly and repeatedly maintained. In fact, conservatism, by its very nature, constitutes an anti-ideology. In support of this argument,

---

32. The Keith Feiling quote is actually a paraphrase of Feiling's definition in *What Is Conservatism?* (1930), 8, by F. J. C. Hearnshaw, *Conservatism in England,* 18. Kirk, *A Program for Conservatives,* 2. Kirk was frequently attacked by reviewers of *The Conservative Mind* for his apparent failure to provide a specific outline of conservative programs. A typical example is the following: "Conservatives were once characterized by John Stuart Mill as 'the stupid party.' Much that conservative politicians have advocated in our day entitles them still to the name. If a new conservatism is to be forthcoming in theory, it will not win the respect of intelligent people unless its criticism is responsible, its ideas clear, and its programs exact." Ralph Gilbert Ross, "Campaign against Liberalism, Continued," 575. Kirk, "The Conservative Cast of American Society," in *Conservatism: Waxing and Waning?* 29; Kirk, *A Program for Conservatives,* 7 (Kirk's emphasis).

he frequently cited H. Stuart Hughes's famous description of conservatism as "the negation of ideology." Since many students of modern political ideas have sharply disagreed with Kirk on this point, it is important to understand precisely his meaning. His critics, I believe, have employed a substantially different definition of ideology than did Kirk. A practice common among scholars of modern ideologies is to call any set of political ideas or beliefs upon which people act an ideology. According to this view, communism, socialism, fascism, conservatism, or liberalism are all equally examples of ideologies. Ideology is any set of beliefs. As the author of one popular undergraduate college textbook put it—whether they know it or not, everyone has an ideology. Insofar as people believe in something, value something, have ideas about things, they possess an ideology.[33] This all-inclusive definition, though, is so conceptually vague, so broad, that analytically useful distinctions between various modes of thought cannot be made. Ideology, to follow the logic of this argument, is indistinguishable from genuine political philosophy. Further, a position of moral relativism is implicit

33. For Kirk's citations of Hughes's "negation of ideology" description of conservatism, see *Enemies of the Permanent Things: Observations of Abnormality in Literature and Politics,* 154; Kirk, *Confessions of a Bohemian Tory,* 284; "The Birchites I: Conservatives and Fantastics," *America* 106 (February 17, 1962): 643. For an opposing view from a European conservative, see Erik Ritter von Kuehnelt-Leddihn, who argued that to define conservatism as an anti-ideology reflects the anti-intellectualism of Britain and America and therefore has "only local significance." Reflecting a continental European perspective, he defined an ideology as "a coherent set of ideas"; he therefore concluded that it is not "completely illegitimate to talk, *horrible dictu* about an ideology." See von Kuehnelt-Leddihn, *Leftism: From de Sade and Marx to Hitler and Marcuse,* 384, 386–87. In the Portland Declaration, Kuehnelt-Leddihn summarized his basic principles and beliefs. He used here the terms "philosophy," "world-view," and "ideology" interchangeably. The triumph of the free world, he wrote, over "sets of ideas which will either reduce man to a purely materialistic animal, or present a philosophy of doubt, if not despair" depends on presenting a counterideology "well grounded in a great tradition" of Western values "for which we ought to be ready to make sacrifices." Further, "our ideology must be based on the Living God." The Portland Declaration was published in 1982 by the National Committee of Catholic Laymen, Inc. Retrieved April 25, 2002 from the World Wide Web: http://www.town.com/phillysoc/Portland.htm. For critical views of Kirk's description of conservatism, see Freund, "The American Conservatism and European Conservatism," 11; Peter Gay, review of *The Conservative Mind,* 587. The undergraduate textbook described is Roy C. Macridis, *Contemporary Political Ideologies: Movements and Regimes,* 1.

in this definition. Without being explicit, the proponent is assuming that all moral judgments, and hence all prescriptive political statements, are equally based upon subjective judgments, or, to put it another way, all are rationalizations of economic or political interests. Without considering here the issue of the moral basis of Kirk's conservatism, let it suffice to say that Kirk affirmed the existence of an objective universal moral order. From this premise, he argued that conservatism should be defined as the defense of this moral order against its ideological adversaries of both the Left and the Right. Given this stance, which Kirk made explicit, his argument that conservatism is the opposite of ideology is logically consistent.[34]

To Kirk, this issue was of no small importance given his conviction that ideology threatens the civilized order of the Western world. Ideology means, he observed, political fanaticism or, more precisely, a Christian heresy that asserts "that this world of ours may be converted into the Terrestrial Paradise through the operation of positive law and positive planning. The ideologue—Communist or Nazi or of whatever affiliation—maintains that human nature and society may be perfected by mundane, secular means, though these means ordinarily involve a violent social revolution. The ideologue immanentizes religious symbols and inverts religious doctrines." "As a fanatical political religion, it can brook no challenge. What religion promises to the believer in a realm beyond time and space, ideology promises to everyone—except those who have been 'liquidated' in the process—in society." Ideology is, hence, inherently inimical to the civilized social order because it amounts to "a passionate endeavor to overthrow" that order. The ideologue rebels against God and his order. In an ideologue's system, "there is no room left for Providence, or chance, or free will, or prudence. He is the devotee, often, of what Burke called 'an armed doctrine.' His ancestor was Procrustes, and he is resolved to stretch or hack all the world until it fits his bed."[35]

34. The problem with the term "ideology," Kenneth R. Minogue notes, is that it is not only vague but also often used as a tactic to dunk "false" beliefs. Those who "conclude that all thinking is ideological . . . destroy the usefulness of the concept." Kenneth R. Minogue, *The Liberal Mind,* 15–16.

35. Kirk, *Enemies of the Permanent Things,* 154, 164; "Ideology and Political Economy," *America* 96 (January 5, 1957): 388; Kirk, *A Program for Conservatives,* 4.

Napoleon is credited with coining the term "ideology." His description, in 1812, of the baneful effects of the ideologues' excesses—their hopeless ignorance of the realities of politics and human nature—is still apt today and captures the spirit of John Adams's views, which were also Kirk's, of the ideologue's fanciful utopia: "It is to ideology, that obscure metaphysics, which searching with subtlety after first causes, wishes to found upon the legislation of nations, instead of adapting the laws to the knowledge of the human heart and to the lessons of history, that we are to attribute all the calamities that our beloved France has experienced. Those errors necessarily produced the government of the men of blood."[36]

Abstract ideas, whether a priori or a posteriori, which fail to give prudent consideration to fact and circumstance, according to Kirk, stand in opposition to conservative principles. The conservative, by contrast, "looks with deep suspicion on the cult of Reason—the worship of an abstract rationality" that would force "men and societies into a pre-conceived pattern divorced from the special circumstances of different times and countries." Burke had condemned the ideology of his day, that of the Jacobins, as advancing a "barbarous philosophy, the off-spring of cold hearts and muddy understandings . . ." which by its defective reasoning dissolved all "the pleasing illusions, which made power gentle and obedience liberal, which harmonized the different shades of life." The art of politics, then, can never be, the conservative would argue, an exact science of inflexible and unchanging principles. As Fisher Ames, the Federalist aristocrat, wrote, "Politicks is the science of good sense, applied to public affairs, and, as those are forever changing, what is wisdom to-day would be folly and perhaps, ruin to-morrow. Politicks is not a science so properly as a business. It cannot have fixed principles, from which a wise man would never swerve, unless the inconstancy of men's view of interest and the capriciousness of the tempers could be fixed."[37] An exact science of politics would be an impossibility, and baneful in its implications, given the passionate and fluctuating nature of man, which defies all efforts to create a perfectly organized society.

36. John Adams, *The Works of John Adams,* vol. 6, 402.
37. Kirk, *A Program for Conservatives,* 6; Edmund Burke, *Reflections on the Revolution in France,* 171; Fisher Ames, *Works,* 357.

Although conservatism may be the negation of ideology, it was clearly not for Kirk the negation of principle. The genuine conservative, he maintained, "believes in Principle, or enduring values ascertained through appreciation of the wisdom of dead generations, the study of history and the reconciliation of authority with the altered circumstances of our present life." What, then, are the principles to which the genuine conservative subscribes? Kirk was reluctant to draw up a list of conservative principles for fear that the process of condensation itself might transform conservative principles into rigid abstractions. "Any informed conservative is reluctant to condense profound and intricate intellectual systems to a few pretentious phrases; he prefers to leave that technique to enthusiasm of the radicals. Conservatism is not a fixed and immutable body of dogma, and conservatives inherit from Burke a talent for re-expressing their convictions to fit the time." Even so, Kirk felt compelled, for the sake of convenience and clarity, to list the basic principles of the genuine conservative tradition. He reduced the dozen principles found in F. J. C. Hearnshaw's *Conservatism in England* (1933) to just six canons of conservative thought.[38] This list of the tenets of conservatism along with the catalogue of principles of the five major schools of radical thought formed for Kirk a preliminary working definition of the essence of conservatism. Later, in *A Program for Conservatives,* he again outlined the principles of conservatism, which although limited to the American experience, are broadly similar:

(1) "Belief in a transcendent order, a body of natural law, which rules society as well as conscience." The conservative realizes that for humane social existence to be possible, man must agree upon certain moral ultimates. A community, as Cicero and St. Augustine agreed, is a group united by commonly held principles of justice. The apprehension and application of these principles is a prerequisite for order in both commonwealth and soul.

(2) "Affection for the proliferating variety and mystery of human existence, as opposed to the narrowing uniformity, equalitarianism,

38. Kirk, *A Program for Conservatives,* 6, 41–44; Kirk, *The Conservative Mind,* 7; Hearnshaw, *Conservatism in England,* 22–33. Kirk's canons of conservatism, as well as the beliefs of five radical schools of thought, are cataloged in his *The Conservative Mind,* 7–9.

and utilitarian aims of most radical systems..." The common characteristic of radical systems is the tendency to exaggerate one aspect of human experience at the expense of all others. Rather than accept and acknowledge the infinite variety of human diversity and experience, radicals attempt to reduce everyone to a bland uniformity. In slavish obedience to their ideological schemes, the ideologists use their Procrustean bed of political abstractions to remold people into identical versions of one another.

(3) "Conviction that civilized society requires orders and classes, as against the notion of a 'classless society.'" As Burke wrote, "A true natural aristocracy is not a separate interest in the state, or separable from it. It is an essential integral part of any large body rightly constituted." Conservatives accept the unequal distribution of talent, character, and wealth among men as an unalterable fact. All efforts to level humanity down to some equal social and economic level violate the natural order of society. Further, the existence of an aristocracy is an effective and beneficial check upon both the centralizing tendencies of government and the assaults of the transient majority, as both Alexis de Tocqueville and John Adams, for example, had affirmed.[39]

(4) "Persuasion that freedom and property are closely linked..." The conservative would insist that private property is the basis of all civilization. The right to property is an effective barrier against the intrusion of the state into the private affairs of the individual.[40] Economic leveling eviscerates the artistic and intellectual freedoms necessary for the development and perpetuation of civilized society.

(5) "Faith in prescription and distrust of sophisters, calculators, and economists who would reconstruct society upon abstract designs." A conservative relies upon "tradition, sound prejudice, and old prescription" as "checks both upon man's anarchic impulse and upon the innovator's lust for power."

(6) "Recognition that change may not be salutary reform: Hasty innovation may be a devouring conflagration, rather than a torch of progress."

39. Edmund Burke, "Appeal from New Whigs," *The Works of the Right Honourable Edmund Burke,* vol. 3, 85; Adams, *Works,* vol. 4, 85; and Alexis de Tocqueville, *Memoir,* ii. 25 (February 24, 1854).
40. Paul Elmer More, *Aristocracy and Justice,* vol. 9 of *Shelburne Essays,* 133, 136.

The conservative does not reject change, of course, but is profoundly concerned with the direction and pace of alteration.

Since Burke, five major schools of radical thought "have competed for public favor" with conservatism: the rationalism of the French philosophes; the moral skepticism of David Hume, and Rousseau and his allies; Benthamite utilitarianism; the positivism of Auguste Comte's school; and the "collectivistic materialism of Marx and other socialists." In these diverse schools of thought, with very different intentions and recommendations, Kirk discerned five principles that the radicals have employed since 1790 to attack "the prescriptive arrangement of society":

(1) "The perfectibility of man and the illimitable progress of society: meliorism." Radicals would affirm that man is either good, or can be made perfectible, through the positive legislation of the government. They reject the conservative principle that man has a natural proclivity toward violence and sin.

(2) "Contempt for tradition." The radicals hold that the past, with its superstitions and prejudices, should be discarded as an unhelpful guide to the future. Unshackled from the chains of the past, man will soar to unprecedented creativity.

(3) "Political leveling." By stripping everyone of distinctions or associations that might be construed as "privileges," the radical would level everyone down to a "tapioca pudding" society. Egalitarianism would inevitably lead, the conservative believes, to both the abolition of the natural hierarchical order of society and to the consolidation of the power of the state.

(4) "Economic leveling." The radicals strongly condemn the institution of private property as the cause of the numerous unjustified social inequities.

(5) The radicals "unite in detesting Burke's description of the state as ordained of God, and his concept of society as joined in perpetuity by a moral bond among the dead, the living, and those yet to be born—the community of souls." For radicals, the state is merely an artificial creation of man to be molded to fit the desires of the present generation.

Like Aristotle's virtuous man *(spoudaios),* the conservative lives a life of moderation, avoiding both political and moral excess. Conservatism, Kirk maintained, "does not breed fanatics. It does not try to excite the enthusiasm of a secular religion. If you want men who will sacrifice their past and present and future to a set of abstract ideas, you must go to Communism, or Fascism, or Benthamism, but if you want men who seek, reasonably and prudently, to reconcile the best in the wisdom of our ancestors with the change which is essential to a vigorous civil social existence, then you will do well to turn to conservative principles."[41]

41. Kirk, *A Program for Conservatives,* 6.

2 THE MORAL BASIS OF CONSERVATIVISM

*The faith in one's natural goodness is a
constant encouragement to evade moral
responsibility.*

—Irving Babbitt, *Rousseau and Romanticism*

*We are conscious of our self as both the inner
check and the flux, one and the many, the
same and different.*

—Paul Elmer More, *Definitions in Dualism*

FUNDAMENTAL TO KIRK'S POLITICS is the conviction that the order of the soul and
commonwealth has been severely shaken by a growing indifference
and hostility to the moral teachings of the Classical and Judeo-Christian
tradition. A "new morality" professing a radical new vision of the human
condition and moral reality has arisen to challenge this older moral
tradition. Consequently, it has become, he noted, "fashionable to deride
authority and prescription." Authority has come to imply "arbitrary restraint," and prescription "has been equated with cultural lag and superstition." These "emancipated notions" have created a "generation of
young people reared according to 'permissive' tenets" who have "grown
up bored, sullen, and in revolt against the very lack of order which was
supposed to ensure the full development of their personalities." If people
are to associate peacefully at all, Kirk stressed, then "some authority
must govern them; if they throw off traditional authority, the authority
of church and precept and old educational disciplines and parents, then
very soon they find themselves subjected to some new and merciless
authority."[1] In reaction to modern moral nihilism and relativism, there-

1. Kirk, *Enemies of the Permanent Things*, 282.

fore, Kirk sought in his work to rediscover, articulate, and defend those enduring moral norms, now blurred in our consciousness, by which civilized peoples have governed their conduct.

To explain and critically assess the ethical position upon which Kirk's defense of order and authority depends, I will rely heavily on the contributions of Irving Babbitt (1865–1933), the Harvard literary scholar and cultural thinker; Paul Elmer More (1864–1937), the American essayist and critic; and Swedish philosopher Folke Leander (1910–1981), who have given definitions of "dualism" and "inner check," two concepts central to my explication. The themes of Babbitt and More are useful for understanding Kirk, not least because he is clearly allied with their "New Humanism" in the development of his own ethical position. Leander, for his part, was involved for the last thirty years or more of his life in the critical interpretation and explanation of Babbitt's and More's concepts of imagination, ethical dualism, and the inner check. A certain degree of philosophical imprecision exists in Kirk's thought that complicates the explication of his ideas. Kirk was not a philosopher in the technical sense of that word (as he readily admitted), and therefore was not concerned in his work with the formal analysis of basic philosophical concepts. Although the concepts I have named are wholly consistent with his teaching, he never attempted to develop them systematically. The works of Babbitt, More, and Leander, then, are indispensable aids toward understanding Kirk's moral principles in areas where he is least precise.

This chapter will define in a preliminary fashion the concepts of duality of human nature and the inner check, which will take on additional significance in later chapters as they are related to Kirk's position on the moral imagination, the ethical role of tradition, order in soul and commonwealth, community, and education.

ETHICAL DUALISM AND HUMAN NATURE

"Men's appetites are voracious and sanguinary," Kirk affirmed, and must be "restrained by this collective and immemorial wisdom we call prejudice, tradition, customary morality." Strongly influenced by Christian views, he frequently made use of Christian terminology to express his moral vision. In his account of human nature, he described man as a flawed creature—his fixed character mingled with both good and evil tendencies. Although capable of choosing to act virtuously, man possesses simultaneously a strong inherent tendency to do evil. Original Sin, or what Babbitt and More preferred to call the lower self, accounts for man's proclivity toward selfish, arbitrary, socially destructive behavior.[2] The immutable flawed character of man is the chief obstacle to utopian reformers who seek to perfect man by altering external social institutions.

Central to Kirk's ethical teaching is the concept of ethical dualism in which man's moral predicament is understood in terms of two contrary potentialities within his soul—what Babbitt and More described as the opposition of his higher and lower self. The higher self refers to that aspect of our being which pulls us in the direction of our true humanity, or ultimate spiritual purpose—"towards the realization of our highest potential as defined by a universally valid standard."[3] As Leander observed, the "higher will is a quality of will which wills itself." It "wills its own perpetuation, its continued existence as an end in itself, as the very *telos* of human life, and all other aspects of life are viewed as means of its continued existence."[4] It constitutes our will to goodness. The lower self, on the other hand, refers to that aspect of our being, our animal self, distinguished by selfish, self-indulgent, temperamental, arbitrary desires. We are pulled constantly between these two simultaneously existing potentialities.

This inner duality means that we exist in effect in two worlds. We experience as an immediate datum of consciousness a dialectical tension between order and disorder, the "One and the Many," permanence and flux, the universal and the particular, or as Babbitt expressed, this "paradox of dualism"—"*a oneness that is always changing.*"[5] Because of our dualistic natures, we need not be merely creatures propelled along helplessly by our undisciplined desires. We can pull ourselves in a contrary direction by structuring our impulses to accord with the governing power of a transcendent good. As More described the moral dimension of this tension at the core of existence in his "Definitions of Dualism," there exists, on the one hand, the "sum of desires and impressions we call the self-moving incessant flux." On the other hand, beside "the flux of life there is also that within man which displays itself

2. Kirk, *The Conservative Mind,* 39; Kirk, *A Program for Conservatives,* 4, 41.
3. Claes Ryn, *Democracy and the Ethical Life: A Philosophy of Politics and Community,* 58, 62.
4. Leander, *The Inner Check,* 3.
5. Irving Babbitt, *Rousseau and Romanticism,* 7 (emphasis added).

intermittently as an inhibition upon this or that impulse, preventing its prolongation in activity, and making a pause or eddy, so to speak, in the stream. This negation of the flux we call the inner check. It is not the mere blocking of one impulse by another, which is a quality of the confusion of the flux itself, but a restraint upon the flux exercised by a force contrary to it."[6]

The moral life, understood in these terms, requires us to be unceasingly vigilant in resisting the temptation to surrender to the impulses of the moment by exercising our higher will. In relation to man's merely selfish inclinations, this exercise of a disciplining will is experienced as an inner check. This higher will becomes for the individual of virtuous character a directive sense of moral reassurance. When the individual experiences a series of impulses toward a particular object, this is called desire. If an ethically inspired person desires that which is not in accord with his ultimate spiritual purposes, then the will to refrain ("the inner check") will block him from satisfying that desire. By exercising this will, the individual blocks the influence of these "disturbing and thwarting impulses," bringing himself into conformity with his ultimate spiritual purposes.[7] This act of checking may involve considerable immediate pain since it may entail giving up satisfying a temptation of the moment. However, as Aristotle taught, genuine happiness is experienced when one brings his or her self into conformity with that which makes life meaningful in the long run. The truly happy man, as will be explained below, is one who lives his life in harmony with the ethical ultimate.

The inner check in one of its aspects is a moral inhibition that forces us to stop and think, eliciting a pause for deliberation, before resolving our will. This pause can be evoked by memories or religious symbols that, because of the presence of the higher will, have an ethical significance for us. For example, as Leander pointed out, a "boy may be restrained from doing mischief by the sudden memory of his mother, followed perhaps by memories of the Ten Commandments, the church, and Sunday school teacher, and so on." This does not mean, Leander added, "that memories and symbols . . . have their inspirational force in themselves: they are just like other ingredients in the stream that runs

6. Paul Elmer More, *The Drift of Romanticism,* vol. 8 of *Shelburne Essays,* 247–48.
7. More, *The Drift of Romanticism,* 274.

from the past toward the future. The flux remains uninfluenced by any moral force." These symbols and memories have acquired inspirational force only because a moral force governs the individual. Because the boy felt an immediate sense of the Good, his impulse to do mischief was checked by memories that had ethical significance for him.[8]

In his description of this faculty, Leander used an analogous example of an artist governed by his aesthetic inner check. The artist is guided in his work by an intuitive sense of beauty to which he surrenders his purely arbitrary whims. Likewise, in its ethical function, the moral inner check responds to our own intuitive sense of the moral universal.

> Every artist has his own sense of beauty as a guide in his creative work. Within him there is something to tell him: "No, not like that—not like that—that's it!" His sense of beauty finds its way by a series of eliminations, a series of esthetic "inner checks." Do these "inner checks" act at random? Does the artist decide arbitrarily when his sense of beauty should protest? No, evidently not. Every artist has surrendered his own sense of beauty; and in the very act of asserting his "freedom"; he would no longer be an artist. If he follows the directions of his sense of beauty step by step, a work of art will gradually emerge. When this creative process began, he had no idea of the final result but only followed by steps the inner guide which directed him, exactly the way a rider guides his horse: by using the reins. It almost seems that the artist had a deity above him, who knew the result beforehand and only leads him towards it. But the "spirit" that leads him is no transcendent personal being but his very self, his own sense of beauty. Our sense of beauty can be compared to a compass needle, which first has to oscillate in various directions before it finally comes to a halt. The oscillations must be eliminated before we can entirely depend upon our compass to find our way. In the same way the creative artist must patiently allow his sense of beauty plenty of time to achieve something and must not hurry along too quickly. By listening humbly he must find out the reactions of his own sense of beauty and he must not let his own self-will take the lead.

Leander added that if "we examine our sense of truth, the same description will be applicable."[9]

8. Leander, *Inner Check*, 6–10.
9. Leander, *Irving Babbitt and Benedetto Croce: The Philosophical Basis of the New Humanism in American Criticism,* 150.

The concept of the inner check hence obviously presupposes the existence of individual free will and responsibility. "Since the inner check is the same potentially in all men and differs only in effect as it acts or remains quiescent," More observed, "each man is certainly responsible for his character or lack of character."[10] Man's behavior, then, is not determined, as the naturalists believe, solely by external natural forces. Man can elect to drift with his momentary impulses, or he can exercise his will to refrain from acting on the promptings of his lower inclinations.

While "[i]ndividual morality is conduct controlled by the check," wrote More, "Social morality is conduct controlled by the external check of society."[11] Society plays an indispensable role in fostering the development of the moral nature of man. It has an interest in diminishing these lower destructive impulses (that is, the natural proclivity toward violence and selfishness), thereby enabling man to participate in the higher good that he potentially shares with the rest of humanity. A person's moral character is developed by his activity in those social groups in which he is a member, for example family, church, community, etc., through which he acquires concrete knowledge of the purpose and meaning of life. His higher disposition to live in accordance with universally accepted norms rather than to pursue merely selfish, momentary desires is thereby strengthened. Guided by a will that by its nature is good, man's natural inclination toward violence and partisanship is thereby disciplined by the moral authority of a transcendent good. To submit primarily to one's selfish impulses would mean a life of isolation and disharmony with others. A society composed merely of selfish, calculating egotists would not long survive. Their conflicting, irresolvable interests would quickly shatter social harmony. But a society where each is disciplined by the promptings of their higher will, which pulls all in the same direction, would be harmoniously united by their shared awareness of an ethical ultimate toward which all would feel commonly obligated to obey.[12]

10. More, *The Drift of Romanticism,* 284.
11. Ibid.
12. See chap. 6, and Ryn, *Democracy and the Ethical Life,* chap. 2, for a discussion of community as an ethical goal of society.

The Challenge of the "New Morality"

This philosophy of individual ethical restraint and the duality of human nature accords with the teachings of the Classical and Judeo-Christian tradition.[13] During the eighteenth and nineteenth centuries, though, Europe witnessed the emergence of various doctrines that challenged these older views of life and morality. Moral innovators strove to replace this emphasis on the inner life of the individual, man's intuitive awareness of an inner power of moral ordering, with an emphasis on something else—natural forces external to the individual's will, but believed to account for the totality of his actions. This denial of the reality of the duality of human nature represented for Babbitt a confusion between two laws which he held must remain discrete: The Law for Man and the Law for Thing. The naturalists, especially of the "Baconian" or utilitarian variety, as will be defined, treat man not as having a law of his own, but "as entirely subject to the same methods that have won for science such triumphs over phenomenal nature."[14]

Babbitt identified two categories of thinkers who fall within the naturalistic school of thought: the Rousseauists, who place their main emphasis upon the sentimental temperament of man, and the positivists and utilitarians, the origin of whose ideas he traced back to the positivistic doctrines of the Renaissance thinker Francis Bacon (1561–1626). The scientific naturalism of Bacon and the sentimental humanitarianism of Rousseau "represent between them," Babbitt maintained, "the main tendencies that are at present disintegrating the traditional disciplines, whether humanistic or religious."[15]

While the naturalists objected to the notion of an ethical ultimate and strove to describe man's behavior wholly in terms of the physical laws of nature, Babbitt held that the unique characteristic of man, which places him above the brutes, is his capacity to check his natural

---

13. Christianity posits as a fundamental principle the existence of an ineradicable tension within man's soul between two conflicting orientations. Social conflict is caused by man's spiritual disorder. Although he knows the good, his lusts and passions nevertheless tempt him to do evil. "So then, with the mind I myself serve the law of God," explained St. Paul, "but with the flesh the law of sin" (Romans 7:25).

14. Babbitt, *Literature and the American College,* 19–20; also see Babbitt, *Democracy and Leadership,* 3.

15. Babbitt, *Literature and the American College,* 24.

impulses and act in accordance with the promptings of higher will. Naturalistic doctrines, such as Marxism, pragmatism, behavioralism, Freudianism, and Social Darwinism, for example, explicitly reject the reality of the inner life, which Babbitt defined as the "recognition in some form or other of a force in man that moves in an opposite direction from the outer impressions and expansive desires that together make up his ordinary or temperamental self." Naturalism amounts to a denial of the insight of the Greeks that "man is the creature of two laws: he has an ordinary self of impulse and desire and a human self that is known practically as a power of control over impulse and desire." The law for man ceases to have significance, and scientific laws that explain the phenomenal world are considered sufficient explanations of man's actions. Having denied the existence of the inner self, the naturalists distort human nature, sensing only a part of the totality of the human experience (the outer phenomena).[16]

With the triumph of these naturalistic doctrines, a transformation in the first principles of moral thought occurred. A new dualism replaced the old, as evidenced in the writings of Rousseau. Man is basically good, proclaimed Rousseau, but corrupted by external social institutions and the environment. "The assertion of man's natural goodness is plainly something very fundamental in Rousseau," Babbitt observed, "but there is something still more fundamental and that is the shifting of dualism itself, the virtual denial of a struggle between good and evil in the breast of the individual." According to the Rousseauistic vision, the source of man's woe is that there once existed a natural man in a prepolitical state of nature into whom society, by way of its inhibiting restrictions ("Man is born free, but everywhere he is in chains"), introduced an artificial man. Artificial man is unhappy man, burdened with guilt and frustrations associated with society's moral strictures. He can escape the pain that society has inflicted on him only by letting himself flow with his natural, momentary impulses. Babbitt vividly describes the effect that this new morality has upon the quality of moral judgment: "The denial of the reality of the 'civil war in the cave' involves an entire transformation of the conscience. The conscience ceases to be a power that sits in judgment on the ordinary self and inhibits the

16. Babbitt, *Democracy and Leadership;* Babbitt, *Rousseau and Romanticism,* 26–27, 14.

impulses. It tends, so far as it is recognized at all, to become itself an instinct and an emotion . . . Conscience is ceasing to be an inner check on the impulses of the individual and becoming a moral sense, a sort of expansive instinct for doing good to others."[17]

The battle between good and evil is thus shifted from the individual to society. If man fails to live up to the potential of his natural goodness, to be the "beautiful soul" of the Rousseauistic vision, then it follows that society has "perverted" him. The responsibility for evil rests not with the individual but with society. The possibilities for moral reform do not come through the difficult, arduous, and often painful task of individual self-reformation, but only from the transformation of society as a whole. Rousseauistic moralists prefer the task of reforming others, uplifting mankind in a lump, to the Christian obligation of self-reform. Eager to point out moral defects in others and society, they are themselves strikingly lacking, Babbitt charged, in moral self-awareness: "Inasmuch as there is no conflict between good and evil in the breast of the beautiful soul, he is free to devote all his efforts to the improvement of mankind, and he proposes to achieve this great end by diffusing the spirit of brotherhood. All the traditional forms that stand in the way of this free emotional expansion he denounces as mere 'prejudices,' and inclines to look on those who administer these forms as a gang of conspirators who are imposing an arbitrary and artificial restraint on the natural goodness of man and so keeping it from manifesting itself." Unable to account adequately for the reality of evil and having denied the existence of man's dualistic nature, the Rousseauistic moralist can never really know the good. Yet he is driven by a humanitarian impulse to impose his conception of the good on others. This instinctive, expansive individual altruism replaces the inner check. Emancipated from society's allegedly arbitrary and artificial restraints, the result is not the "beautiful soul" of Rousseau's idyllic imagination, but the unleashing of all sorts of terrible and sometimes diabolic passions formerly restrained in the breasts of man by custom, habit, religious sanctions, etc. Ugly things "have a way of happening," Babbitt warned, "when impulse is . . . left uncontrolled." Barbarism and savagery is the inevitable result when the doctrines preached by the romantic emotionalist, celebrating the individual's expansive emotions dictated by

17. Babbitt, *Rousseau and Romanticism,* 111–12.

the "voice of nature," are encouraged. To make society the "universal scapegoat" while professing an uncritical faith in man's natural goodness is, according to Babbitt, "a constant encouragement to evade moral responsibility."[18]

The major emphasis of Bacon's thought, on the other hand, was toward a scientific positivism that set up "purely quantitative and dynamic standards of conduct." The intellectual descendant of Baconian positivism is utilitarianism. Denying the existence of any standard of conduct above that of individual feeling, the utilitarian system of thought is rooted in a hedonistic psychology. As John Stuart Mill wrote, the criterion of moral judgment for the utilitarian creed is based on the principle of utility, or the "Greatest Happiness Principle," which "holds that actions are right in proportion as they tend to promote happiness, wrong as they tend to produce the reverse of happiness. By happiness is intended pleasure, and the absence of pain; by unhappiness, pain, and the privation of pleasure." Pleasure and freedom from pain "are the only things desirable as ends." All "desirable things . . . are desirable either for the pleasure inherent in themselves, or as means to the promotion of pleasure and the prevention of pain." The *summum bonum,* therefore, of the utilitarian is the pleasure of the individual. The ultimate sanction of utilitarian morality is the "subjective feeling in our own minds," with the final consequence that society is left with no standards whatsoever to resolve conflicts between various competing interests—save perhaps that of the will of the strongest. According to James Fitzjames Stephen, a Victorian critic of Mill's utilitarianism, utilitarianism "proposes no external standard to which disputants can appeal, and its adoption would involve as a necessary consequence the hopeless perpetuation of all moral controversies."[19]

Responding to the criticism that utilitarian morality would result in moral nihilism and social anarchy, Mill answered by proposing that education could inculcate into the minds of citizens a "moral sense," defined as a feeling of concern for the well-being of others. This "moral sense" amounts to a sophisticated egotism or enlightened self-interest. Through education, citizens would acquire a sense of unity whereby

18. Ibid., 115–16, 128–29.
19. Ibid., 27; John Stuart Mill, *Utilitarianism, Liberty and Representative Government,* 8, 14, 35; James Fitzjames Stephen, *Liberty, Equality, Fraternity,* 347.

they would come to rationally prefer to act in harmony than to pursue preferences at odds with the general happiness. The feelings of unity and harmony with our fellow creatures would become, Mill predicted, "as deeply rooted in our character, and to our own consciousness as completely a part of our nature, as the horror of crime is in an ordinarily well brought up young person."[20]

The proponent of enlightened self-interest places his faith in the capacity of the rational individual to apprehend the undeniable truth that cooperation, order, and harmony are preferable to social anarchy. Therefore, from a purely selfish point of view, he realizes that an ordered society, based on rule of law, agreed upon rules, and mutual cooperation, is preferable to ruthless interminable conflict in which the condition of everyone's life would be indisputably worse. Purely rational self-interest, then, is all that is necessary to control man's immoderate and social-disruptive desires.

Claes Ryn, a Catholic University of America professor of politics who has written extensively on Babbitt and the New Humanism, contends that the faith in the capacity of rational self-interest alone to ethically govern conduct is rooted in a flawed understanding of human nature. When men lose sight of an ethical ultimate that transcends private advantage, "their enlightened self-interest, too, will be increasingly difficult to discern. As their ethical vision is blurred, there is less to restrain their cruder inclinations. Men will become more indiscriminate in their choice of ends and means." Enlightened self-interest alone is an insufficient check upon the wolfish appetites of man. A sense of sympathy for the feelings and interests of others provides a weak antidote to self-serving impulses. More warned that the moral sentiment of sympathy, "when put to the test, becomes a mere veneer upon the law of absolute self-interest." The recognition of a transcendent good has the power of pulling one away from purely arbitrary selfish desires. When its existence is in question, the tendency will be for one to look to one's immediate self-interest, and as Ryn points out, "to look at the laws with less reverence and not be as predisposed against breaking them."[21]

20. Mill, *Utilitarianism,* 33.
21. Ryn, *Democracy and the Ethical Life,* 25; Paul Elmer More, *On Being Human,* 149.

Of the two major schools of naturalism that challenge ethical dualism (that is, the romantic humanitarianism of Rousseau and the utilitarian rationalism of Jeremy Bentham and John Stuart Mill), Kirk attacked more fiercely the doctrines of utilitarianism manifest in modern ideological movements. Even though Kirk's antipathy toward Rousseauistic morality is certainly no less than Babbitt's, the reason that the bulk of his literary ammunition was directed at those doctrines he perceived as primarily utilitarian in inspiration no doubt resulted from his conviction that the emotional romanticism of Rousseau has either largely lost its force in an age where utility has become the basis of politics and morality, or has been absorbed by utilitarian ideas. Another possibility could be that he considered Rousseauism less of a threat to the intellect and moral understanding than utilitarianism because, at least, some sort of imagination inspires it, albeit of the flawed, idyllic type.

The mind of the utilitarian, defective in understanding of morality and the realities of human nature, charged Kirk, is always on the level of the merely useful. Utilitarians deny the existence of an ethical ultimate and exalt private rationality. Like Rousseau, they are oblivious to the darker side of man, his proclivity toward violence and sin. For them, man is simply a creature rationally striving to increase his pleasures and diminish his pain. They profess no sense of warmth for others or a sense of consecration for the virtuous, noble, or sacred. The motive for the utilitarian is not love, the "object of civil social existence, and the one reality which makes life worth living," but mere utility. Because of the influence of utilitarian doctrines upon American ideas, Kirk warned that presently "we Americans are in danger of neglecting the profound reasons of the heart, and so condemning ourselves either to the sterile existence of private aggrandizement, or to the internal and external anarchy which commonly follows close upon the divorce of the heart from the mind." Modern man is thus ultimately left defenseless against "the hard knot of special interests."[22] As a result of the failure of the utilitarian to recognize what lies above subjective interests, he ultimately lacks any principle except the resolutions of the marketplace or

22. Kirk, *A Program for Conservatives,* 82, 56; Kirk, "The Unbought Grace of Life," 19; Kirk, *The Conservative Mind,* 250; Kirk, *The Roots of American Order,* 28.

mere majoritarianism for discriminating between the competing claims of self-serving interests.

In conclusion, man possesses, Kirk believed, a mysterious faculty of moral perception that permits him to escape from this moral solipsism. Through the moral imagination, as he called this faculty, man can perceive a moral order larger than his present circumstances or private experiences. The ethical role of imagination and its relationship to the concepts of ethical dualism and the inner check form the subject of the next chapter.

3 THE MORAL IMAGINATION, REASON, AND THE NATURAL LAW

> *[T]his distrust of human nature is closely connected with another and more positive factor of conservatism—its trust in the controlling power of the imagination.*
>
> —Paul Elmer More, *Aristocracy and Justice*

THE ROLE OF LITERATURE and humane letters in reawakening the normative consciousness grew integral to Kirk's social and moral thought by the 1960s. His work began to exhibit an evolving appreciation of the "moral imagination" and its significance apropos of revival of reflective conservative thought. No doubt his growing interest in the moral principles of T. S. Eliot opened this avenue to him. Kirk's ethico-aesthetical approach first played a central role in his literary and social criticism in *Enemies of the Permanent Things* (1969), and would become his most distinctive and enduring contribution to modern conservative thought.

Kirk described the moral imagination as "that power of ethical perception which strides beyond the barriers of private experience and events of the moment," especially "the higher form of this power exercised in poetry and art." A uniquely human faculty, not shared with the lower forms of life, the moral imagination comprises "man's power to perceive ethical truth, abiding law, in the seeming chaos of many events." Without "the moral imagination, man would live merely from day to day, or rather moment to moment, as dogs do. It is the strange faculty—inexplicable if men are assumed to have an animal nature only—of discerning greatness, justice, and order, beyond the bars of appetite and self-interest."[1] In any civilized society, the moral imagination reigns

---

1. Russell Kirk, *Eliot and His Age: T. S. Eliot's Moral Imagination in the Twentieth Century*, 7–8; Kirk, *Enemies of the Permanent Things*, 119.

supreme. When it functions in an impaired manner or ceases to function altogether, communication between generations becomes difficult and distorted views of human nature arise and moral character erodes. The result is moral decadence throughout society.

As noted in the previous chapter, Kirk's social and political thought presupposes the reality of ethical universals beyond the economic calculus of private advantage. The most important guide to living in accord with these universals is the imaginative absorption of the totality of man's experience. Man possesses a higher self, of which the imagination is a part, that allows him to apprehend intuitively that which is the source of his enduring good and happiness. This awareness of the ultimate good common to all mankind forms the basis of the final end of politics, namely, genuine community. Kirk insisted that personal experience and individual rationality, whether separately or in combination, cannot account for the most important things in life. It is the nonconceptual and nondefinitional power of the moral imagination, not the faculty of reason, that gives rise to the ultimate norms by which the soul and commonwealth are ordered.

Donald Atwell Zoll was the first of Kirk's critics to recognize in print the central importance of the moral imagination and its aesthetic components to his thought. "The roots of conservatism, as seen in *The Conservative Mind*," Zoll noted in a lengthy essay examining Kirk's social and political thought, "are to be found in high humanism, a release of what Burke called the 'moral imagination.'" More than Kirk's previous critics, Zoll understood that Kirk's pronounced aesthetic orientation was not a literary affectation but rather an integral part of his social and cultural criticism. The "heart of his social philosophy is ultimately aesthetic," Zoll explained. Kirk's "historical commentary, quite apart from his literary criticism shows that his basic judgmental criterion is an aesthetic one; those whom he admires most in the history of social thought are those imbued with an intense aesthetic orientation and a corresponding artistic talent."[2] Zoll recognized that central to Kirk's social and political commentary was the conviction that ethical and normative truths are often best conveyed through a symbolic veil, as found, for example, in the medium of great poetry, rather than by the

2. Zoll, "The Social Thought of Russell Kirk," 112–13, 121.

means of discursive explication. Regrettably, Zoll only briefly mentioned the moral imagination and failed to examine its importance to Kirk's ethical position as an alternative to the narrow abstract reasoning of the utilitarians of both the Left and the Right.

The present chapter goes beyond Zoll's study by clarifying the concept of the moral imagination and demonstrating its central importance to Kirk's moral and social thought. To these ends, I draw upon Burke, who coined the phrase "moral imagination"; Babbitt, who raised it to a conceptual level; and Leander, who borrowed from Burke and Babbitt to further develop it. Various intellectual threads come together in this chapter's six sections. The first section examines the definition and application of the moral imagination in Kirk's work. The second describes its original use by Burke and later development by Babbitt. In the third section, I analyze the relative roles of "reason" and "intuition" in Kirk's moral thought. The fourth section distinguishes between the moral imagination and the natural-law tradition and demonstrates why the ontological basis of Kirk's moral position precluded him from fitting comfortably within the natural-law tradition. The final section of this chapter explores different aspects of utilitarianism's baleful effect on the moral imagination's wellspring. Here I explicate Kirk's critique of the morally and socially corrosive consequences of the "rationalism" typified by ideologies of both the Left and the Right and examine his critique of the scientistic utilitarian reasoning employed by the behavioralist movement in the social sciences.

THE ROLE OF THE MORAL IMAGINATION IN KIRK'S THOUGHT

The moral imagination forms the core of Kirk's ethical teaching. While one may argue that he did not significantly expand Babbitt's theory of the moral imagination, Kirk did apply the principle in an innovative fashion to counter the pseudoscientific formulations of contemporary ideologues, for example, the neo-Benthamite libertarians, the social engineers, and the behavioralists. Kirk further recognized its importance to the revival of an enduring conservatism in an age of "Mass, Speed, and Whirl" when the very sources of imaginative inspiration were withering. If conservatism were to become an enduring intellectual, moral, and political force against the discordant impulses of our age, Kirk consistently stressed, it would have to be rooted in a faith in the power of imagination to control man's lower impulses.[3]

This faculty of ethical perception makes use of such resources as historical studies, humane letters, fable, myth, and religion. The work of a gifted historian, for example, proves imaginatively stimulating and morally salutary because the historian has fashioned intuitive ethical universals out of the myriad, fragmentary historical facts he has examined. Ethical universals embody truths about human nature from which we derive self-knowledge about our potentialities and limitations. The imagination further enables us to escape from the confining limits of our personal experience to become conscious of what is beyond ourselves. By perceiving what we hold in common with others, or imaginatively seeing things from the perspective of others unlike ourselves, we become aware of ourselves as members of a community. "Through the moral imagination, one may escape from the pit of solipsism." The "moral order is perceived to be something larger than the circumstances of one's time or one's private experience; one becomes aware of membership in a community of souls; one learns that consciousness and rationality did not commence with one's self or with one's contemporaries." Further, the imaginative faculty enables us to regain order in our souls as we become aware of our personal failings of "concupiscence, error, and ennui . . . including the sins of omissions," an awareness of which "the average sensual man is spared."[4]

Kirk likened the moral imagination to John Henry Cardinal Newman's concept of "Illative Sense," as set forth in Newman's *The Grammar of Assent.* From our Illative Sense, Newman believed, come the ultimate values that govern our lives. Newman called this faculty of intuitive reasoning the power of "judging and concluding." Since, as Newman knew, the Illative Sense is not infallible, its assumptions must be corrected by reference to the authority of conscience, the Bible, the church, ancient customs, ethical truths, historical memories, old maxims, proverbs, legal saws, etc. Our moral sense, Kirk explained, is "constituted by impressions that are borne in upon us, from a source deeper

3. Kirk, *Confessions of a Bohemian Tory,* 208; Paul Elmer More, "Disraeli and Conservatism" and "Natural Aristocracy," essays in *Aristocracy and Justice,* vol. 9 of *Shelbourne Essays.* More's writings strengthened Kirk's appreciation of the concept of the moral imagination.
4. Kirk, *Eliot and His Age,* 45–47, 172.

than our conscious and formal reason. It is the combined product of intuition, instinct, imagination, and long and intricate experience."[5]

Kirk placed perhaps his strongest emphasis on history as a source of imaginative insight and self-knowledge. History is, after all, the record of human experience from which we gain insights into the divine design and human nature. From the study of history we can learn "about the significance of human existence: about the splendor and the misery of our condition." The role of the historian is especially important nowadays. Because "historical studies may become the principal literary form and way to wisdom in the dawning age," Kirk predicted, the historian might well "supplant the novelist as culture's guardian." The historian's profession, in Kirk's estimation, is charged with a special responsibility to be "engaged in a labor of moral imagination." The great weight, which Kirk accorded to the importance of historical studies, does not imply that he would have subscribed to the notion, such as found in Hegel or Marx, that the process of historical events can be predetermined. He specifically rejected the doctrine of historical determinism as a violation of two basic Christian principles: free will and Providence. A so-called scientific knowledge of history cannot "enable people to predict tomorrow's events or the next century's events. Yet a knowledge of human nature derived from historical thinking may enable a talented historian, or indeed any person well schooled historically, to foresee with reasonable prospect of fulfillment the consequences of certain tendencies of courses of action—supposing, always, that such tendencies or courses are not interrupted or diverted by other influences (whether contrived or seemingly happenstance)." Seen from a genuinely historical perspective, the nature of man cannot be reduced to the simple pseudo-scientific assertions of the positivists or the historic determinists, who view man as a passive creature governed by phenomenal forces.

The great literary works of a civilization likewise powerfully contribute to the healthy arousal of the imagination. The poetic consciousness reveals "moral insights which are sources of human normality, and which make possible order and justice and freedom." The influence of great literature makes possible the linking of one generation to another. Literature "is the breath of society, transmitting to successive rising generations, century upon century, a body of ethical principles and crit-

5. Kirk, *The Conservative Mind*, 285. See also Kirk, *Eliot and His Age*, 47.

ical standards and imaginative creations that constitutes a kind of collective intellect of humanity, the formalized wisdom of our ancestors."
The impact of poets of great imaginative powers far surpasses and
endures, Kirk insisted, beyond that of ordinary statesmen, "No less than
politicians do great poets move nations, even though the generality of
men may not know the poets' names. When the chief poet and critic of
the age sets his hand to 'redeeming the time: so that Faith may be preserved alive through the dark ages before us; to renew and rebuild civilization, and save the World from suicide'—why, it is possible that he
may undo Marx and Freud, not to mention captains and kings."[6]

Kirk would likewise have endorsed Peter Viereck's observation that
great literature provides a powerful antidote to collectivist ideologies.
Although Kirk accused Viereck of having commended spontaneity, orig-
inality, and eccentricity to the detriment of norms,[7] they agreed that the
moral inspiration of great literature nurtures a sense of individual self-
awareness and worth that the "blueprint mentality" of the ideologist
cannot understand. Elaborating on the impact of great literature, Viereck
wrote, "There is no intellectual gesture, no matter how intimate, which
is not by implication a moral and political act. The Soviets recognize
this in reverse. They condemn the lyric poetry of Akhmatova and Paster-
nak for the crime of expressing emotions of private love and loneli-
ness. These emotions are presented as a thorn in the side of a collectivist utopia. From their viewpoint, the Soviets are right in resenting
and hating this. Whatever expresses ethics, beauty, and love with genuine human individuality is thereby a blow against tyrants (whether
communists, fascists, or domestic American thought-controllers). For
it aspires beyond the propagandistic, the expedient, and the temporary
to the true and lasting aspect of things."[8]

The poet, moreover, possesses the power to alter the social consciousness of an age. Among the great poets of the present century who have
contributed to normative consciousness, Kirk cited Frost, Faulkner,
Waugh, and Yeats. He singled out Eliot, though, as the "principal cham-

---

6. Kirk, "Returning Humanity to History: The Example of John Lukacs," 24–
27; Kirk, "History and the Moral Imagination," 352; See also Kirk, *Redeeming
the Time,* 102. Kirk, *Eliot and His Age,* 8; Kirk, *Enemies of the Permanent Things,*
68; Kirk, *The Conservative Mind,* 495–96.
7. Kirk, *Enemies of the Permanent Things,* 23.
8. Peter Viereck, *Dream and Responsibility,* 42–43.

pion of the moral imagination in the twentieth century." Through Eliot's poetic imagination, Kirk saw the present age as acquiring a revived awareness of "the permanent things"—those norms indispensable to a humane order but presently threatened by the onrush of modernity.[9]

Myth, fable, allegory, parable, and fantasy are poetic instruments to arouse our imagination by bringing us back to the central concerns of life. They "are not falsehoods," Kirk assured us; "on the contrary, they are means for penetrating to the truth by appealing to the moral imagination." A myth "is the symbolic representation of reality" in which the teller attempts to explain "the operation of natural forces and the events of history as the work of supernatural or living beings." Far from being false, "the great and ancient myths are profoundly true," because if they did not in some way reflect on our vices and virtues, they would not interest us. The great myths of a civilization which are "religious in origin and purpose," then, teach us the ethical concerns of our existence, foster a sense of veneration for long-established institutions, and provide a body of common experience that ties a people closer together. Fantasy represents things "strangely, so as to rouse our wonder; yet the shock of the fantastic is intended to wake us from dullness and complacency. That is precisely what the modern creators of fable, allegory, and parable are doing with some success. They show us the norms for man and society through conjuring up fanciful episodes in which virtues and vices glimmer as in a looking glass."[10] The influence of myth and fantasy, according to Kirk, cannot be escaped. Political and religious movements activate their followers more through their visionary aspects than by reasoned argument. In this sense, imagination, not reason, governs the world.

Dogmas, authority, rituals, and the symbols of religion, finally, are perhaps the primary means by which civilizations transmit truths basic to the social and moral order. Without the strong authority of the religion, Kirk claimed, most individuals would be left with unrestrained appetites. Religion's "chief benefit," observed Kirk, "is the ordering of

9. Kirk, *Eliot and His Age,* 7–9.

10. Ibid., 81; Kirk, *Beyond the Dreams of Avarice: Essays of a Social Critic,* 32; Kirk, *Enemies of the Permanent Things,* 111–12. See also Vigen Guroian's excellent essay in which he examines the importance of using fairy tales and fantasy stories to awaken the moral imagination in young people. Vigen Guroian, "Awakening the Moral Imagination: Teaching Virtues through Fairy Tales," 3–13.

the soul—that is, the subordination of one's life and appetites to divine will, and the harmonious arrangement of mind and conscience which produces the genuinely humane person." This conviction explains in great part his conversion in 1964 to the Catholic Church. "The greatest power for order the world has ever known," he affirmed, "is the Catholic Church."[11]

THE CONTRIBUTIONS OF BURKE AND BABBITT

As Kirk noted, the principle of the moral imagination was "first clearly expressed by Edmund Burke." Indeed, although Plato, Virgil, St. Augustine, Dante, and T. S. Eliot implicitly recognized the moral imagination, Burke is rightly credited with having coined the phrase. He intuitively grasped its central importance as a means of ethical insight. However, it was Babbitt and More who raised this intuition to the level of a philosophical concept that they wielded against the incomplete accounts of man's nature and experiences found in positivism and naturalism. As Kirk rightly pointed out, the idea was "adapted by More and Babbitt to the twentieth-century discussion."[12]

Burke had invoked the moral imagination to defend the traditional moral and social order of Europe against the challenge posed by the contemporaries and disciples of Rousseau—the philosophes and the revolutionary Jacobins—whom he contemptuously dismissed as "sophisters, oeconomists, and calculators." He praised England for her resistance to these moral innovators. "We are not the converts of Rousseau; we are not the disciples of Voltaire," roared Burke. "Helvetius has made no progress amongst us. Atheists are not our preachers; madmen are not our lawgivers. We know that *we* have made no discoveries, and we think that no discoveries are to be made, in morality; nor many in the great principles of government, nor in the ideas of liberty, which were understood long before we were born, altogether as well as they will be after the grave has heaped its mould upon our presumption, and the silent tomb shall have imposed its law on our pert loquacity."[13]

11. Kirk, *Confessions of a Bohemian Tory;* 208; Christine Richert, "Russell Kirk Surveys Catholic Church," 3; also see Russell Kirk, "Influence of Religion on Contemporary Society," in *Great,* 3–14.

12. Kirk, foreword to *The Inner Check: A Concept of Paul Elmer More with Reference to Benedetto Croce,* iii.

13. Burke, *Reflections on the Revolution,* 169, 181 (Burke's emphasis).

Burke condemned as a "barbarous philosophy" the rational skepticism of the radicals, who scoffed at the public's veneration of long-established institutions and customs. The doctrines of French philosophes struck Burke as a challenge to Western civilization of unprecedented proportions. Everything that was admirable and generous in the European culture depended upon the existence of the spirit of religion and the spirit of the gentleman. With the radical French thinkers, Burke believed, there had arisen a new speculative rationalism that "detests piety, manners, the traditional morality, and all the ancient usages."[14] The old supports of civilized order were to be rudely torn away by the "armed doctrines" of the Jacobins. Everything would be judged, Burke predicted, in accordance with the abstract speculative reasoning of the radical innovators and, if found wanting, would be contemptuously destroyed. The consequences of the loss of prescriptive institutions and inherited traditions for a well-ordered society would be, in his opinion, incalculable. Long-established institutions evoke a natural affection from the mass of men, he held, and once destroyed, would have their place taken by grudging compliance with brute force. Civilized existence requires imagery and illusion to enrich our lives in community:

> But now all is to be changed. All the pleasing illusions, which made power gentle and obedience liberal, which harmonized the different shades of life, and which, by a bland assimilation, incorporated into politics the sentiments which beautify and soften private society, are to be dissolved by this new conquering empire of light and reason. All the decent drapery of life is to be rudely torn off. All the superadded ideas, furnished from the wardrobe of a moral imagination, which the heart owns, and the understanding ratifies, as necessary to cover the defects of our naked, shivering nature, and to raise it to dignity in our own estimation, are to be exploded as a ridiculous, absurd, and antiquated fashion.[15]

By "evoking images," Kirk explained, "Burke sought to persuade by his appeal to the moral imagination—not by setting his own abstractions against the abstractions of the philosophes."[16] Burke recognized

14. Kirk, *Edmund Burke: A Genius Reconsidered,* 164.
15. Burke, *Reflections on the Revolution,* 170–71. Although Burke's political thought is certainly a labor of the moral imagination, he never developed this idea as a concept. This quotation contains the only mention of the phrase in his entire work.
16. Kirk, *Edmund Burke,* 159.

that man is born into a social context in which past, present, and future cannot be separated. History then is a guide to the moral imagination. The imagination can seize upon multiple climactic episodes in history, episodes of struggle to attain man's highest moral purpose, to merge them into a compelling image. We are thus able to draw from our historical experience a vast body of wisdom that provides us with insight and standards. The more comprehensive our grasp of history, the more we will understand the present as mirrored by our history in which the limitations and potentialities of human nature are constant.

No previous student of Burke had grasped as well as Irving Babbitt the critical importance of moral imagination for his political thought. Babbitt believed that Burke saw, perhaps better than anyone else of his era, how much of "the wisdom of life consists in an imaginative assumption of the experience of the past in such a fashion as to bring it to bear as a living force upon the present." Man's private stock of wisdom and experience, contrary to the notions of the rationalists who possess an unbounded faith in the rational faculties of the individual, is an insufficient basis on which man can morally order his existence. By giving a generous respect to the "wisdom of our ancestors"—that collective wisdom of the ages bound up in great literary works, sayings, axioms, morals, and customs—man will have at his disposal, Babbitt argued, a considerable body of experience upon which he can imaginatively draw for moral guides amidst the changing circumstances of his existence. The civilized man can defend prejudice, habit, and custom because "they are not arbitrary but are convenient summings up of a vast body of past experiences."[17]

Babbitt conceptualized the idea of the imagination as a check on the lower impulses. Against the utilitarian imagination, which is incapable of rising above the here and now, and the idyllic imagination of the Rousseauist, which evades the moral conflict in man and leaves the appetites unchecked, Babbitt proposed an ethical imagination disciplined by the veto power of the inner check over the arbitrary will of man. The inner check, as the awareness of a universal good that cannot be violated, inspires man's moral imagination to bring forth concrete images of his true purpose.

17. Babbitt, *Democracy and Leadership,* 103, 109.

Babbitt maintained that the imagination is both necessary and, when properly disciplined, good. Only through imagination can man come to perceive what is abiding in his existence. The perception of ethical norms in an imaginative vision is indispensable to civilization. From these norms derive laws, standards of justice, customs, and other moral beliefs that bind people into community. Central to this ethical stance is a dualistic interpretation of human nature according to which the soul has two opposing wills, the baser of which the inner check censures to mitigate its selfish, arbitrary impulses that, if left unchecked, would insinuate disharmony into the soul and the commonwealth. Man must "do an inner obeisance to something higher than his ordinary self, whether he calls this something God, or, like the man of the Far East, calls it his higher Self, or simply the Law. Without this inner principle of restraint man can only oscillate violently between the opposite extremes" of anarchical individualism and utopian collectivism. The moral imagination, then, draws man back to the "ethical centre," or what Kirk would later call the "permanent things," which supplies a "standard with reference to which the individual may set bounds to the lawless expansion of his natural self (which includes his intellect as well as his emotions)."[18]

REASON, INTUITION, AND THE MORAL IMAGINATION

The weight that Kirk gave to the role of imagination as the primary means by which we gain insight into the human condition and knowledge of transcendent norms left him open to the charge that he unduly deprecated reason. Willmoore Kendall (1909–1967), an important figure in the postwar conservative intellectual moment, pointed to apparent contradictions in Kirk's teaching regarding "where his conservatives stand with regard to *reason.*" While Kirk condemned "narrow rationality," he elsewhere called upon conservatives to "distrust" reason itself, Kendall claimed, only to reverse himself again by declaring that "reason" rather than emotion should govern human affairs because reason is "a *good* thing presumably because reason *is* to be trusted." Frank S. Meyer, a former Communist who moved to the Right and became a

18. Babbitt, *Literature and the American College,* 40–41; Babbitt, *Democracy and Leadership,* 109.

senior editor at *National Review,* alleged that one of the chief weaknesses of Kirk was his "refusal to recognize the role of reason" as a means to distinguish between moral possibilities. Ronald Lora complained that Kirk contradicted himself because he "continues to attack the presumed rationality—the 'metaphysic sophistry'—of contemporary liberals while at the same time noting that man no longer has the capacity for rational decision-making." James F. Pontuso, after making similar objections about Kirk's "depreciation of the human faculty of reason," accused him of being "a historicist" because, by abandoning "theory altogether," he "leaves us with little choice but to throw ourselves into the arms of historical inevitability."[19]

Kirk's apparent hostility to reason and his readiness to rely upon intuition made him an easy target for such criticism. Indeed, he was clearly skeptical of the power of intellectual analysis alone to determine right from wrong or to provide a basis for the good life. The norms that should govern our lives are conveyed to us more reliably, Kirk maintained, through the accumulated wisdom of our ancestors, the lessons of history, prescriptive institutions, religious dogmas, and the visions of poets.

In spite of his strong reliance on intuition as a surer guide to ultimate values, Kirk did not disparage reason per se. The target of his criticism was a particular type or quality of reason or, one may say, the misuse of reasoning he called "defecated rationality." This infelicitous phrase alludes to a type of reason that, as a result of its boundless faith in the intellect and in benevolent progress, is "arrogantly severed from larger sources of wisdom," such as tradition, customs, religious faith, and the visions of great poets, prophets, and philosophers.[20] Kirk's ani-

19. Willmoore Kendall, "The Benevolent Sage of Mecosta," in *Willmore Kendall: Contra Mundum,* 32–33 (Kendall's emphasis). Kirk's meaning in the passages cited by Kendall is not as confusing as Kendall claimed. Kendall misrepresented Kirk's understanding of the role of reason by failing to clarify what Kirk meant by "narrow rationality" and by suggesting that Kirk even believed that reason alone could be a sufficient check in the absence of other factors on man's "anarchic impulse." See Kirk, *The Conservative Mind,* 8–9. Frank S. Meyer, *In Defense of Freedom: A Conservative Credo,* 44; Ronald Lora, *Conservative Minds in America,* 182; James F. Pontuso, "Russell Kirk: The Conservatism of Tradition," 42.

20. Kirk, *Eliot and His Age,* 45.

madversions against reason are thus reserved for the formal and abstract notions of logic found in positivistic and pragmatic rationality.

The British philosopher Michael Oakeshott, in one of his most enduring contributions to modern philosophy, took an equally harsh view of what he described as "the most remarkable intellectual fashion of post-Renaissance Europe," namely, "modern Rationalism." The distinguishing attribute of modern Rationalism is the tendency of its adherents to regard themselves as enemies of authority, prejudice, tradition, custom, and habit. The Rationalist is relentlessly skeptical of all opinions and beliefs and confidently optimistic that all social problems and moral differences of opinion can be eventually resolved by the power of reason. Utilitarianism, Marxism, and socialism are examples of modern ideologies that purport to have discovered through rational cogitation the laws of behavior that account for all of man's actions. From these laws Rationalists derive their schemes and policies for perfecting man and society. Left out of their calculations, though, are the truths of man's inner life, that is, the inner check and his dual nature, which, although they constitute a part of the universal experience of mankind, as Babbitt pointed out, "are not clear in the logical or any other sense. These truths are rather a matter of elusive intuition."[21]

Intuition is that faculty which enables us to perceive truths without logical proofs. It represented, for Kirk, certain insights or "leaps of being" which men of special, remarkable vision possess. In our age, Kirk believed that poets are especially endowed with the power to intuit truths by which man may come "to redeem the time." Poetry "rouses the imagination and shapes our ends." By means of the poets' vision, such as that of Virgil, Dante, and Eliot, we gain knowledge of ourselves (our limits and potentialities) and of the realities of the world. The mental images that poets evoke allow us to perceive in a prelogical manner the norms that should govern our existences.[22]

Kirk's most extensive discussion of the distinction between "abstract reasoning" of the Benthamite variety and the genuine conservative's "intuitive reasoning" is found in his summary of Samuel Taylor Cole-

---

21. Michael Oakeshott, *Rationalism in Politics,* 1; Babbitt, *Democracy and Leadership,* 322.
22. Kirk, *Eliot and His Age,* 141, 149–50.

ridge's views. Whereas Jeremy Bentham "believed that certitudes may be secured by scientific analysis and statistical methods," Coleridge denied "that truth could ever be settled on abstract grounds." Truths that are concerned with our ultimate ends, Coleridge believed, require us to employ our powers of faith and intuition, "the organ of the supersenuous." When a civilization opts for the supremacy of abstract reason as opposed to reason illuminated by intuition, Kirk added, it will "lose any standard for determining what is good and what is bad, and therefore cannot possibly know how to do good to people, or how to seek their own good."[23]

The most important things in life, that is, knowledge of our ultimate spiritual ends and moral principles, cannot be apprehended by the intellect alone. In moral epistemology, reason's role is subordinate to that of intuition. Reason can play the modest role of helping us determine the most efficient and economic means for reaching or avoiding a particular end, and predicting what the likely consequences of a decision would be. But it is incapable, by its very nature, of ascertaining whether any end has moral value. Ethical action originates in a certain orientation of will, not in the intellect as many wrongly presume. Before acting, a person is inspired by his higher will and has a vision of what life ought to be. After this precognitive experience of the good, drawing upon the widest possible experience available to him, he censures those impulses that stir a moral uneasiness within him; he simultaneously permits those intentions that conform to his higher will to flow into action. Whether the anticipated act will bring him enduring happiness and satisfaction will be the question guiding his moral deliberation. Since intuition, like other human faculties, is fallible, the authority of faith, ancient wisdom, and long-established customs must discipline it. Moral universals do not exist in some abstract sense, outside of human experience, to be apprehended by intellectual prowess; rather, they come to life in acts of ethical will. Our reason raises intuitions of the good into conceptual awareness by which they can be articulated and explained. But reason is always a product of a particular volitional orientation. For a person of hedonistic orientation, for example, reason is his ally in the pursuit of pleasure. His imagination, corrupted by

23. Kirk, *The Conservative Mind,* 134–35, 137–38.

a pleasure-seeking will, draws him deeper into an illusionary vision of reality.[24]

Because Kirk's interests were literary and historical rather than narrowly philosophical, he never developed a rigorous epistemological base for his social and moral thought. While this omission is not an insuperable obstacle to grasping and appreciating his moral insights, it makes for certain difficulties in the critical understanding and acceptance of his work. For example, Zoll has commented on Kirk's "lack of philosophical precision." Zoll found himself, more than once, "agreeing with Kirk's judgments but often feeling that he was supporting them with second-best evidence." Kirk's speculations would benefit, Zoll suggested, "from an amplified philosophical rigor."[25]

The strong emphasis that Kirk placed on intuition, in preference to reason, as a sanction for moral truths strongly suggests that he had fallen victim to the same weakness in explicating his ethical positions that Claes Ryn detected in Babbitt. Abstract, pragmatic types of reasoning, characterized by an exaggerated notion of their ability to understand life and an inability to account for the facts of moral experience, have fostered moral confusion. Although Kirk was convincing in his analysis of reason's limitations, he failed to provide a logic for systematically discussing his preferred alternative to reason, namely, intuitions of "the permanent things." Like Babbitt, he was not fully aware of a type of reason, although he unwittingly used it, which supplants the rationalism that he rejected. When he made arguments in defense of "the permanent things," he was indeed employing this type of reason, albeit without recognizing it as such. If Kirk had acknowledged that he was employing a logic capable of giving a faithful account of the immediate experiences of the human self (that is, its dualistic nature and the inner check), he would not have had to overtly rely exclusively on his intuitions to explain his insights into man's essential nature.[26] The insights that are incorporated in tradition, religion, the wisdom of our ancestors, the lessons of history, and "the permanent things" should not be under-

24. See Claes G. Ryn, *Will, Imagination and Reason: Irving Babbitt and the Problem of Reality,* chap. 13 for a discussion of the relationship between reason, intuition, and will.

25. Zoll, "The Social Thought of Russell Kirk," 128–29.

26. See Ryn, "The Humanism of Irving Babbitt Revisited," 261.

stood as mere intuitions, but as realities suitable for discussion on the conceptual level. Kirk's characteristic philosophical ambiguity accounts in part for the failure of most of his critics to give sufficient attention to his idea of the moral imagination, and further explains why in some circles he is regarded as a popularizer of ideas or an intellectual and literary historian rather than a serious philosopher. If Kirk had been explicit in defining his ethical concepts and providing a philosophic defense for his positions, he would have been less vulnerable to those who accuse him of nostalgic, antiquarian romanticism.[27]

The Moral Imagination and the Natural Law

Was Russell Kirk a natural law thinker? Most of his strongest admirers certainly believe that he was. Yet, a close examination of his work reveals aspects of his thought inconsistent with the consensual Christian natural law position typically attributed to him. Although the moral principles to which Kirk appealed may in most cases be compatible with natural law postulates, his moral epistemology significantly differed from that employed by natural law theorists. Now has come the time to take a broader view of Kirk that deals with not only the ambivalence in his thought with regard to natural law but also the role of other traditions on the formulation of his thinking.

In reaction to the moral relativism intrinsic to such ideological movements as liberalism, socialism, and Marxism, many conservatives in the 1950s sought to establish the existence of an objective moral order from which there would flow a body of ethical absolutes capable of forever defining man's moral obligations. The natural law tradition of Cicero, St. Thomas Aquinas, and Richard Hooker appeared to provide the ideal solution. Natural law precepts, it was alleged, offered a viable alternative to the modern tendency, originating with Machiavelli and Hobbes, "to equate right with will and justice with power." Faith in natural law convictions became, for many conservatives, the hallmark

27. See Ryn, *Will, Imagination and Reason,* especially chaps. 3–7 and 13, for a more extensive and thorough explication of the relationship between will, imagination, and reason. Ryn makes important strides in this work, drawing on the thought of Babbitt, More, and Benedetto Croce (1896–1952) toward developing a philosophical logic capable of giving a complete account of the duality of existence. In this endeavor, he supplements Kirk's moral thought in areas where Kirk is most vulnerable to criticism.

of conservative thought. Stephen Tonsor, a conservative historian from the University of Michigan, declared more than twenty years ago that the leaders of the postwar conservative movement "are clearly identified with natural law philosophy and revealed religion."[28]

Even though Kirk consistently maintained during the last forty years of his life that the moral basis of conservatism was composed of natural law principles, he never explicitly defined them nor explained how man apprehends the dictates of natural law. Kirk appeared satisfied that the moral principles embodied in the natural law tradition are compatible with and supportive of what he calls "the permanent things." He never devoted himself to the task of deciding whether the moral imperative, as he ordinarily understood it, is consistent with natural law precepts conceived as a body of immutable rules. In respect to natural law, the epistemological problems raised by the concepts of "intuition" and "reason" did not deeply concern him.

Consequently, Kirk's self-identification with the natural law tradition makes for some exegetic difficulties. Zoll, for example, expressed his uneasiness with Kirk's natural law assertions by arguing that neither Kirk nor his mentor, Burke, were proponents "of an orthodox conception of natural law." To deduce "a corpus of theological orthodoxy as a philosophical foundation" for their social and ethical positions would be unwarranted. Kirk's views were "only in part the logical offspring of his Catholic or neo-Thomist metaphysics." Although one of the major themes in Kirk's moral thinking that "remained relatively constant" throughout all of his works was his "preference for a natural law orientation," he "devotes little time to the ontological character of value, with its obligatory aspects, but, rather, provides a historicistic defense; like Burke, he is a teleologist who assumes that moral models emerge as representative of the underlying valuational character of existence."[29] Zoll regrettably stopped short of drawing a distinction between Kirk's stress on the historicity of moral value and the moral legalism typical of conventional natural law theory.

For Kirk, Zoll continued, an "ethical mandate emerges from moral actions of notable men in which a certain consistency and continuity

28. Nash, *The Conservative Intellectual Movement,* 152–53, 136 (quoted by Nash from Stephen J. Tonsor to the editor, *Reporter,* August 11, 1955, 8).

29. Zoll, "The Social Thought of Russell Kirk," 129, 118.

can be witnessed." In other words, moral values are seen as deriving from the unfolding of history in which originate those images or models of perfection that give evidence of what Zoll variously calls a "moral tradition," "historical 'decorum,'" or a "pattern in the civilized experience." While Zoll's interpretation of Kirk's moral position is correct insofar as it goes, it leaves the false impression that Kirk was a crude historicist who equated the good with what history has wrought. Although history and tradition enrich the imagination, as Kirk always stressed, they cannot speak with final authority on the content of the ethical ultimate. The lessons of history can serve as a guide, or authority to our conscience, but they are incapable, if severed from the intuitively perceived sources of enduring truth, of imparting certitude regarding moral imperatives. As Burke wrote, "History is a preceptor of prudence, not of principles." The past, as Vigen Guroian pointed out in a discussion of Burke's insight, "instructs us in the relativities and contingencies of political life." History "is the record of human existence under God," Kirk explained, "meaningful only so far as it reflects and explains and illustrates the order in character and society which emanates from divine purpose." The "ends of man and society," he affirmed, "are not to be found in history: those ends are transcendent, attaining fruition only beyond the limits of time and space."[30]

Zoll noted that Kirk's ethical reactions were "aesthetic at root," meaning that for Kirk ugliness and vulgarity "loom as the personifications of moral corruption."[31] But Zoll did not elaborate on the crucial relationship in Kirk's thought between aesthetic judgments and moral convictions.

Kirk's preference for natural law explanations of his moral position can perhaps be attributed to three factors. First, there was what Zoll called his "unabashed theism." Kirk was "often content to defend a premise by reference to its compatibility with Christian principles or concepts." His conversion to Catholicism in 1964 probably strengthened his already strong sympathy for its doctrines and institutions. His well-known regard for the Catholic Church's historic role as a civiliz-

---

30. Ibid., 118; Burke to Markham, November 9, 1771, *The Correspondence of Edmund Burke,* vol 2: 1960, 282, quoted by Vigen Guroian, "Natural Law and Historicity: Burke and Niebuhr," 164; Kirk, "Behind the Veil of History," 467–69.

31. Zoll, "The Social Thought of Russell Kirk," 118.

ing force certainly helps to explain his willingness to accept neo-Thomistic natural law formulations. Second, Peter J. Stanlis's *Edmund Burke and the Natural Law,* for which Kirk wrote the foreword, probably reinforced this leaning. Any inclination in Kirk to read into Burke's observations a full-blown natural law tradition seemed confirmed by Stanlis's arguments.[32] Third, Kirk's assumption about the indistinguishability of the moral imagination and the natural law made him even more receptive to the natural law tradition. The last two explanations deserve further comment.

In response to the view that Burke worshipped only the expedient and denied the existence of abiding ethical norms, Stanlis contended that Burke was an exponent of the natural law tradition of Richard Hooker, St. Thomas Aquinas, and Cicero. From "at least 1857–1861, when Buckle's *The History of Civilization in England* appeared, until the present, it has been the almost universal conviction of utilitarian and positivist scholars and critics that Burke had a strong contempt for the Natural Law," wrote Stanlis, "and that the ultimate basis of his political philosophy was to be found in a conservative utilitarianism." Stanlis, on the other hand, argued that "Burke regarded the Natural Law as a divinely ordained imperative ethical norm which, without consulting man, fixed forever his moral duties in civil society." Against the charge that Burke was a relativist, Stanlis defended him as "one of the most eloquent and profound defenders of Natural Law morality and politics in Western Civilization." Kirk came to endorse this thesis. In his review of the book, he approvingly cited a passage in which Stanlis equated Burke's moral imagination with the Thomistic natural law tradition: "Acceptance of the Natural Law made Burke's moral imagination transcend sectarian differences. He is the perfect bridge between utilitarians or positivists and Christians, and between Catholics and Protestants. Essentially a Thomist in his political philosophy he is the embodiment of all that is best in the Anglican tradition. For a vast number of people, therefore, Burke is a restorative of the Christian-humanist wisdom of Europe, based on Natural Law."[33]

32. Ibid., 128, 133; Peter J. Stanlis, *Edmund Burke and the Natural Law,* see especially chap. 3. The first edition was published in 1958.

33. Stanlis, *Edmund Burke and Natural Law,* 29, 73, ix, 249; Kirk, "The Conservative Revolution of Edmund Burke," *Catholic World* 5 (August 1958): 342 (emphasis added).

It should be noted that Kirk did not identify Burke with Thomistic natural law principles in the first edition of *The Conservative Mind* (1953), written before Stanlis's book appeared. In fact, Kirk mentioned natural law in reference to Burke in that edition only briefly as a sense of harmony with the providential order. Moreover, in the 1953 edition, his first canon of conservative thought reads: "Belief that a divine intent rules society as well as conscience." In the later editions that appeared after the publication of Stanlis's book, this statement was revised to read: "Belief in a transcendent order, or *body of natural law*, which rules society as well as conscience." This revision suggests that Stanlis apparently had persuaded Kirk to think of Burke as a champion of natural law and to conclude that the conservative tradition and natural law principles were inseparably linked.[34]

Nowhere did Stanlis make any mention of Burke's "moral imagination," aside from identifying it with natural law; nor did he ever discuss it as a concept. Moreover, Stanlis did not raise the issues concerning the imagination discussed in Babbitt's classic chapter in *Democracy and Leadership*, "Burke and the Moral Imagination."

Kirk, for his part, made no distinction between the moral imagination and natural law. In fact, in his discussion of Cicero's natural law doctrines, he defined the natural law without equivocation as the moral imagination. The natural law "is not a fixed code in opposition to the laws of the state," but is rather an "ethical principle interpreting the

34. Kirk, *The Conservative Mind* (1978), 56, 7 (emphasis added). Historian Paul Gottfried drew similar conclusions concerning the influence of Stanlis's book on Kirk: "In *The Conservative Mind,* Kirk praised Burke, in the tradition of Babbitt, for his conception of the moral imagination, but only after he had read Stanlis in the late fifties did Kirk present Burke as a Christian Aristotelian teacher of natural law. This interpretive shift suggests how fluid was even Kirk's conception of the thinker to whom he tried to give a central role in the postwar conservative movement." The reason for this "shift," assumed Gottfried, was because Kirk, before establishing himself as a political thinker, had not yet studied Burke "deeply." See Paul Edward Gottfried, *The Search for Historical Meaning,* 130, 161. On the contrary, as I shall argue later in this chapter, Kirk arrived at his conclusion that Burke was a natural law theorist not because he was insufficiently read in Burke, but because of his strong attraction to the natural law doctrine. As I have already stated, Kirk acknowledged the formative influence of Babbitt on his work. Kirk never questioned whether Babbitt's and Stanlis's interpretations of Burke's moral thought were compatible.

rules by which men live together in society" and which is, in part, derived "from the long experience of mankind in community."[35] But as
we shall see, the proponents of natural law conceive of the ethical imperative as a body of immutable truths in which reason rather than experience plays the dominant role in confirming their validity.

Kirk's affinity for the natural law tradition tends to obscure the fact
that his moral epistemology deviates in two significant respects from
the usual natural law approach. The first involves the role of reason.
St. Thomas Aquinas, who is regarded as the preeminently authoritative
Christian natural law theorist, defined natural law as "the rational creature's participation [in] eternal law." In other words, man apprehends
the precepts of natural law through his faculty of reason, which all
men possess, but not in equal proportions. Reason for St. Thomas, as
A. P. d'Éntreves argued, "is the essence of man, the divine spark which
makes for his greatness. It is the 'light of natural reason' which enables
us 'to discern good from evil.'" Kirk, of course, did not assign such primacy to reason. Vivas observed that natural law's proponents wrongly
assert that the physical universe "exhibits a moral law which men are
expected or, more precisely, are commanded, to use as a guide for their
conduct." This assertion is based upon a misconception of the status of
moral law. Physical laws and moral laws are entirely different entities.
According to Vivas, physical laws refer "to aspects of that which is."
Moral laws, on the other hand, refer "to what ought to be." Therefore,
Vivas concluded, it is impossible to "conceive of the natural law of the
moralist as we conceive of the laws of the physicists." Starting with the

35. Kirk, *The Roots of American Order,* 112. Nearly twenty years later, Kirk
repeated this argument: "Natural law is not a harsh code that we thrust upon other
people: rather, it is an ethical knowledge, innate perhaps, but made more clearly
known to us through the operation of right reason. And the more imagination with
which a person is endowed, the more will he apprehend the essence of the natural
law, and understand its necessity." Kirk, "The Case For and Against Natural Law,"
in *Redeeming the Time,* 200. This essay, which is a revision of a lecture delivered
to the Heritage Foundation, Washington, D.C., on March 4, 1993, was an attempt
to clarify and further explicate his natural law position. However, Kirk was primarily here making a case for the importance of natural law in jurisprudential thinking and attacking the arguments of natural law's legal positivist critics. Since Kirk
did not attempt to clarify the problems in his moral epistemology that I am raising
here, it is apparent that the blurring of distinctions between reason and imagination did not deeply trouble him.

Eternal Verities that are seized through ratiocination, he pointed out, the natural law theorist presumes to "know quite clearly and adequately what man is, what his virtues and vices are, and what are the principles or laws that can guide him safely through life." Vivas rejected this approach as "a paternalistic misconception of moral experience." The good is conceived of as static and predefined because the precepts of natural law are viewed as unchanging and universal. A rigid adherence to the prescriptions of natural law—which is precisely what Kirk eschewed—can itself become a form of abstract morality, especially if it is divorced from immediate circumstances that, Burke wrote, "give in reality to every political principle its distinguishing colour, and discriminating effect."[36]

Kirk could not accept a natural law that predefines the good for all time and formulates a code that transcends all other codes. Many advocates of natural law take a legalistic and intellectualistic view of morality because they perceive the moral ultimate to be a precept of reason that can be applied to particular cases in a casuistic manner. But, as Vivas pointed out, "moral law cannot be enacted in advance of experience, enacted into law by decree prior to specific human action."[37] Man's finite mind is incapable of grasping all the infinite possibilities that

36. Although there are many competing interpretations of natural law derived from the various schools, my analysis deals only with the Thomistic natural law tradition that Kirk embraced. St. Thomas Aquinas, *Treatise on Law,* 16, 65–67; A. P. d'Éntreves, *Natural Law: An Historical Survey,* 38–40; Eliseo Vivas, "Animadversions upon the Doctrine of Natural Law," 151, 153; Burke, *Reflections on the Revolution,* 93.

37. "The introduction of legal valuations into the field of morality can give rise to serious misgivings. Yet the moment we conceive of moral values as expressed in terms of law, as indeed the very notion of natural law requires us to do, it is difficult to see how these misgivings can be avoided. For this can mean only that, in passing judgement on the moral quality of action, we do nothing more than pronounce upon the conformity of that action to a legal pattern. If morality consists solely in respect for the law, then the Pharisee is a perfect example of moral behaviour. If moral duties can be couched in legal terms, they can best specified with code-like precision. Casuistry will set in and forecast all possible alternatives. Probabilism will help men to solve their doubts about the most appropriate role to choose for their conduct. Moral experience is reduced to narrow legal categories. The task of the moralist is for all purposes identical with that of the lawyer. He must expound and interpret the law." d'Éntreves, *Natural Law,* 83; Vivas, "Animadversions upon the Doctrine of Natural Law," 155.

will emerge. Man, then, must be given the freedom, which natural law apparently denies him, to adjust moral prescriptions creatively to emerging, unique situations.

The moral imagination, on the other hand, as Burke and Babbitt understood it, and as Kirk used it, presupposes a decidedly different conception of moral experience. The good is seen as dynamic, living, and organic; it has particulars that cannot be conceptually predefined but are grasped by an intuitive vision. This conforms to Kirk's understanding of the actual experience of moral decision-making. As explained in the earlier discussion of reason and intuition, reason plays a secondary role to intuition in Kirk's moral thought. In his search for the good life and ethical universals, man is aided by intuitive knowledge supplied by the moral imagination. A body of images conjured up by the imagination shapes his moral deliberation as he weighs the probable effects of acting on particular impulses. Therefore, "a genuine moral decision," as Vivas explained, "is creative in its nature." Its parallels to aesthetics are apparent: moral judgment is an art, the ability to apply creatively the universal good (which is permanent), the One, to the ever-changing flux of existence, the Many. Reason cannot instruct us as to whether our values are correct; it can only give us evidence of what the likely consequences of a particular act will be. "Reason is not itself the evaluative function," Claes Ryn noted. "It is the *reflective awareness* of the moral reality, without which the latter would remain conceptually inarticulate."[38]

As an ethical dualist, Kirk asked us to act in a particular spirit: to put our expansive, lower selves under the disciplining influence of the ethical will. By striving to will that which is good for its own sake, the individual brings about a transformation of his character. The morally disciplined individual prefers virtuous activity, having experienced the peace and happiness it brings. Here, the virtuous quality of particular acts is tested by the direct experience of life, not simply on the basis of intellectual deliberation.

Are acts of courage, charity, or honesty to be preferred to cowardice, greed, and mendacity? Such a question cannot be answered in the absence of experience acquired by observing the fruits of the acts

38. Vivas, "Animadversions upon the Doctrine of Natural Law," 151; Claes G. Ryn, "History and the Moral Order," 99 (Ryn's emphasis).

that flow from these various qualities of will. Reasoning about alternative moral choices in an experiential vacuum would be a fruitless endeavor. In Kirk's inchoate moral epistemology, the primary emphasis is placed upon the quality of will rather than upon reason. Insofar as the individual is inspired by his higher will, he will prefer ethical action. Volumes of moral teaching will have little effect upon an individual corrupted by hedonistic, selfish impulses. Socrates was wrong, then, to believe that virtue is knowledge. As we know from experience, to know the good is not always to do it. Sound habits, prejudices, and traditions influence the development of moral character far more than formal instruction. In fact, as the popularity of ethical speculation spread in the ancient world, it brought in its wake "a general decay of public and private morals." "When first I read Socrates' argument, I being then a college freshman, this seemed to me an insupportable thesis; for we all have known human beings of much intelligence and cleverness whose light is as darkness," Kirk wrote. "After considerable experience of the world and the passage of more than four decades, to me Socrates' argument seems yet more feeble."[39]

Appealing to intuition, the moral imagination brings to bear upon a particular moral problem the accumulated wisdom and experience of civilization. Here the natural law tradition is only a component. Its precepts are part of the vast body of traditional moral wisdom that Kirk called the "wisdom of the ages." While there exists a certain presumption in favor of these natural law precepts—based on what Zoll identified as their "historicistic defense" of value—they are discovered or inspired not by reason, but by the imagination. These precepts serve as aids to the imagination. By illuminating a particular situation with the "wisdom of the ages," which the individual has worked up into intuitive ethical wholes, he is able to check his immediate impulses, his

39. Kirk, "Can Virtue Be Taught?" In *Redeeming the Time,* 55–57. The great Jewish philosopher Martin Buber reached an identical conclusion when he attempted to morally instruct his pupils. He soon discovered that teaching ethics as formal rules and principles did not result in his charges becoming more virtuous. In fact, they frequently would twist the lessons they had learned to rationalize selfish behavior. Buber, *Between Man and Man* (New York: Macmillan Publishing Company, Inc., 1978), 105, quoted by Guroian, "Awakening the Moral Imagination," 4–5.

expansive self, with reference to a steadily evolving view of the social good. While the good is eternal, it is not in the form of a singular precept or definition. It cannot be predefined since it is always emerging. Each new situation presents a unique set of circumstances. The individual, hence, must be open to what the good may be in any particular circumstance.

Similarly, the ideal society cannot be predefined. It is a matter of no small significance that both Burke and Kirk regarded with horror all attempts to outline the perfect society into which all men could be fitted forever. Kirk emphatically stressed that

> [T]here exists no single best form of government for the happiness of all mankind. The most suitable form of government necessarily depends upon the historic experience, the customs, the beliefs, the state of culture, the ancient laws, and the material circumstances of a people, and all these things vary from land to land and age to age. Monarchy may defend the highest possible degree of order, justice, and freedom for a people—as, despite shortcomings, the Abyssinian monarchy did in Ethiopia, until the Marxist revolution there. Aristocracy, under other circumstances, may be found most advantageous for the general welfare. The Swiss form of democracy may work very well in twentieth-century Switzerland; yet it does not follow that the Swiss pattern, imposed abruptly upon Brazil, say would function at all. Nor would the American pattern of politics, developed through an intricate process extending over several centuries, be readily transplanted to Uganda or Indonesia.[40]

The good society, then, can never be solely a design of deliberate creation. Rather, as Burke and Kirk maintained, it is the product of organic growth and the accumulated wisdom of innumerable generations as transmitted through their cultural achievements, mores, traditions, and institutions. Because the good cannot be predefined and codified for all time, any effort to freeze a society into a preconceived mold or to impose upon it a static concept of the good is doomed to fail. The task of knowing the good is always unfinished because its possibilities are never exhausted. Life is always presenting us with new possibilities, and hence our applications of the good must be constantly adjusted to emerging circumstances. The ethically ordered society is realized by

40. Kirk, "Popular Government and Intemperate Minds," 596–97.

the creative acts of successive generations of virtuous people striving to apply universal standards of the good to concrete situations. In this process, as traditions are preserved and renewed, society maintains a healthy balance between the twin necessities of change and preservation.[41]

Kirk's affirmation of the natural law tradition was intellectually confusing because he overlooked the fact that natural law theorists such as St. Thomas Aquinas understood natural law as the law of reason discovered by rational cogitation. Kirk's moral imagination, by contrast, is the power of intuition, which is nonconceptual and nondefinitional. Intuition and reason are distinctive modes of apprehending the good that cannot be subsumed into each other.[42] The moral imagination is a direct, concrete perception of a standard of life, of moral experience, which is not arrived at through discursive reasoning. Literature, music, and historical studies, inter alia, fertilize intuition. Through such literature as poetry, fiction, fantasy, and parable, we can experience, by way of images that an author has created, the moral quality of different types of life. Charles Dickens's character Uriah Heep, for example, provides a vivid and compelling image of a soul deformed by pride and avarice. T. S. Eliot's poem "The Wasteland," a favorite of Kirk's, enables us to feel directly the disintegrative forces of spiritual confusion upon Western civilization. The power of Eliot's poetry to move and convince us does not depend on rational proofs of his depiction of reality, but upon the ability of his images to arouse our moral imagination and to enlighten us in a merely intuitive way.[43]

41. Leo Strauss, for his part, could find little merit in this view as applied to prescriptive constitutions. Contrary to Kirk or Burke, Strauss conceived of the "best constitution" as "a contrivance of reason, i.e., of conscious activity or of planning on the part of an individual or of a few individuals." Leo Strauss, *Natural Right and History*, 314. Strauss apparently had little faith in the value of historical or customary wisdom; for him the "good" was predefined and universal. As we will see in chap. 4, the principles of prudence and prescription in Burke's conservatism represented for Strauss a denial of universal norms. See Strauss's discussion of Burke's view of the British constitution, 313–23.

42. In addition to works of Ryn and Babbitt, my interpretation of the moral imagination owes much to Leander, *Irving Babbitt and Benedetto Croce.*

43. Gerald J. Russello sharply criticizes my analysis of Kirk's natural law position as it appeared in earlier published versions. Russello claims that my criticisms of Kirk for being overly "intuitive" and "for not providing a proper 'philosophic' defense of [Kirk's] moral and legal thought" simplify "Kirk's view more than . . . is warranted." Russello's critique, though, is marred by his failure to

THE CHALLENGE OF IDEOLOGY

In the age of ideology, the moral imagination necessarily suffers. The ideologue's imagination gives rise to flawed and distorted visions of reality that in turn create social and moral disorder. Thus, the mind of the ideologue and that of the man of moral imagination are always at opposite poles. The ideologue formulates abstract static doctrines that are severed from historical experience and moral authority. He deduces, in a casuistic fashion, vast schemes for social and political improvement. The complex nature of man is thereby reduced to abstract formulae that allegedly hold potential for manipulating human nature and bringing forth an earthly paradise.[44] Lacking a conception of the inner life, the ideologue perceives man as a being whose behavior is wholly determined by the forces of nature. Once these forces are fully understood, the ideologue imagines, he and his cohorts will have within their grasp the means to control man's destiny.

Because the imagination of the ideologue is impoverished, the reason it begets will lead him deep into false views of reality, for example, utopian expectations or political fanaticism. The root cause of these moral and political errors lies not in the faulty reason behind them, Kirk argued, but in the still more basic defective imagination that fails to give a complete account of man's universal experience. Kirk cited three ideologies, or constellations of ideological notions, as primarily responsible for working the most mischief in our times: liberalism and

---

adequately understand the point of my arguments. He believes that I am mainly criticizing Kirk for being overly "intuitive" and for failing to be more of a natural law theorist. In reality, I fault Kirk for blurring the distinctions between reason, imagination, and natural law.

Russello's arguments, furthermore, unwittingly confirm my contention that Kirk cannot be adequately described as a natural law theorist. "Reason is the only active mode of knowing; it is interpenetrated by *intellectus,*" Russello contends, "the passive capacity to receive truth which Kirk calls 'intuition.'" Russello fails to understand that, for Kirk, it is not reason but the intuitive power of the moral imagination that is the ultimate moral authority. The intuition, rather than being "passive," is a creative force by which man grasps knowledge of moral universals. Reason alone is incapable of being a sure guide to either truth or goodness. Gerald J. Russello, "The Jurisprudence of Russell Kirk," 359–60.

44. Kirk defined the ideology of "reductionism" as "the deliberate attempt to reduce our understanding of human nature to a 'realistic'—and lowered—assessment." Kirk, "The End of Learning," 25.

its numerous collectivist variants, libertarianism, and the behavioralist persuasion as manifested in the social sciences.

The presumptuous rationality characteristic of liberals from John Locke onward struck Kirk as liberalism's major flaw. The Lockean liberal proclaims that tradition, authority, and wisdom "must now expect to exist upon sufferance." Hence, he desires that "everything in heaven and earth would come under the critical scrutiny of dispassionate private rationality."[45] Breaking even more sharply with classical and biblical views, the Benthamite utilitarian liberal expresses a pride and an unlimited confidence in the power of individual reason. His mentality is always on the level of the purely useful, of means and ends, because he is unable to comprehend the higher imagination or to understand the complexity of the motives of man. Utility, rather than love, is his main motive. He lacks warmth and a "sense of consecration" toward community, authority, inherited values, and institutions.[46]

Doubting all things in heaven and on earth, accepting only what can be validated by empirico-quantitative reason, utilitarianism is "a philosophy of death: its morbidity is the consequence of Benthamite emphasis upon Doubt . . . and this is consummate folly. For Doubt is a surly, envious, egotistic emotion, a bitter denial of everything but the sullen self; and one learns nothing by doubting. Doubt never can be wholly assuaged in many things, but we must manage to live despite our doubts (which are a condition of our imperfect temporal nature)."[47] We must recognize, admonished Kirk, that we are ignorant of much and must accept much on faith. To doubt everything results in a paralysis of will and the impoverishment of one's spiritual existence. Such is the fate of the doctrinaire liberal who would follow Bentham in repudiating authority, tradition, and the prescriptive wisdom of his ancestors. He has succumbed to the Benthamite folly of believing that "private rationality henceforth would emancipate mankind from obedience to tradition, authority, and the past experience of humanity." Without faith and standards to check his arbitrary will, the Benthamite liberal

45. Kirk, "John Locke Reconsidered," 300; see also Kirk, *The Conservative Mind* (1978), 251; Kirk, *The Roots of American Order*, 290, and Kirk, preface to *An Essay Concerning Human Understanding*, by John Locke (Chicago: Gateway Editions/Henry Regnery Company, 1956), vii.

46. Kirk, "John Locke Reconsidered," 297.

47. Kirk, *The Conservative Mind* (1986), 287.

comes to believe, in his pride, that he has the right to judge everything according to his own private taste. The modern mind, having made utility the essence of politics and having thereby lost sight of the higher ends of existence, Kirk charged, "has thought of men as the flies of a summer, and so has deprived itself of the wisdom of our ancestors, and laid waste that portion of posterity."[48] The result is a weakening of the social bonds that hold a community intact. A community lacking the restraining power of tradition or prescriptive institutions is rendered defenseless against the demands of special interests and selfish passions.

Lacking historical perspective and imagination, modern liberalism proceeds from Benthamite assumptions to the delusion that scientific reason can solve all of mankind's complex problems and thereby guarantee a golden age of prosperity and plenty. This abstract, utopian mentality, Kirk predicted, will be the ultimate undoing of liberalism.[49]

In light of his vigorous attack upon the abstract reasoning of liberals, Kirk's equally strong criticism of similar deficiencies in libertarian thought is not surprising. Although many observers have regarded libertarians and traditional conservatives as natural allies because of their common opposition to the growth of the modern collectivist state, Kirk vehemently and consistently opposed all attempts to form an alliance. Genuine conservatism would suffer as a consequence of such a merging of what he considered to be antithetical positions. The atomistic individualism and ahistorical rationality of the libertarians, reflecting their utilitarian mentality, would corrupt conservative thinking. Their exaltation of reason uninformed by the moral imagination precludes any understanding of values beyond utility and self-interest. A conservatism incorporating old Benthamite or social Darwinist tenets would be worse than no conservatism at all. Like liberalism, its lack of imagination would be its undoing.[50]

48. Kirk, "The Unbought Grace of Life," 19.

49. Kirk, *A Program for Conservatives,* 6; Kirk, *Beyond the Dreams of Avarice,* 33.

50. Kirk, *Confessions of a Bohemian Tory,* 293. See chap. 7 for additional discussion of Kirk's critique of libertarianism. In 1982, for a series of lectures delivered at the Heritage Foundation, Kirk reiterated his criticisms of libertarians, calling them "chirping sectaries." Conservatives must disassociate themselves entirely from the libertarians, or else they run the risk of being discredited. See Russell Kirk, "Libertarians: Chirping Sectaries," in *Reclaiming a Patrimony,* 25–34.

The deficient rationality that characterizes the Benthamite mind has infected as well, in Kirk's estimation, the social sciences where the ascendance of the behavioralist persuasion has done much to distort the modern understanding of man's complex nature. Behavioralists assume that the scientific methods appropriate to the natural sciences can and should be applied to the study of politics. That study would be then value-free and exhibit the same sort of objectivity apparently found in the natural sciences. This new positivism (now accompanied by computers and modern statistical methods), because it concentrates solely on the outer workings of man while denying the existence of his inner life, is the direct descendant of "the incomplete positivism" that Babbitt had earlier attacked. With its hostility to traditional norms and ancient wisdom, and with its faith in narrow rationality, it brings forth, according to Kirk, not a new understanding of the nature of man, but only darkness and confusion. Deficient in imagination, the behavioralists "mistake fact-accumulation for wisdom." Having never experienced real wonder at the mysterious complexity of human experience, they resent the imagination as lacking utility, and prefer surveys and statistical compliance. But "facts" alone have no real meaning unless accompanied by the imagination that gives them concrete meaning. What would be more useless than, for example, statistical demographic data without a theory to explain and interpret these numbers in a manner indicating their importance to the human experience? Without imagination, from which theory is derived, knowledge cannot be gathered from purely statistical data. "The 'fact-value' distinction is alien to human self-knowledge, for the facts accounted for in such knowledge are value-realities, namely, actions having, or not having, a moral inspiration," as Claes Ryn stressed.[51] The old issue of the fact/value dichotomy in the social sciences, then, is based on a naive, simplistic notion about the nature of knowledge.

Although the behavioralist lacks the capacity to create normative standards, he has a vague humanitarian sentiment that compels him to think "man should be made with the help of science to behave as he should." At this point, both the Baconian and Rousseauistic components of naturalism become evident. The earlier doctrine persuades the

---

51. Kirk, *Enemies of the Permanent Things,* 213; Ryn, "History and the Moral Order," 100.

behavioralist that he is objective and scientific in his judgments, while the latter drives him to do good to others. Both tendencies fill him with an arrogant faith in the validity of his prescriptions. He is convinced of both the rightness of his beliefs and his humanitarian duty to reform others. Although opposed to prejudice, he is "unaware of his own." Cut off from "theological, humane, and historical disciplines, he often mistakes his petty private rationality for self-evident truth."[52] As the behavioralist movement spreads, Kirk warned, the moral imagination will wither, constricting our understanding of the nature of man, and the moral prerequisites of freedom and social order.

52. Kirk, *Enemies of the Permanent Things*, 213, 217–18.

4 Tradition and the "Permanent Things"

*Ask for the old paths, where is the good way,
and walk therein, and ye shall find rest for
your souls.*

—Jeremiah 6:16

*What is conservatism? Is it not adherence to
the old and tried, against the new and
untried?*

—Abraham Lincoln

No ASPECT OF CONSERVATIVE THOUGHT better defines its essence than the conviction that the search for the good life involves looking to historical experience as a valued source of moral and practical guidance and insight. The characteristic conservative esteem for sound habits, customs, traditions, prescriptive institutions, and continuity bespeaks conservatism's highly developed sense of historical consciousness. By contrast, liberals typically dismiss these conservative touchstones as unworthy of special veneration. For liberals, the past consists only of the hoary old days of socially inequitable institutions, injustice, superstition, and ignorance. Traditions are regarded merely as obstacles to be overcome in the march of mankind toward ever greater technical, scientific, and social achievements. Philosophically and in practical politics, liberals and more extreme radicals of the Left exhibit a strong sympathy for "the feelings of glory in the future" and "the forces of change in society." The temperaments of all meliorist ideologues toward prospects of change, Kirk observed, stand in marked contrast to that of the conservative. While the liberal ordinarily "writes polemical tracts and organizes mass movements, the conservative, except when he is aroused by dread of radical change or alarmed by the decay of his society, tends to rely upon the powerful and stable forces of custom and habit."[1]

The reactionary, for his part, opposes all change, but the conservative recognizes that unyielding resistance to the pressures for change would be futile. In his social, cultural, and moral thought, the conservative instead strives to balance the competing needs for permanence and change by endeavoring "to conserve the best in our traditions and our institutions" and "reconciling that best with necessary reform from time to time." The standard for a statesman must be, as Burke wrote, the "disposition to preserve," combined with "an ability to improve." Whether the conservative should be an advocate of reform or an opponent of change depends on the specific circumstances. Change can either renew a society or bring about its ruination. "Our modern peril...is that of vertiginous speed: the traditions of civility may be swallowed up by will and appetite," Kirk declared; "with us, the expectation of change is greater than the expectation of continuity, and generation scarcely links with generation." Contemporary society is not characterized by social and cultural stagnation such as existed "in an ancient Egyptian or Peruvian culture, where the dead hand of the past seems to lie mercilessly upon a whole people, and where the only change is corruption," but by a rapidly accelerating pace of change that threatens social stability. Modern man seeks to be modern on principle, exalting the present over past achievements and worshipping at the shire of material self-aggrandizement, do-it-yourself ethics, and secularism.[2]

Maintaining this delicate balance between tradition and modernity creates especially complex and bewildering problems for the thoughtful conservative. The traditions venerated by conservatives, as Clinton Rossiter rightly pointed out, are continually being overthrown by the intrusion of new institutions and new arrangements:

> In the abstract the conservative is a man who announces that this, the here and now, is the best of all possible worlds; in the concrete he is a man for whom this simple formula means one surrender after another to the whimsicalities of change and aggressions of reform. Unwilling to surrender, yet buffeted by the dizzy pace of events, he is forced to be

1. Kirk, *The Intelligent Woman's Guide to Conservatism,* 92.
2. Ibid., 12.; Burke, *Reflections on the Revolution,* 262; Kirk, *Enemies of the Permanent Things,* 26; see also Kirk, *A Program for Conservatives,* 305; Kirk, "Obdurate Adversaries of Modernity," 203.

more and more selective about those events of the past and institutions of the present he will choose to celebrate; and how much veneration can a man display, we are bound to ask, when he really puts his mind to work in this analytical manner? When a conservative once decides, as many articulate conservatives seem to have decided in explosive America, that his best of all possible worlds was here yesterday and is gone today, he begins the fateful move toward reaction and ratiocination that turns him from a prudent traditionalist into an angry ideologue. What history shall I venerate? What traditions shall I uphold? What institutions shall I protect against the reformers?—these are hard questions for conservatives, and the answers may be as numerous as the men who make them.[3]

Rossiter's observations seem to be borne out by certain principles that conservatives have tended to accept as axiomatic. The following quotations, randomly selected but generally recognized as statements of sound conservative views, illustrate the point:

Unless it is necessary to change, it is necessary not to change.—Viscount Falkland[4]

Most schemes of political improvement are very laughable things.—Samuel Johnson.[5]

This is a cardinal principle, that should govern all statesmen—never, without the strongest necessity, to disturb that which is at rest. . . . Change is not reform.—John Randolph of Roanoke.[6]

While the above statements reflect a predisposition against change, they do not qualify as philosophical arguments. By themselves, they provide no standard, other than to caution against change, by which the statesman can discriminate between what must be preserved and what must be reformed. If the conservative position toward the prob-

---

3. Rossiter, *Conservatism in America,* 257–58. Rossiter unfairly characterized the views of most thoughtful conservatives. Cultural conservatives, such as Kirk, Eliseo Vivas, Stephen Tonsor, and Thomas Molnar, have never subscribed to the Panglossian view that the present "is the best of all possible worlds." In their social criticism, they display a profound dissatisfaction with the dominant culture and the prevailing contemporary social and political trends.

4. Quoted by Hearnshaw, *Conservatism in England,* 18.

5. James Boswell, *Boswell's Life of Johnson,* edited by George Birkbeck Hill (New York: Harper and Brothers, 1904), vol. 2, 118.

6. Quoted by Kirk, *John Randolph of Roanoke: A Study in American Politics,* 192, 208.

lem of modernity amounts to no more than blind resistance to change, as Rossiter suggests, then conservatism truly is, despite Kirk's disclaimers, an ideology—a set of rigidly held, a priori abstractions.

The perception that Kirk's conservatism represents a form of inert traditionalism, an uncritical acceptance of the past or existing institutions, has provoked sharp attacks from his detractors. His conservatism consists, they argued, entirely of a futile attempt to either preserve traditions irrelevant to contemporary needs or impose an alien feudal European tradition upon American institutions and politics. A similar line of attack dismissed Kirk as a captive of the past. As a historicist who equated the ancestral with the good, Kirk lacked, his critics charged, a moral standard for distinguishing between good and evil traditions. The most noteworthy of these attacks appeared in the 1950s and 1960s. While self-proclaimed liberals such as Harvey Wheeler, Arthur Schlesinger, and William J. Newman were unsurprisingly relentless critics of Kirk's traditionalism, some of his sharpest attacks came from those who considered themselves to be part of the revival of conservative ideas in America.

Peter Viereck and Clinton Rossiter, historians and self-identified conservatives, pointed to alleged weaknesses in Kirk's traditionalism. Viereck charged that the "main defect" in the "new conservatism" of Kirk, "threatening to make it a transient fad irrelevant to real needs, is its rootless nostalgia for roots." Because Kirk frequently appealed to principles derived from the European aristocratic tradition, Viereck concluded that his conservatism "is based on roots either never existent or no longer existent." Concluding that the traditions to which Kirk appealed were alien imports from outside the American political experience, Viereck excoriated him for his "unhistorical appeal to history" and "traditionless worship of tradition."[7]

Rossiter was likewise uneasy with Kirk's traditionalism, which he considered to be as out of touch with the times. While Kirk hated "change as heartily as reform," he nevertheless, Rossiter charged, was inconsistently "passionately intent on restoration rather than conservation." Hence, Kirk sought "to cultivate the Conservative mood of reverence and contentment, yet sounds like a radical in his attacks on what is now, for better or worse, the American way of life." His conservatism

7. Viereck, *Conservatism Revisited,* 124–25.

is irrelevant to the modern situation, Rossiter concluded, because he is "a man born one hundred and fifty years too late and in the wrong country."[8]

Another line of criticism was launched in the early 1960s by Frank S. Meyer (1909–1972), once a Communist party member and later an editor and columnist for *National Review*. Always suspicious of any encroachments by the state or society on individual freedom, he made the primacy of the autonomous individual a central focus of his political thought. He bitterly attacked the so-called New Conservatives, of which he considered Kirk to be the foremost spokesman, for denigrating individual reason and subordinating freedom to the claims of society. Traditionalism appeared to Meyer to be a weak reed upon which to establish a philosophical alternative to the prevailing liberal orthodoxy. Kirk's devaluation of the faculty of reason and exaltation of tradition as the ultimate sanction for the good and moral truth had the effect, in Meyer's view, of intellectually disarming conservatives in their struggle against the forces of collectivism. Intellectual appeals to Burke's principles of prescription and history as providential dispensation in an age when liberal-collectivist doctrines have become the tradition leave "New Conservatives" with "no justification for their stand as an opposition." The task of defending tradition, Meyer contended, has grown considerably more complex since 1793 when Burke wrote *Reflections on the Revolution in France*. The British government then had, Meyer alleged, "a powerful, a solid constitution, not seriously challenged at home." By contrast, the "New Conservatives" led by Kirk "are concerned with the salvation of their civilization and their country from positivist and liberal-collectivist doctrines which are already far advanced in authority over the minds and hearts of men. The values they purport to defend *are* seriously challenged at home."[9] Kirkean conservatives are hence caught in a dilemma: "Either the whole

8. Rossiter, *Conservatism in America,* 220–21.
9. Meyer, *In Defense of Freedom,* 1, 40–48 passim (Meyer's emphasis). Meyer's assertion, though, that the threats to the American constitutional order during the 1960s far outstripped anything experienced by the British during the high-water mark of the French revolutionary fever does not stand up to close examination. Burke certainly believed that the existence of civilization itself was at stake in the struggle with the "armed doctrines" of the Jacobins. Although the anti-Catholic Gordon riots took place nine years before the Parisian mobs stormed the Bastille,

historical and social situation in which they find themselves, including the development of collectivism, statism, and intellectual anarchy, is Providential, and all prescriptive attitudes, including the orthodox collectivist attitudes of the day, are right and true. Or, there is a higher sanction than prescription and tradition; there are standards of truth and good by which men must make their ultimate judgments of ideas and institutions, in which case, reason, operating against the background of tradition, is the faculty upon which they must depend in making that judgment."[10]

Meyer could discover no principle in Kirk's political thought from which he could escape the politically eviscerating consequences of the Hegelian dictum: "all that is real is rational." Lacking clear rational principles, the "New Conservatives" are doomed, according to Meyer, to descend into ethical relativism, expediency, and accommodation with the dominant liberal tendencies of their age.[11]

The eminent libertarian European economist Friedrich A. von Hayek similarly complained that his "decisive objection" to conservatism was

---

the violence of the British mob that Burke witnessed in the streets of London no doubt made a great impression on his imagination as he contemplated the even greater horrors erupting in Paris. Burke must have felt that, given the right inspiration, the London mobs could be worked up to an equal intensity of frenzy and rage. Commenting on the possibility of a similar revolutionary movement sweeping England, Burke wrote: "The beginnings of confusion with us in England are at present feeble enough; but, with you [referring to France], we have seen an infancy, still more feeble, growing by moments into a strength to heap mountains upon mountains, and to wage war with heaven itself. Whenever our neighbour's house is on fire, it cannot be amiss for engines to play a little on our own. Better to be despised for too anxious apprehensions, than ruined by too confident a security." See Burke, *Reflections on the Revolution,* 75.

In addition, Burke was troubled by the radical sentiments expressed in the sermon of Dr. Richard Price, who asserted a "new, and hitherto unheard of, bill of rights." Burke, *Reflections on the Revolution,* 96–102. Quite clearly, Burke had concluded that what Meyer called the "solid constitution" of England could also be shaken by the revolutionary doctrines of Jacobin France.

10. Ibid., 41.

11. Ibid., 41–42; Willmoore Kendall's criticism of Kirk's use of tradition echoes that of Meyer. "Mr. Kirk's teaching on tradition is, on the face of it, an assertion of the very relativism and positivism that, in other contexts, he abhors.... Contemporary conservatism, one of whose basic quarrels *must* be the quarrel with relativism and positivism *in all their forms,* must give [Kirk's] teaching a wide berth." Kendall, "The Benevolent Sage of Mecosta," 45–46 (Kendall's emphasis).

its inability to "offer an alternative to the direction in which we are moving." Conservatism fears new ideas "because it has no distinctive principles of its own to oppose to them, and, by its distrust of theory and its lack of imagination concerning anything except that which experience has already proved, it deprives itself of the weapons needed in the struggle of ideas." Hence, Hayek concluded, while conservatism "may often be a useful practical maxim," it "does not give us any guiding principles which can influence long-range developments."[12]

Richard Weaver (1910–1963) and Leo Strauss (1899–1973) were, like Meyer, less than enthusiastic about grounding opposition to liberal doctrines in the political philosophy of Burke. They considered Burke's politics to be insufficiently informed by a moral standard beyond the order of the British constitution. "Burke should not," advised Weaver, "be taken as a prophet by the political conservatives." Weaver claimed that Burke never rooted his political thought in principle. Rather, Burke made an "argument from circumstances" that was "the nearest of all arguments to pure expediency." Further, because of the ethical relativism implicit in this form of argumentation, it was an "argument philosophically appropriate to the liberal."[13] Strauss, for his part, claimed that the consequences of Burke's principles of prescription and providence constituted an even more radical departure from the classical political tradition than the radical doctrines of the French revolutionaries. Burke's thought was not about what a civil society ought to be, but "is, or tends to become identical with a theory of the British constitution." His sole standard in measuring the wisdom of the constitution is prescription. "Prescription," though, Strauss retorted, "cannot be the sole authority for a constitution, and therefore recourse to rights anterior to the constitution, i.e., to natural rights, cannot be superfluous unless prescription by itself is a sufficient guaranty of goodness. Transcendent standards can be dispensed with if the standard is inherent in the process. . . . What could appear as a return to the primeval equation of the good with the ancestral is, in fact, a preparation for Hegel." Burke's view of providence led to the conclusion that men should submit to immoral forces rather than oppose history. In one of his most controversial as-

12. F. A. Hayek, "Why I Am Not a Conservative," in *What Is Conservatism?* edited by Frank S. Meyer, 89, 95, 103. Hayek's essay originally appeared in his *The Constitution of Liberty,* 397–411.
13. Richard M. Weaver, *The Ethics of Rhetoric,* 83, 57–58.

sessments, Strauss declared that Burke "comes close to suggesting that to oppose a thoroughly evil current in human affairs is perverse if that current is sufficiently powerful." If Burke's theory was not grounded in enduring moral principles, as Strauss argued, then the vicissitudes of history should have compelled Burke to repeatedly shift grounds in his utterances on political principle. Yet, as Strauss himself admitted, Burke "adhered throughout his career to the same principles." Strauss did not explain this inconsistency.[14]

Such attacks on Burke can be taken as indirect criticisms of Kirk, the leading contemporary Burkean conservative. Traditionalism, seen from this prospective, conceals its own form of ethical relativism. It develops out of a kind of conservative positivism such as found in the

14. Strauss, *Natural Right and History,* 295, 318–19. Strauss selectively and misleadingly misquoted Burke. Quoting Burke, who in this passage was envisioning one possible consequence of the triumph of the French Revolution, Strauss wrote: "'if the system of Europe, taking in laws, manners, religion and politics' is doomed, 'they, who persist in opposing this mighty current in human affairs ... will not be resolute and firm, but perverse and obstinate.'" From this quotation, Strauss drew the erroneous conclusion that Burke was advocating surrender before these powerful ideological forces. Left out of the text, which concludes Burke's *Thoughts on the French Revolution,* is a portion that significantly alters its meaning. In the restored version, it reads: Those "who persist in opposing this mighty current in human affairs, *will appear rather to resist the decrees of Providence itself, than the mere designs of men.* They will not be resolute and firm, but perverse and obstinate." The emphasized words are missing from Strauss's quotation of Burke. It is clear, therefore, that Burke never intended to say that he considered those who resisted the forces of revolution to be "perverse and obstinate," but rather that, to some, their persistent opposition "will appear" as "perverse and obstinate." Kirk later responded to Strauss's criticism of Burke. Kirk denied that Burke in this passage had suggested that the defenders of moral order should permit themselves to be swept away by the advocates of revolutionary change. "On the contrary, he says that effectual opposition to the Revolution must be the work of many people," Kirk replied, "acting together intelligently." Although personally "vehemently opposed to any compromise with Jacobinism," Burke had warned that "if mankind neglects the laws for human conduct, then a vengeful providence may begin to operate." Burke was not recommending, then, as Strauss argued, a cowardly surrender to the "mighty current" of revolutionary change, but was attempting to awaken the informed sector of the British public to the magnitude of the evil that the French Revolution presented to them. See Kirk, "Three Pillars of Order: Edmund Burke, Samuel Johnson, Adam Smith," in *Reclaiming a Patrimony,* 15–16. This essay was reprinted in Kirk, *Redeeming the Time,* 258–59. "Also Burke still thought it possible that men's minds might be moved by Providence to resist the Revolution; he was endeavoring to be a Providential instrument

work of David Hume, who denied the reality of an ethical ultimate or, at least, deemed it purely a matter of subjective judgment. In a world of infinite possibilities, Hume thought it preferable to cling to things as they are rather than to risk the unanticipated consequences of alteration. All change is risky since no uniformly accepted ethical standards exist by which the process of change can be restrained. Even small modifications of existing structures may open the floodgates to unrestrained upheavals. Conservatism, then, based on these suppositions would amount to no more than fearful inertia, perhaps followed by an abject surrender to the forces of change, if they are judged to be "sufficiently powerful." Being unable to discriminate between what must be preserved and what must be changed in order to preserve a tolerable social order, conservative inertia invites its own destruction.

We are compelled then to examine a central issue to Kirk's definition of conservatism. How does he propose that paradoxes and dilemmas inherent in balancing the competing demands of change and permanence in society be resolved? By what standard can good and bad traditions be distinguished? If no standard can be found, then his conservatism is not a principled defense of a particular vision of moral and social order, but merely a disgruntled resistance to change. Accordingly, the accusation of Kirk's critics that his position amounts to no more than a Fafnir-like conservatism ("I lie in possession, let me sleep") and the gibe of John Stuart Mill that conservatives are "the stupid party" ("stupid" because they lack the imagination to formulate principles) would appear to have validity.

The answer to our question necessitates an exploration of Kirk's conception of the manner by which tradition gives guidance and support to the good life and aids man in the task of apprehending moral universals. Since, as was demonstrated in the previous chapter, the moral imagination plays a central role in Kirk's moral thought, much

---

of that cause." Kirk, *Edmund Burke: A Genius Reconsidered,* 185. Strauss's disciples, on the other hand, were especially hostile to Kirk's argument that the American Republic rests on Burkean rather than Lockean principles. "Less learned and less amiable than their master," Kirk wrote of them, "many of the latter-day Straussites demand ideological conformity to a 'Lockian interpretation' of the Constitution and American history and politics generally." Kirk, *The Conservative Constitution,* 65. Among the disciples of Strauss that Kirk had in mind were Harry Jaffa, Charles R. Kessler, Willmoore Kendall, and Walter Berns.

of the following discussion constitutes a specific application of the principles already explicated there in more general terms.

The Ethical Role of Tradition

If men could learn from history, what lessons it might teach us! But passion and party blind our eyes, and the light which experience gives is a lantern on the stern, which shines only on the waves behind us!

—Samuel Taylor Coleridge, *Table Talk*

When we speak of traditions, Kirk explained, "we mean prescriptive social habits, prejudices, customs and political usages which most people accept with little question, as an intellectual legacy from their ancestors." The vast majority of people accept traditions as good because of their long standing. Because previous generations have preserved and transmitted them, they enjoy a presumption in their favor. Most people inquire little into "the origins or sanctions for these traditions." Such conventions and customs are usually accepted with unreflecting confidence.[15]

This transmittal of traditions occurs not so much through formal schooling or books as "through the life of the family and the observances of the church." Children acquire from their parents and from other authorities a deferential attitude toward established ways of life. Tradition, then, is a body of knowledge, but of a different sort from "scientific knowledge," which Kirk judged to be of an inferior quality because of its inherent limitations. "Almost nothing of importance really can be irrefutably demonstrated by finally ascertained 'facts.'" Knowledge based purely upon scientifically demonstrable facts is grossly incomplete. In fact, if man were to restrict himself purely to scientifically demonstrable facts, emancipating himself from his spiritual heritage, he would actually be separating himself from his richest source of social and moral wisdom, "which is bound up with presumption and prejudice and authority, the accepted beliefs of a people." Prejudice, prescription, and presumption direct the individual conscience. Describing Burke's

15. Kirk, "What Are American Traditions?" 284.

definition of prejudice, Kirk wrote that it "is prejudgment, the answer with which intuition and ancestral consensus of opinion supply a man when he lacks either time or knowledge to arrive at a decision predicated upon pure reason." Hence, man must often rely on this body of ancestral wisdom because, as Burke told us, "We are afraid to put men to live and trade each on his own private stock of reason; because we suspect that this stock in each man is small, and that the individuals would do better to avail themselves of the general bank and capital of nations and of ages." Prejudice, moreover, "is of ready application in the emergency; it previously engages the mind in a steady course of wisdom and virtue, and does not leave the man hesitating in the moment of decision, skeptical, puzzled, and unresolved. Prejudice renders a man's virtue his habit; and not a series of unconnected acts. Through just prejudice, his duty becomes a part of his nature."[16] Far from being merely arbitrary judgments, prejudices are derived from the accumulated wisdom of the many generations who have passed before us. Prejudices should be looked upon as indispensable guides in our social and moral decisions. We should cling to our prejudices to avoid the pitfalls of moral confusion, doubt, and error.

Prescription is "the customary right which grows out of the conventions and compacts of many successive generations." The English constitution, for example, as Kirk pointed out, "is prescriptive, and, said Burke, 'its sole authority is that it has existed time out of mind. Your king, your lords, your juries, grand and little, are all prescriptive.'" Burke had furiously attacked in the name of prescription the abstract doctrines embodied in the French Jacobins' "Rights of Man." The real rights of man, Burke held, are rooted not in rational speculation but convention. Civil society, as well, is "the offspring of convention." Consequently, the science of government cannot be "taught a priori," because its mastery requires "even more experience than any person can gain in his whole life, however sagacious and observing he may be." The reformer should always proceed cautiously before venturing to tear down any existing structure of government, "which has answered in any tolerable degree for ages the common purposes of society" and

16. Kirk, *A Program for Conservatives,* 302; Kirk, *The Conservative Mind,* 38; Burke, *Reflections on the Revolution,* 182.

he should be cautious about rebuilding governmental structures "without having models and patterns of approved utility before his eyes."[17]

Burke's idea of prescriptive rights entails a "presumption" in favor of settled usages, conventional wisdom, and existing customs and mores. This is, according to Kirk, an "inference in accordance with the common experience of mankind." While it may be possible that things have changed and innovation is required, and "past experience in that particular is invalid," the "presumption ordinarily is to the contrary; and in any case, it may be wiser to continue an old practice, even though it seem the child of error, than to break radically with custom and run the risk of poisoning the body social, out of doctrinaire affection for mathematical precision or bluebook uniformity." To force alteration upon society, without considering the existing patterns of social behavior, Burke condemned as a positive evil. The "rage and phrensy" displayed during the French Revolution, he declared, "will pull down more in half an hour, than prudence, deliberation, and foresight can build up in a hundred years." Prescription, prejudice, and presumption, all of which embody a society's traditions, help to sustain and direct man's ethical thought and actions. Without them, Kirk believed, a powerful check upon man's proclivity for selfish, destructive, and arbitrary behavior would be lacking.[18]

The "principles of the good life tend to be reflected in tradition," Claes Ryn explained, "for they represent the permanent element in history amid the flux of continual change." There are universal dimensions of human existence. Natural law, the Eternal Verities, or what the Chinese called the *Tao,* or the Hindus *Rta,* are all attempts by different civilizations to give expression to this intuitive grasp of an ethical ultimate that transcends mere private advantage. Despite the variations of time, place, and circumstance, they have universal validity. These "permanent things," defined by Kirk as immutable and universal norms, "are derived from the experience of the species, the ancient usages of humanity, and from the perceptions of genius, of those rare men who have seen profoundly into the human condition—and whose wisdom

17. Burke, *Reflections on the Revolution,* 151–53.
18. Kirk, *The Conservative Mind,* 42–43; Burke, *Reflections on the Revolution,* 274.

soon is accepted by the mass of men, down the generations."[19] They amount to the sum total of man's efforts in thought and action through the ages to achieve standards of moral perfection.

A dualistic view of existence is integral to this perspective. The classical Greek philosophers and the leading Christian thinkers were united in their view of man as "a creature of two worlds." They saw man as partaking "of two intimately related and yet distinct orders of reality, one immanent and finite, one transcendent and infinite." This insight has been expressed as "the paradox of the one and the many, the coexistence in life of unity and multiplicity, order and disorder." We experience in life an everlasting flow of impressions, impulses, changes, actions, while also being aware of something central, unchanging, which gives order to what would otherwise be a "chaos of multiplicity." In terms of our perception of social reality, the "many" is experienced as an awareness of the multiplicity of individual personalities, belief systems, customs, habits, cultures, and conventions. We also experience history as a dynamic process. Individuals and institutions cannot be frozen in time—circumstances, events, and the natural progression of the law of growth and decay make change inevitable. But we are simultaneously conscious of certain constant aspects of man's nature, and his moral obligations are part of the universal experience of mankind. Reality consists, then, as Babbitt put it, "both of oneness and change." In the ethical life of man, "this fundamental dualism of human existence can be defined as a tension between the universal good and all that thwarts its purpose in the world." Thus, to "build up a sound model for imitation," the civilized man must grasp, as Babbitt advised, the "element of oneness that is inextricably blended with the manifoldness of change." To discover the "unity at the heart of change," that is, standards by which existence is ordered, requires the aid of the imagination.[20]

By employing our imagination, we can tease moral universals out of manifold history. Intuitively, we can experience life in the broadest sense and formulate concepts describing what is universal in history.

19. Ryn, *Democracy and the Ethical Life,* 89; see C. S. Lewis, *The Abolition of Man,* 11; Kirk, *Enemies of the Permanent Things,* 35.
20. Babbitt, *Rousseau and Romanticism,* 7–9; Ryn, *Democracy and the Ethical Life,* 58.

The "moral precepts and the social conventions which we obey represent the considered judgments and filtered experience of many generations of prudent and dutiful human beings—the most sagacious of our species." By reflecting upon the trials and errors of our ancestors' struggles to achieve moral perfection, to fulfill their ultimate spiritual destinies, and to give expression to the ethical imperative, we bring the past as a living presence to bear on the present situation. Particular acts of courage, charity, honesty, faith, and duty offer concrete examples of attempts to rise above personal bias and advantage. When we adopt the perspective "of the ages," ethical truths that personal experience alone could never reveal arise in our awareness because we are drawing from a well of knowledge infinitely broader than that which is available to our own intellects or even the combined intellects of a whole generation of individuals. A tradition is a summation of previous concrete efforts to achieve the common good; our tradition, in turn, inspires us to additional acts of morality. To whatever degree society has a concern for the common good, its traditions will be a source of formative good, directing and supporting its efforts to achieve the highest possible purpose. Insofar as our ethical or higher selves prevail, we will be brought into harmony—that is, genuine community—with others similarly motivated. Traditions provide, further, an ethical check on our merely arbitrary, socially disruptive, momentary impulses by bringing us under the control of standards external to our individual wills. "A people," then, observed Kirk, "who have exhausted their traditions are starved for imagination and devoid of any general assumptions to give coherence to their life."[21]

We must respect "the moral traditions and immemorial customs of mankind," warned Kirk, "for men who ignore the past are condemned to repeat it." The price we pay for neglecting the lessons of our accumulated historical experience is to be thrown back upon our "meager resources of private judgment, having run recklessly through the bank and capital that is the wisdom of our ancestors." Private judgment alone can never replace the authority of moral judgments handed down by traditional culture. Strip a person of this body of wisdom and he will

21. Kirk, *Enemies of the Permanent Things,* 209; Kirk, *A Program for Conservatives,* 305.

find his options and power of creativity not enhanced, but greatly constricted. He would be "most like an artist who begins without perspective, and ignores all that has been learned and felt of color." Not able to express himself through the written word, he would have to start over learning the letters of the alphabet, basic grammar, and syntax before he could even begin to develop great literature. And, without "the religious history of the race behind us, not one of us is likely to achieve anything, either in his own religious life or in his thinking."[22]

Kirk, then, adopted as axiomatic Burke's famous aphorism: the "individual is foolish; but the species is wise." Because none of us can experience all the possibilities of life, our personal accumulation of knowledge is deficient and fragmentary. So, in important matters, we must rely upon "'the wisdom of ancestors'—who as a whole are infinitely wiser than any individual." No one today could possibly build from scratch, for example, even a simple gasoline engine without the aid of the vast technical knowledge accumulated during the last century. Moral and social concerns, by contrast, are infinitely "more delicate and complex than a mere mechanical contrivance."[23]

Obedience to traditions also permits man, Kirk believed, to live in conformity with God's will as it unfolds in history. Because the "temporal order is only part of a larger supernatural order," the first duty of society is "obedience to God and the dispensations of Providence." Kirk deemed the collective wisdom found chiefly in tradition, prejudice, and prescription and gathered from thousands of years of experience and meditation to be providentially available for the sake of humanity. "God's purpose among men is revealed through the unrolling of history. How are we to know God's mind and will? Through the prejudices and traditions which millenniums of human experience with Divine means and judgments have implanted in the mind of the species." In addition, by knowing history, "the gradual revelation of a supreme design," and human nature, "the springs of conduct common to civilized people," men "may humbly aspire to apprehend providential dis-

22. Kirk, *A Program for Conservatives,* 305, 43, 298; Kirk, *Eliot and His Age,* 82. This is, of course, a paraphrase of the famous aphorism of the American philosopher George Santayana. See also Joseph F. Baldacchino, Jr.'s "The Value-Centered Historicism of Edmund Burke," 139–45, for an insightful discussion of the ethical role of tradition; Kirk, "What Are American Traditions?" 289.
23. Kirk, *The Roots of American Order,* 8.

pensations." Warning against the prideful temptation to place too much trust in these human sources of knowledge, however, Kirk added, "the study of history and human character never can encompass the greater part of human wisdom." Books and theoretical speculation can never replace habit and custom as "surer guides to conduct and conscience." Even the wisest person "cannot live by reason alone; pure arrogant reason, denying the claims of prejudice"; hence, in most matters, we should venerate and follow the dictates of tradition—tempered by experience—and our intuitions.[24] By reflecting upon the vast body of historical knowledge, we undergo self-discovery as we learn about our human nature through a form of enlightenment that only the concrete historical experiences of our species can provide.

Meliorists, by contrast, rightly realize that a highly traditional society offers stubborn resistance to their attempts at sweeping alteration. Prescription, prejudice, and presumption are unhelpful to the march of progress. History constitutes little more than a prologue to a golden age in which man's defective nature will be perfected. When the new man of the revolutionary's dream emerges, all lessons of the past will be rendered useless. The Rousseauistic humanitarian, for example, holds that men will follow their immediate impulses of the moment, which are judged to be always good and moral. The utilitarian (through different reasoning that nonetheless still abrogates tradition) fashions the touchstone of his moral thought out of his private judgments and self-interest projected onto society.

Jean-Jacques Rousseau looked upon all social and cultural inhibitions to man's spontaneous will as perversions of his essential good nature. In his manual of education, *Emile,* Rousseau emphatically stated that the "only habit the child should be allowed to acquire is to contract none." No law is so fundamental to Rousseau that cannot be revoked, when the will of the sovereign (the will of the people expressed through the General Will) demands it. The state, he asserted, "knows no laws that are basic in the sense that they cannot be revoked, not even the social contract. If, then, all the citizens of the state were to assemble and resolve unanimously to break the contract, it would be impossible for anyone to raise questions as to whether it had been broken in a fully lawful manner." When the sovereign fails to act to alter

24. Ibid., 58–59, 33, 26, 36.

the existing law, it means that the laws are good. "Yesterday's law is not binding today at all," proclaimed Rousseau; "what happens is, rather, that the silence of the sovereign is considered as tacit consent."[25]

Likewise, the English utilitarian John Stuart Mill contended that the "despotism of custom is everywhere the standing hindrance to human advancement, being an unceasing antagonism to that disposition to aim at something better than customary, which is called, according to circumstance, the spirit of liberty, of that of progress or improvement." According to this view, by sloughing off the dead weight of tradition, man, through the exercise of his private and now liberated intellect, will put an end to all the miseries that have historically plagued mankind. As the late American historian Louis Hartz advised, "instead of recapturing our past, we have got to transcend it." Kirk noted, referring to Hartz and other self-proclaimed progressives, that for them, "tradition is a devil-term: it is something you try to transcend as fast as you can, tugging dull conservatives along behind you." Progressives believe that "we ought to throw off the hand of this dead ancestry and march away in some rational new direction, with our modern pragmatic rationality for guide and governor."[26]

Traditions are not, Kirk averred, abstractions, and, hence, are the very opposite of ideology. There cannot be a communist, a fascist, or a democratic tradition. Ideology is a set of general beliefs that are either imposed upon a people or consciously adopted by them. Traditions, on the other hand, grow out of their accumulated experiences. The process by which a society adopts a tradition is almost unconscious, never by design or by imposition upon an unwilling people. No person, party, or government can be solely responsible for the creation of a tradition. Rather, customs and traditions transmitted down through the generations acquire over time "by prescription almost the force of law."[27]

Unlike the efforts of utopian ideologues to capture the good permanently in a rational scheme, Kirk believed that no tradition could totally exhaust the good. These are not static; they are dynamic entities.

25. Ryn, *Democracy and the Ethical Life,* 98–99; Babbitt, *Rousseau and Romanticism,* 110–13; Jean Jacques Rousseau, *Emile,* 22; Rousseau, *The Social Contract,* 161, 139.

26. John Stuart Mill, *On Liberty,* 102; Hartz, *The Liberal Tradition in America,* 32; Kirk, *Enemies of the Permanent Things,* 176.

27. Kirk, "What Are American Traditions?" 284.

Critics err by presuming the defense of traditional social and moral arrangements precludes the possibility for change. Traditionalists are often profoundly dissatisfied with the status quo. Tradition, as Burke argued and Kirk reiterated, is continually alive and bringing forth new meanings and possibilities. People have new experiences and gain new images of perfection that they can apply to emerging circumstances: "Traditions do take on new meanings with the growing experience of a people. And simply to appeal to the wisdom of the species, to tradition, will not of itself provide solutions of all problems. The endeavor of the intelligent believer in tradition is so to blend ancient usage with necessary amendment that society never is wholly old and never wholly new." Therefore, in a healthy nation, "tradition must be balanced by some strong element of curiosity and individual dissent. Some people who today are conservatives because they protest against the tyranny of neoterism, in another age or nation would be radicals, because they could not endure the tyranny of tradition. It is a question of degree and balance." Kirk was not being ambivalent here. The people who value a cultural tradition are often the same people "who stress the need for an imaginative and critical assessment of contemporary society." The principle of discrimination must be rooted in a judgment on whether a particular tradition enhances those things that are central and abiding in a culture. Society's task is to evaluate a challenge to a long-standing tradition in terms of whether it represents "a superior insight" or "a slackening of the will and the ability to live up to the high demands of true civilization."[28]

Some critics have contended that Kirk's appeals to tradition amount to merely a nostalgic longing for a vanished past. But, he would reply that the good life cannot be realized by a people who are incapable of venerating the achievements of their past. Given man's dualistic nature, tradition plays an invaluable and necessary civilizing role by helping to direct man's will and imagination toward his enduring purpose. Reform, which brings improvement, must occur within the context of tradition. Mere social experimentation may unleash uncontrollable passions and energies previously restrained by long-established customs and habits. Without the experience of communal traditions, it would be

28. Kirk, *Enemies of the Permanent Things*, 181; Kirk, *A Program for Conservatives*, 305; Ryn, *Democracy and the Ethical Life*, 88–89.

impossible, in Kirk's judgment, for a people to live together without repressive controls on their will and appetites.

The Contract of Eternal Society

By the latter part of the eighteenth century, the idea that civil society is the product of a voluntary agreement by equal people living in the state of nature became popular in many intellectual circles. According to the social-contract theorists, government comes into being when people decide to freely transfer their prepolitical rights of self-protection to a sovereign body. Since government, according to Hobbes, Locke, and Rousseau, exists to serve the interests of the living, the social contract does not include deference to the "wisdom of the ancestors." The legitimacy of government and its laws rests entirely upon the people's temporary sufferance. People are bound together in civil society not by love or duty, but rational, enlightened self-interest.[29]

Against this conception of civil society as merely an aggregation of discrete individuals, Burke posited "the contract of eternal society." According to his view, society is a spiritual unity in which generation links to generation in mutual obligation. Burke's understanding of this contract can be easily misconstrued, though, because he appeared at one point in his *Reflections on the Revolution in France* to agree with popular Enlightenment ideas on the social compact:

> Society is indeed a contract. Subordinate contracts for objects of mere occasional interest may be dissolved at pleasure—but the state ought not to be considered as nothing better than a partnership agreement in a trade of pepper and coffee, calico or tobacco, or some other such low concern, to be taken up for a little temporary interest, and to be dissolved by the fancy of the parties. It is to be looked on with other reverence; because it is not a partnership in things subservient only to the gross animal existence of a temporary and perishable nature. It is a partnership in all science; a partnership in all art; in every virtue, and in all perfection. As the ends of such a partnership cannot be obtained in many generations, it becomes a partnership not only between those who are living,

29. Louis I. Brevold, *The Brave New World of The Enlightenment,* 140; Sterling Power Lamprecht, *The Moral and Political Philosophy of John Locke,* chap. 2; Charles Parkin, *The Moral Basis of Burke's Political Thought,* 6–10; Kathleen M. Squadrito, *John Locke,* 106–8; J. W. Gough, *The Social Contract,* 137–46; Ryn, *Democracy and the Ethical Life,* 111–13.

but between those who are living, those who are dead, and those who are to be born. Each contract of each particular state is but a clause in the great primaeval contract of eternal society, linking the lower with the higher nature, connecting the visible and invisible world, according to a fixed compact sanctioned by the inviolable oath which holds all physical and all moral natures, each in their appointed place.[30]

A careful reading of this passage readily demonstrates that Burke's "contract of eternal society" is wholly at odds with the precepts of the social-contract theorists. Although he did adopt their language when it was useful to him, he consistently objected to the substance of their speculations. Comparing Burke's and Locke's views on the social contract, Kirk concluded that Burke "transcended Locke and touched upon an idea of community infinitely warmer and richer than Locke's aggregation of individuals."[31] Burke's eternal society, which is a permanent entity containing transitory parts, is the ultimate authority from which are derived all the subordinate contracts of communities and governments. It is a moral essence, a higher unity, the permanent element in human social existence transcending time and place. Communities and governments must obey the law of decay and growth, but this higher law possesses "unchangeable constancy." Expressed in terms of ethical dualism, this concept reflects Burke's intuitive grasp of the "One," that which is permanent and constant in man's nature, the mystical unity of which all of man's social creations partake, amid the flux (the "Many") of continual change. The disposition of men, therefore, should be to look upon improvements "with due caution," and "with pious awe and trembling solicitude," because all people, Burke argued, are morally obligated not to tear asunder the "great primaeval contract of eternal society." Such an act Burke considered tantamount to a rebellion against the order of the universe itself.[32]

The same ideas of permanence, continuity, and change that run so strongly in Burke's moral and social idea form the kernel of Kirk's thought as well. The notion of past and present generations linked together in spiritual unity accords with Judeo-Christian moral convictions. We have no right, Kirk claimed, "to break this contract of eternal

30. Burke, *Reflections on the Revolution,* 192–93; Parkin, *The Moral Basis of Burke's Political Thought,* 24–25.
31. Russell Kirk, "John Locke Reconsidered," 298.
32. Burke, *Reflections on the Revolution,* 192, 193–94.

society; and if we do, we are cast out of this world of love and order into the antagonist world of hate and discord." The contract, made between man and God, "is the free promise of God, and its terms are obeyed by man in gratitude and in fear." This "consciousness of our spiritual inheritance," however, can take place only in "an atmosphere of diffuse gratitude: gratitude not merely to the generations that have preceded us in this life, but gratitude toward the eternal order, and the source of that order, which raises man above the brutes, and makes art man's nature." But, this *pietas,* "the veneration of man's sacred associations and of the wisdom of man's ancestors, is presently breaking down. Industrialization and urbanization of our society are breaking the sense of continuity which links generation to generation." The present crisis of modernity has arisen because we have neglected this principle of continuity "so that with us, as Aristophanes said of his own generation, 'Whirl is king, having overthrown Zeus.'" A just and well-ordered society requires that continuity be preserved in religious and ethical convictions, literature and schooling, political and economic affairs, and the physical fabric of life. The principle of continuity expresses the present generation's solicitude to the wisdom of the past and also its "concern for the future of the race." In an age when traditions are being cast aside with reckless abandon, Kirk warned that we must return to the principle of continuity "out of simple anxiety for self-preservation."[33]

To preserve continuity, Burke advised a cautious approach to reform. Although change is necessary to conservation, the alteration of present institutions and customs should proceed only after careful deliberation. Change in society should occur like the growth of a great oak tree. A human observer hardly senses any change at all, but the oak does grow. Burke saw that reform carried out in a civilized spirit was absolutely necessary to the continued vitality of society: "A state without the means of some change is without the means of its conservation. Without such means it might even risk the loss of that part of the constitution which it wished the most religiously to preserve." On the other hand, whirlwind alteration in which the past is rudely cast aside precipitates de-

33. Kirk, *A Program for Conservatives,* 295–97. See also Burke, *Reflections on the Revolution,* 193–94.

structive social upheavals. Prudent reform, which entails preserving and reforming at the same time, "is quite another thing. When the useful parts of an old establishment are kept, and what is superadded is to be fitted to what is retained, a vigorous mind, steady, persevering attention, various powers of comparison and combination, and the resources of an understanding fruitful in expedients, are to be exercised; they are to be exercised in a continued conflict with the combined force of opposite vices, with the obstinacy that rejects all improvement, and the levity that is fatigued and disgusted with everything of which it is in possession." But, some may object, Burke acknowledged: "'Such a mode of reforming, possibly might take up too many years.' Without question it might and it ought." It is part of the duty of the statesman to carry out alteration with caution and a veneration toward long-established institutions. Burke felt that the admirable principles of conservation and correction operated strongly in the British Constitution. Reform was carried out, not by dissolving the whole constitution, but by retaining those parts that were not impaired while dispensing with those which were deficient:

> Our political system is placed in a just correspondence and symmetry with the order of the world, and with the mode of existence decreed to a permanent body composed of transitory parts; wherein, by the disposition of a stupendous wisdom, moulding together the great mysterious incorporation of the human race, the whole, at one time, is never old, or middle-aged, or young, but, in a condition of unchangeable constancy moves on through the tenor of perpetual decay, fall, renovation, and progression. Thus, by preserving the method of nature in the conduct of the state, in what we improve, we are never wholly new; in what we retain, we are never wholly obsolete.[34]

The abstract doctrines of the French Jacobins were in sharp contrast to Burke's politics of prescription. He opposed no doctrine more violently than the belief that rights, liberties, and the forms of government are the proper objects of abstract reason.[35] No man, Burke knew, is so wise or knowledgeable that he can constructively act in matters of

---

34. Burke, *Reflections on the Revolution,* 108–9, 274–75, 122.
35. Ibid., 150–51.

morals and government without resorting to the collective wisdom of the species.

A widespread respect for this filtered experience of mankind will spare society the social and political disorders attributable to the spread of pernicious "rights of man" doctrines and the glorification of "reason." For example, with respect to the issue of individual liberty about which there has been much abstract speculation resulting in bitter conflicts, Burke declared that liberties should be transmitted as an entailed inheritance, much like property is transmitted, from one generation to the next. Each generation, while enjoying its legacy of freedom, should feel obligated to preserve and transmit its liberties to the rising generation. There is no need, Burke added, to make "any reference whatever to any other more general or prior right."[36]

Government, as well, should not be devised "in virtue of natural rights, which may and do exist in total independence of it; and exist in much greater clearness, and in a much greater degree of abstract perfection: but their abstract perfection is their practical defect. By having a right to everything they want everything. Government is a contrivance of human wisdom to provide for human *wants*. Men have a right that these wants should be provided for by this wisdom."[37]

What, then, are the real rights of men, according to Burke? They are derived from long usage and convention, unlike the merely pretended rights of the French revolutionaries. Burke stressed the concrete rights afforded men by a civil society respectful of its past:

> a right to live by the rule; they have a right to do justice, as between their fellows, whether their fellows are in public function or in ordinary occupation. They have a right to the fruits of their industry; and to the means of making their industry fruitful. They have a right to the acquisitions of their parents; to the nourishment and improvement of their offspring; to instruction in life, and to consolation in death. Whatever each man can separately do, without trespassing upon others, he has a right to do for himself; and he has a right to a fair portion of all which society, with all its combinations of skill and force, can do in his favour. In this partnership all men have equal rights; but not to equal things.[38]

36. Ibid., 151–52, 121; Kirk, *The Conservative Mind,* 47–48, 57.
37. Burke, *Reflections on the Revolution,* 57 (Burke's emphasis).
38. Ibid., 150.

On the other hand, the "pretended rights" of the abstract theorists "are all extremes: and in proportion as they are metaphysically true, they are morally and politically false. The rights of men are in a sort of middle, incapable of definition, but not impossible to be discovered. The rights of men in governments are their advantages; and these are often in balances between differences of good, in compromises sometimes between good and evil, and sometimes evil and evil." Men have "no right to what is not reasonable, and to what is not for their benefit."[39] Rights, then, are not derived from the abstract premises of the social-contract theorists, but from custom, usage, and convention.

In the wisely governed society, the presumption is against hasty alterations arrogantly disregarding past achievements. Better to bear present ills than to incur unwittingly, in a fit of hurried impatience for change, unanticipated consequences that could make things worse. Kirk appealed to G. K. Chesterton's principle of "the democracy of the dead," by which the present generation expresses its debt to its ancestors. Like Burke, Chesterton affirmed the ethical value of a society governed by an eternal contract linking generations in a spiritual bond:

> Tradition may be defined as an extension of the franchise. Tradition means giving votes to the most obscure of all classes, our ancestors. It is the democracy of the dead. Tradition refuses to submit to the small and arrogant oligarchy of those who merely happen to be walking about. All democrats object to men being disqualified by the accident of birth; tradition objects to their being disqualified by the accident of death. Democracy tells us not to neglect a good man's opinion, even if he is our groom; tradition asks us not to neglect a good man's opinion, even if he is our father.[40]

In the traditional society, the will of ancestors operates as a living force in the present.

Challenges to America's Traditions

Kirk was confident that the "American political tradition has given the American people a higher degree of justice and order and freedom—taking society as a whole—than any other political tradition, with the

---

39. Ibid., 154.
40. Kirk, *The Conservative Mind,* 436; Gilbert K. Chesterton, *Orthodoxy,* 48.

exception of the English, has conferred upon any other people." As a large geographical entity with great ethnic and regional differences, America also "has room aplenty for a variety of traditions; diversity and freedom of choice, indeed, are themselves American traditions."[41]

But, very few of these traditions actually originated on American soil. Most came from the Old World and were modified "somewhat to suit the American experience." The American political tradition is rooted in two main sources of opinion and custom: the Christian religion and the colonial historical experience. Since nearly all the population, excepting "some million American Jews," are either "professed Christians or people strongly influenced by Christianity," Kirk concluded that America is a "Christian nation." Christianity also provides the underlying moral ethos for society: "Christian morality is the cement of American life and Christian concepts of natural law for man, natural rights for man, and necessary limitations to human ambitions all govern our politics and even our economic system." The other foundation of the American tradition, the English colonial experience, gave us the "fruits of representative institutions, local government, private rights, and the supremacy of law." When Americans consider the principles upon which their government is erected, they do not think of some newly conceived, abstract political doctrines. Rather, they have in mind a body of traditions originating in England or elsewhere in Europe and tested by long, civilized experience in America.[42]

But even so, he feared that America's respect for the legacy of its past, the continuity of American tradition, and the wisdom of Ameri-

41. Kirk, "The American Political Tradition," 134–35; Kirk, "What Are American Traditions?" 283, 287.

42. Kirk, "What Are American Traditions?" 285; Kirk, *The American Cause,* 21, 32, 48. The United States has become, of course, a far more religiously diverse country since; see also Kirk, "What Are American Traditions?" 285–86, 134, 48; Kirk, "The American Political Tradition," 134. "American attitudes toward representative government, private property, local and private rights, political community, decent manners, family relationships and even the physical pattern of civilized life, all are derived principally from British custom; and these constitute true traditions, accepted unquestioningly by the mass of Americans as 'the American way of life,' even though they were originally imported from Britain in the seventeenth century, and have been strengthened by borrowings from British society ever since." Kirk, "What Are American Traditions?" 286; Kirk expanded on this argument years later in his *America's British Culture.*

cans' ancestors was dangerously evaporating. "Modern men and women live in an age in which the expectation of change often seems greater than the expectation of continuity." There is in public opinion a growing "expectation of change." Not only are our morals, social mores, and religion undergoing rapid and bewildering alterations, but, as a consequence of technological development and urban renewal, so too is our physical environment. "The annihilation of our traditional architecture and town patterns, indeed is only part of a larger revolutionary movement calculated to efface the Past and establish a new society Utilitarian in its principles, so far as it owns any principles." Modern society is threatened with the prospect of the total breakdown of that continuity which links generation with generation.[43]

The greatest enemy of tradition today is industrialization and urbanization. The impulse for change comes primarily from the cities, where people tend to be detached from a community where close bonds of kinship and common experience give structure and meaning to life. Kirk agreed with T. S. Eliot's observation that the "tendency of unlimited industrialism is to create bodies of men and women—of all classes—detached from tradition, alienated from religion and susceptible to mass suggestions: in other words, a mob." By contrast, the agrarian life, partly because it is closely connected with the cyclical change of seasons, is a mode of existence less yielding to the temptations for innovation. "Tradition thrives where men follow naturally in the ways of their fathers, and live in the same houses and experience in their lives that continuity of existence which assures them that the great things in human nature do not alter much from one generation to another." To such people, the perception of change itself seems almost illusionary. "One generation passeth away, and another generation cometh: but the earth abideth for ever," proclaimed the preacher in Ecclesiastes, what "hath been, it is that what shall be; and that which is done is that which shall be done: and *there is* no new *thing* under the sun."[44] Therefore, such people would not anticipate vast improvements

43. Kirk, *America's British Culture,* 85; Kirk, *A Program for Conservatives,* 295; Kirk, *Enemies of the Permanent Things,* 26.
44. T. S. Eliot, *Christianity and Culture: The Idea of a Christian Society and Notes Towards the Definition of Culture,* 17; Kirk, *A Program for Conservatives,* 303; Ecclesiastes 1:4, 9.

in their lives, nor would they succumb to the rising expectations a technological age instills in them or the discontent that such expectations breed.

Conservatism then flourishes best in stable, rural communities where people are slow to break the old ways. Hence, the guardians of tradition have been "recruited principally, although not wholly from our farms and small towns."[45] But if the healthy influence of tradition within society is dependent upon the preservation of the rural mode of life, then what measures must be taken to check the advances of industrialization and urbanization? The small family farm, for which Kirk has an almost Jeffersonian affection, is threatened with virtual extinction. Farmland is being transformed into more valuable residential property. Furthermore, the small family farm of yesteryear, widely acknowledged today as an economically inefficient method of agricultural production, continues to be replaced by large, more efficient, agribusiness corporations. High inheritance and property taxes and the fluctuations of the agricultural produce market make farming today a precarious and often unprofitable profession.

For the most part, Kirk rarely committed himself to any specific governmental schemes for preserving the agrarian way of life, for example, protective tariffs, price supports, low-density zoning regulations, abolishing inheritance taxes on or other tax write-offs for farmland, crop subsidies, local governmental purchase of the development rights to agricultural land, etc. Yet, he did tellingly decry Parliament's failure to pass Prime Minister George Canning's abortive Corn Bill of 1827 as a missed opportunity for Great Britain to have preserved "a prosperous agriculture and hearty landed gentry and a large rural population." When Robert Peel

> Succumbed through a kind of mental osmosis to the free-trading theories of the Liberals; Cobden and Bright swept everything before them; and Britain became the most thoroughly industrialized country of the world, perilously overpopulated, maddeningly decayed in taste and beauty; more and more, the national tone was set by the Black Country and the swollen seaports, rather than by the rural parishes and tight little towns which had nourished English political stability, English literature, and

45. Kirk, *A Program for Conservatives,* 304.

English charm. The bulk of the population, from the 1840s onward,
slipped toward the condition of a proletariat.

But if Canning had succeeded, all this could have been averted. "Britain
could have retained the comparatively balanced economy of France or
Germany or America. That would have been a magnificent accomplishment for conservatives."[46]

Kirk's critique of the social consequences of the free trade policies
of the Benthamites parallels in significant respects the arguments made
by early-nineteenth-century Tory critics of industrialism such as Robert
Southey and even, intriguingly, some socialist critics.[47] Whether protective tariffs could have preserved the pastoral England of Jane Austen
is dubious. Whatever the economic merits of Kirk's criticism may be,
it vividly underscores the enormous philosophical gap separating him
from the ritualistic advocates of laissez-faire economic policies. Advocates of free trade doctrines adamantly oppose any restrictions on the
free workings of the marketplace as infringements on individual freedom and impediments to material improvement and modernization.
Kirk, while he defended private property as a moral and social good,
did not possess an equally high regard for the unfettered free market
system. Values "beyond the dreams of avarice" must take precedence
over the demands of economic efficiency and prosperity. If a choice
must be made between conserving "the permanent things," through
which men find identity and purpose in their lives, and swelling the
nation's material wealth, he advised sacrificing the latter. He supported
tariffs to protect small farmers against the destructive consequences of
a capricious global market to family and community. He deplored the
ruinous destruction of the environment wrought by corporate greed
and commercial excess. To protect the traditional order against the

46. Kirk, *The Conservative Mind,* 132–33.
47. The late sociologist Robert Nisbet made the intriguing argument that traditional conservatives and socialists in democracies "have . . . a good deal in common." Both use the past to attack the present and "are compelled to live under the
liberal welfare state, which they do not like, though for different reasons." Nisbet
observed, as well, that conservatives are more strongly critical of capitalism than
even Marxist socialists. "The reason is apparent. The Marxians at least accepted
the technical framework of capitalism for their coming socialism. For conservatives in many instances, that was the loathsome part of it." Robert Nisbet, *Conservatism: Dream and Reality,* 65, 109.

destructive and socially disintegrative consequences of the avaricious pursuit of wealth and rapid industrialization, Kirk unquestionably favored appropriate governmental regulation of market forces. The need for order and community always took precedence in his mind over the need to satisfy people's insatiable lust for material aggrandizement.

5 ORDER IN THE SOUL AND COMMONWEALTH

Men are qualified for civil liberty in exact proportions to their disposition to put moral chains upon their own appetites.

—Edmund Burke, *Reflections on the Revolution in France*

The first of the soul's needs, the one which touches most nearly its eternal destiny, is order.

—Simone Weil, *The Need for Roots*

RUSSELL KIRK HAD a "philosophical dream" once. It was a "curious dream," the only one of its sort in his life, he recalled, in which "a vision with some symbolic meaning" came to him. He dreamed that he was seated with members of a men's club debating "the question of whether God is just." Several conflicting opinions were heard. Then, one member, an egalitarian humanitarian, declared that if God had made men unequal—and this seemed a reasonable premise since some men are damned and some are saved—then either God does not exist or else He is "a capricious tyrant." Suddenly, in a flash, the men's club room, in which all had sat conversing so enjoyably, was "suspended—like Mahomet's coffin—between Heaven and Earth." Outside, there "lay the terror of infinite space.... We were marooned forever in nothingness."

Even so, the situation was not entirely disagreeable. All that was required of these men is that they be content to live within the constraints that their present circumstances imposed on them. After all, there were plenty of amenities, such as unlimited time for pleasant discourse, an endless supply of books, magazines, and fine Scotch. They could "spend eternity pleasantly enough in their tidy changelessness." But a few malcontents in the group, unhappy with the restraints and limitations of this little world, rebelled and immediately suffered the unhappy fate of being "flung into infinity" where they were "swallowed by nothingness," the very definition of hell. These restless souls damned themselves by their actions. By rebelling against the divine order, they brought about their own unhappiness and misery. Kirk had a "symbolic glimpse of eternal order."

This allegorical dream succinctly encapsulates the essence of Kirk's teaching on the nature of order. If we live in accordance with the eternal order, we can live in reasonable happiness and peace. If, however, we "demand more from life than life can give," then we will pay an enormous price.[1] Anarchy, misery, and eventual destruction inevitably ensue.

All political doctrines, even anarchism, posit some vision of order. None sanction disorder as an end for its own sake. Kirk's defense of social and moral order did not imply that he attributed a preference for disorder to his adversaries. His goal instead was to understand the causes of disorder and the principles upon which civilized order depends for its existence. To fully explore Kirk's position requires that several interrelated issues be examined. Pursuant to this end, I have divided this chapter into four sections. The first defines and explicates Kirk's concept of order. Section two deals with his concept of justice, its foundational principles, and their ramifications for social order. The discussion here leads into Kirk's stance on the natural aristocracy and the problem of who should rule. Section three examines the relationship between order and freedom. How are moral and legal restraints upon the will of the individual justified? Does genuine freedom, as opposed to mere license, presuppose the existence of moral and social order? To what extent have ideologies, with their doctrines of universal emancipation, contributed to disorder in our time? The final section discusses Kirk's reaction to a development he considered a major threat to contemporary social and moral order: technological innovation.

THE PRINCIPLE OF ORDER

Kirk's most extensive discussion of the concept of order is found in his *The Roots of American Order* (1974), in which he examined the reli-

---

1. Kirk, *Confessions of a Bohemian Tory,* 240–41.

gious and philosophical foundations of the American social and political order. He opened the book's first chapter with an explication of the definition of order found in Simone Weil's classic book, *The Need for Roots*. Writing during the Nazi occupation of her native France, Weil (1910–1943) was painfully conscious of the terrible consequences that ensue to soul and commonwealth alike when the moral and political order disintegrates. The first need of the soul, the need that most closely touches its spiritual destiny, she declared, is order. Order is "a texture of social relationships such that no one is compelled to violate imperative obligations in order to carry out other ones." The norms of our civil social order dictate certain obligations. In an ideal order, our obligations would be so systematically and harmoniously arranged that none would be incompatible. Imagine a life without order, she asked us. Consider a man traveling at night without a guide. His confused wanderings immediately convey to us an image of a life devoid of order. The need for order precedes even the need for food and shelter. Without order, life becomes insufferable—bewildering, frightening, and without love, peace, or certitude. "The individual," observed Kirk, "finds purpose within an order, and security—whether it is the order of the soul or the order of the community. Without order, indeed the life of man is poor, nasty, brutish, and short."[2]

Although the words "law" and "order" are often coupled and are related, they are not identical. "Laws arise of a social order, they are the general rules which make possible the tolerable functioning of an order." Order, however, is "bigger than its laws."[3] The underlying customs, mores, habits, and traditions that constitute the moral ethos of a community establish its order. The positive law alone cannot, in the absence of widespread voluntary public obedience to the moral order, establish true order.

Social order depends on two distinguishable yet inseparably connected factors: the order of the soul and the order of the commonwealth. In the commonwealth, order "signifies the performance of certain duties and the enjoyment of certain rights in a community: thus we use the

---

2. Simone Weil, *The Need for Roots: Prelude to a Declaration of Duties toward Mankind,* 9, 11. See Kirk, *The Roots of American Order,* 10, 474.
3. Weil, *The Need for Roots,* 3.

phrase 'the civil social order.'"[4] In the soul, order entails bringing the passions under the disciplining influence of ethical imperatives.

The connection between the order of the soul and the commonwealth has its roots in classical political thought. As Sir Ernest Barker pointed out, with Plato and Aristotle the virtues of the state are the virtues of the individual writ large. In all the regimes described by Plato in *The Republic,* the dominant spiritual orientation of the citizens determines the order of the state. Since social and political phenomena are products of the soul, the character types within society determine the order of the state. Plato and Aristotle rejected, as did Kirk, the notion (advanced by naturalistic thinkers such as Rousseau, Marx, and the Social Darwinists) that the impersonal forces of nature over which he has no control determine man's character. A well-ordered soul has its natural impulses under the discipline of the higher will. Impersonal economic or social forces external to the will of man do not shape his soul. The roots of social and personal disorder always lie in the defects of the soul; that is, they are found in the characters of persons. "States do not come out of an oak or a rock," Plato reminded us, "but from the characters of the men that dwell therein." Likewise, Kirk maintained that disorder in the soul and state must go hand in hand.[5]

Ideologists characteristically believe, to the contrary, that a just and stable social order can be established merely through economic or political reforms. They exaggerate the potential for creating and maintaining order through the institutional manipulation. Our hope against this intellectual fallacy, according to Kirk, lies in the revival of Edmund Burke's principle of true order, a "consecrated society guided by veneration and prescription." In such a society, order is "the harmonious arrangement of classes and functions which guards justice and gives willing consent to law and ensures that we all shall be safe together." This temporal order, however, is only part of a larger supernatural order. Order in the moral realm "is the realization of a body of transcendent values—indeed, a hierarchy of values—which give purpose to existence and motive to conduct." The foundation of social tranquility is reverence and obedience "to God and the dispensations of Providence,

4. Ibid., 5; see also Kirk, *A Program for Conservatives,* 227.
5. Sir Ernest Barker, *The Political Thought of Plato and Aristotle,* 291; Plato, *The Republic,* 544D, cited by Barker, p. 103; Kirk, *Enemies of the Permanent Things,* 15.

which work through natural processes," such as the duty of a man to provide for his family.[6]

The recognition of transcendent order in the universe is not a utopian illusion, Kirk pointed out. It does not "make the statesman into a dreamer, but a realist. Knowing his theology and his history, [the prudent politician] . . . takes it for granted that man is not a perfect nor a perfectible being." Hence, the statesman "will endeavor to make life tolerable, not impossibly perfect."[7]

JUSTICE AND NORMS

The "malady of normative decay" today, insisted Kirk, "gnaws at order in the person and at order in the republic." Order can be restored only after man comes to understand how and why he has fallen away from old truths. A norm is an "enduring standard" for public and private conduct, "a law of nature which we ignore at our peril." Without widespread respect for norms, men fall into disorder and confusion because they lack common values for ordering their lives. Insofar as people willingly respect the authority of norms, they are able to achieve order in both soul and commonwealth through the self-imposition of restraints upon their selfish wills. The only real way to measure the progress of mankind is to observe the strides man makes toward understanding and obeying norms. Through experiencing intuitively that quality of life which is the opposite of selfishness or by exercising their inner checks, people apprehend the norms that enable them to live in harmony.[8]

Kirk listed three "doors of normative perception: revelation, custom or common sense, and the insights of the seer." The primary "source of knowledge about faith and morals is divine revelation." Direct revelation, God speaking directly to a chosen few, is extremely rare. The Bible lists only a few such occasions, for example, when God spoke directly to Moses on Mount Sinai. Man has had to rely chiefly upon custom and the insights of seers, the sages of the race, as sources of normative perception. For "the most part our norms are derived from the experience of the species, the ancient usages of humanity; and from the perceptions of genius, of those rare men who have seen profoundly into

6. Kirk, *The Conservative Mind,* 66–68; Kirk, *Beyond the Dreams of Avarice,* 166.

7. Kirk, *Beyond the Dreams of Avarice,* 23–24.

8. Kirk, *Enemies of the Permanent Things,* 16–17, 286.

the human condition—and whose wisdom soon is accepted by the mass of men, down the generations."[9] Most truths, which govern our lives, are derived from these sources.

Customs are expressions of the collective experience of civilization. These shared experiences and common-sense judgments constitute a vast body of wisdom that can be called upon when we are in moral doubt. We adhere to these customs, or prejudices, because traditionally all decent men, that is, those who have concerned themselves with the good, have likewise lived in conformity with them. They have the effect, to use Burke's phrase, of making "a man's virtue his habit." Without custom, man would perpetually be paralyzed by agonizing doubt over the most ordinary of moral decisions.[10]

We are governed by the normative insights of our ancestors and by great minds "because we are incapable of inventing better rules for ourselves." Seers, such as Moses, Solon, Isaiah, Sophocles, Plato, St. Paul, Dante, and Pascal, possessing great intuitive gifts, saw truths to which the rest of us are blind. Because of man's unchanging nature, "men of vision are able to describe the norms, the rules, for mankind."[11] Private judgment, unattached to norms or dogmas (Kirk used these terms interchangeably), "is insufficient for the moral order or the social order." Rather, we must rely upon the moral insights that mankind has acquired over thousands of years by painful trial and error and from revelation and the perceptions of men of genius. These represent a body of wisdom "of human nature and of the civil social order which no one individual possibly can supplant by private rationality. The justification for the norms that govern our existence does not depend on whether they give the individual pleasure or upon one's subjective values or needs. Having a more profound basis, norms point us toward our transcendent destiny; they enhance, if acknowledged and obeyed, the possibilities of communal harmony. They are, hence, "the standard against which any alleged value must be measured objectively."[12]

---

9. Ibid., 34–35.
10. Ibid., 36.
11. Ibid., 39; Burke, *Reflections on the Revolution,* 182.
12. Kirk, *Decadence and Renewal in the Higher Learning,* 254; Kirk, "Prescription, Authority, and Ordered Freedom," 28; Kirk, *Enemies of the Permanent Things,* 21.

"Justice," wrote Kirk, "cannot be enforced until a tolerable civil social order is attained."[13] But human social order cannot exist by itself without a widespread consensus of opinion on the principle of justice. Thus, order and justice must go hand in hand. Neither can exist without the other. Order without justice would mean the brutal order of the police state imposed on an unwilling population by threats and punishments. Justice without order is inconceivable since justice by definition stipulates a particular order.

Implicit in Kirk's definition of order as the "harmonious arrangement of classes and functions" is the principle of distributive justice. The ancient Greeks defined justice *(Dike)* as "to each man his due." In other words, everyone "should perform the duties and receive the rewards that accord with his own nature." The distribution of talents and abilities among men is assumed to be unequal. Some men are more capable as scholars; others have greater leadership capabilities, or are best fitted to exercise various practical skills. Those who exhibit superior abilities should be rewarded in proportion to their contributions to the well-being of the community. Ideally, then, every man should obtain that which is best suited to his nature: to do the work for which he is best suited and to receive the appropriate rewards for that work. Given that "talents and desires vary among men," Kirk held that society would be unjust if it rewarded each member uniformly or allotted rights and duties unsuited for them. Justice would forbid murderers from obtaining guns, alcoholics from obtaining spirituous drink, or infants from obtaining freedom from parental supervision. "To each his own" means "to the natural entrepreneur, the fruits of industry; to the natural scholar, the contemplative leisure which is his need and his reward."[14]

The concept of the just society would lead neither to a society of unchecked competition between selfish egos nor to a "sentimental and enervating socialism." The determinants of rewards and privileges in a Benthamite society would be the resolutions of the marketplace or the outcome of a fierce competitive struggle for advantage. Those lacking sufficient competitive skills for success would clearly be disadvantaged. Their claims to justice would be rudely trampled underfoot. On

13. Kirk, *The Roots of American Order,* 6.
14. Ibid., 83, 464–66; Kirk, *Enemies of the Permanent Things,* 287.

the other hand, socialism in its various forms denies the reality of differences in talent and ability. By attempting to impose a uniform equality upon all, socialism discourages those most able to contribute to the well-being of society while rewarding those whose contributions are either slight or destructive. Consequently, socialist policies tend to promote sloth, immorality, and pure selfishness. Kirk wrote:

> Really, men are equal in two ways only: before the judgment-seat of God (who, remember, doesn't assign them all to the same place), and in the eyes of the law. But human beings are not equal otherwise; and because they are unequal, they are not entitled to identical things. Every man is entitled to what is his own; but he has no right to take away from another who has more by his talents or inheritance. For the slothful man is not equal to the diligent man. The brute is not equal to the saint. The fool is not equal to the sage. The traitor is not equal to the loyal man. The selfish is not equal to the loving. The coward is not equal to the hero. The rogue is not equal to the just judge. And nothing could be more unjust than to treat all these, under the lunatic pretext of natural equality, as if they ought to live one life and enjoy the same rewards.[15]

A sound social order further requires the "general acquiescence in social distinctions of duty and privilege." Political equality is unnatural, as Burke held, because experience tells us that moral capacity, talents, and strengths vary greatly among individuals. Not all are mentally, spiritually, or physically capable of exercising moral leadership. Challenging the egalitarian spirit of our age, Kirk reminded us that leadership "by men of ability, birth, and wealth is one of the most natural, and most beneficial, aspects of civilized life." By contrast, egalitarianism, the effort to impose equality upon man, perverts the natural order of things. As Burke wrote in opposition to the dogmas of the radical levelers, "Believe me, Sir, those who attempt to level, never equalize. In all societies, consisting of various descriptions of citizens, some descriptions must be uppermost. The levellers therefore only change and pervert the natural order of things; they load the edifice of society, by setting up in the air what the solidity of the structure requires to

15. Kirk, *Confessions of a Bohemian Tory,* 280; See George Santayana, *Dominations and Powers: Reflections on Liberty, Society and Government,* 366–70 for a discussion of equality based not on treating individuals as mathematically identical units but rather in terms of a "moral identity between souls."

be on the ground."[16] Like Burke and John Adams, Kirk held that a natural aristocracy exercises its authority not solely, nor even primarily, because of wealth nor inherited titles, but due to its possession of virtue and wisdom. Adams defined the basic characteristics of an aristocracy: "By aristocracy, I understand all those men who can command, influence, or procure more than an average number of votes; by an aristocracy every man who can and will influence one man to vote besides himself. Few men will deny that there is a natural aristocracy of virtues and talents in every nation and in every party, in every city and village."[17]

The qualities of character necessary for aristocratic status are best conveyed by James Fenimore Cooper's famous description of a gentleman as "one elevated above the mass of society by his birth, manners, attainments, character, and social condition." When society ceases to honor the high "character, strong intellects, good birth and practical shrewdness" which the natural aristocracy possesses, Kirk added, then the envy of the masses and the oppressive power of the state will assume awesome proportions. The natural aristocracy serves as a socially beneficial brake both on the will of the masses, who without proper leadership are liable to sink to moral dissipation, and the tendency of the state to concentrate its power into a unitary political structure. Destroy the natural aristocracy, and "an administrative corps of ambitious and clever reformers" will replace it. Kirk warned that this "elite" will be "recruited out of conformity to party fanaticism and enthusiastic adherence to venomous intellectual credo." Their loyalty will be totally to the state and its ends, or to whatever political party is responsible for their ascendancy to power and privilege. This super-bureaucracy will be devoted to state planning for its own sake. Power will become increasingly concentrated in the state that will take on all the characteristics of a military organization. An aristocracy, then, is not an enemy of freedom, as some allege, but is absolutely essential to its preservation. It serves freedom because it interposes "barriers between the government and the private concerns of citizens." The "society from which

16. Kirk, *The Conservative Mind,* 67; Burke, *Reflections on the Revolution,* 139.

17. John Adams, *The Works of John Adams,* vol. 6, 451–52.

aristocracy has vanished, never to rise again, is a civilization open to despotism; and tyranny, once established there, maintains itself by pandering to the society's vices. The jealousy for personal liberty which aristocracies possess having been extirpated, omnipotent sovereign and defenseless subject stand face to face." Therefore, Kirk suggested, the policy of the state should be to arrange its honors, lands, and constitutional powers to foster the growth of a natural aristocracy as "defenders of the people against the encroachments of despotism." At the same time, however, the government should be so constructed that it can exercise "vigilance over the swelling ambition of the aristocrats." In this matter, an aristocracy forms part of a checks-and-balance system essential to the preservation of liberty.[18]

Because it is an "incontrovertible fact" that all societies are governed by some sort of an elite, Kirk believed that it is of paramount importance for a society to elevate only those people qualified by their superior virtue and wisdom to the leadership class. A genuine aristocracy provides a worthy model for imitation by the remainder of society. As a body, an aristocracy can exert moral leadership on society, lifting it as a whole away from purely momentary, self-indulgent impulses. A true aristocracy will conform to Coleridge's concept of the "clerisy or clerks" whose primary duty "is the maintenance and advance of the moral cultivation of the people." Through the institutions of education and religion, aristocrats cultivate the national morality and character. By diffusing knowledge among the people and providing moral models worthy of emulation, they uplift the moral tone of society as a whole.[19] The just society further inculcates a widespread and enduring respect for the existing structure of order because the object of its laws is the reconciliation of the claims of various competing social groups. As Aristotle observed, the causes of sedition are rooted primarily in the passion for equality. When any social group in the polis, whether rich or poor, fails to enjoy its just share of constitutional rights, it is ripe for insurgency. In Aristotle's best practical regime, the polity, where the competing claims of all classes are respected, the motives for class conflict are mitigated since both the poor and rich have agreed to live

18. Kirk, *The Conservative Mind,* 67–68, 244, 367–470, 212–13, 98.
19. Ibid., 98, 142–43.

under the self-imposed restraints of the law. The rich have agreed to refrain from the most blatant kinds of exploitation, while the poor have moderated their desire to appropriate the property of the wealthy. By moderating their aspirations, thus permitting others to retain what is their just due, the elements of society can be brought together in a stable and orderly regime. Citizens gradually learn through habits induced by just laws how to check their immediate impulses and how to deal justly with others. Everyone will be, in effect, educated for the middle. This Aristotelian middle, or mean between two extremes (anarchy and authoritarianism in this case), fosters social harmony by encouraging moderation in all things. "This 'mean,'" as Kirk explained, "does not signify the average, the mediocre, or that splitting the difference which Aristotle called 'the disputed middle.' Nor does the 'mean' always signify necessarily, the best. Rather, the mean amounts to that harmony achieved by avoiding excesses and extremes; it is moderation, or balance, in private life and in public."[20]

ORDER AND FREEDOM

The principles of moral and political order embodied in Burke's political thought, revived and defended by Kirk as a challenge to contemporary radical and revolutionary thinking, have frequently been criticized for allegedly having about them the distasteful odor of authoritarianism. A widespread hostility exists, especially among those inspired by utilitarian or Rousseauistic doctrines, toward any body of thought that seeks to impose restraints upon the will of either individuals or popular movements. Unable to bear any norm of conduct above that of individual feeling, critics argue that any external or internal restraints placed on the spontaneous will of the individual by society, government, culture, or religion constitute barriers to the fulfillment of his true humanity. Hence, the removal of all moral, cultural, and legal restraints is a prerequisite to the realization of the full potentiality of the individual. The desire to unleash impulses that have hitherto been restrained by custom, traditional moral codes of behavior, political institutions, religion, habit, or social manners is periodically expressed in society by

20. Aristotle, *Politics,* 1301a19 and see books 4–6; Kirk, *The Roots of American Order,* 86–95. See Aristotle, *Nicomachean Ethics,* book 2, vi–ix.

those who out of boredom are easily excited by the anticipation of novelty or the opportunity to express repressed emotions.

Liberty defined as the absence of limitations placed on the individual will and appetite implies that liberty and order are incompatible. Order in the soul means that a certain quality of impulses, those originating in the arbitrary or selfish will of the individual, must be disciplined with reference to the individual's ultimate spiritual purpose. The order of the commonwealth, likewise, involves a similar disciplining of the arbitrary, unchecked will of the sovereign (regardless of whether sovereignty resides in a single individual or a majority of the citizens) with reference to the basic constitutional law of the regime. But does this disciplining power entail a loss of liberty, or should it be viewed as a necessary precondition for true liberty? Without it, would liberty descend into license? Would the ensuing anarchy become so intolerable that people would eagerly embrace the grim order of the authoritarian state to escape its horrors?

Burke made the case for order as a precondition of liberty. He argued that liberty is possible only when most citizens have disciplined their selfish and antisocial passions. A direct relationship between the range of liberty that a people can beneficially enjoy and their capacity for individual self-discipline was a fundamental principle of Burke: "Society cannot exist unless a controlling power upon will and appetite be placed somewhere and the less of it there is within, the more there must be without. It is ordained in the eternal constitutions of things, that men of intemperate minds cannot be free. Their passions forge their fetters."[21] There must exist control of will and appetite both for the individual and the government. "Society requires not only that the passions of individuals should be subjected, but that even in the mass and body, as well as in individuals, the inclinations of men should frequently be thwarted, their will controlled, and their passions brought into subjection." These passions are disciplined by social, moral, and religious restraints. The ability of the bulk of citizens to bring inner control over their passions seems to determine, as Babbitt pointed out, "the degree to which any community is capable of political liberty."

21. Burke, "A Letter from Mr. Burke to A Member of the National Assembly" (1791) in *Reflections on the Revolution* (New York: E. P. Dutton and Co., 1960), 282. All references to Burke's *Reflections on the Revolution in France,* unless otherwise indicated, refer to the Liberty Fund edition.

The task of the statesman, then, is to mediate between order and liberty. This task, Burke assumed, can never be settled in the abstract but must be adjusted to circumstances. Liberties and restrictions, he wrote, "vary with times and circumstances, and admit of infinite modifications, they cannot be settled upon any abstract rule; and nothing is so foolish as to discuss them upon that principle." An individual is qualified for liberty in proportion to his ability to live a life of self-discipline. No appeal to an abstract principle, divorced from the actual concrete circumstances of a particular situation, can be a sufficient moral basis for granting liberty. "Is it because liberty in the abstract may be classed amongst the blessings of mankind, that I am seriously to felicitate a madman, who has escaped from the protecting restraint and wholesome darkness of his cell, on his restoration to the enjoyment of light and liberty?" asked Burke. "Am I to congratulate a highwayman and murderer, who has broke prison, upon the recovery of his natural rights?" Rights and liberties, then, contrary to the arguments of Lockean liberals, the American Civil Liberties Union, and other advocates of abstract individual rights, do not exist apart or against society since, as Kirk stressed, they "can only exist within a social order—that is, in community." Therefore, when community begins to fail entirely, "the most fundamental civil liberties, including the life, cannot be secured." There are worse things than loss of liberty, as people who have lived through great political and social upheavals know well. In such circumstances, it is not unusual for a desperate people to embrace even a totalitarian master rather than endure continual fear of loss of their property and maybe their lives.[22]

Christianity, too, teaches that moral self-discipline is a precondition for freedom. The soul is in a state of perfect freedom, according to the Christian, when it is obedient to God's will. It is original sin, the rebellion of the individual against God's will, that leads men astray. The essence of sin is "pride: the desire of the human creature to make himself the center of the universe." In this sinful condition, "love lies subordinate to lust, or libido." To lust is to prefer worldly things to the things of God. Drawing on St. Augustine, Kirk cited three forms of lust: the lust

22. Burke, *Reflections on the Revolution,* 152, 93; Babbitt, *Democracy and Leadership,* 110: Kirk, *Rights and Duties: Reflections on Our Conservative Constitution,* 73–74.

of material possessions—the sin of avarice in which the individual desires wealth and worldly possessions beyond what is good for his soul and to the disadvantage of the less privileged in society; "the lust for power, *libido dominandi*," the desire for power for its own sake and to subdue others; and, lastly, sexual lust. All human beings are affected by these lusts, to which Kirk attributed the causes of "crimes, public disorders, and aggressive wars." What, then, is the remedy? The Christian is advised to diminish his personal desires and live in accordance with God's law. "Order your soul; reduce your wants, live in charity; associate in Christian community; obey the laws; trust in Providence—so will we find order, Augustine told his generation, and so will we come to know that service to God which is perfect freedom." As the preacher in Ecclesiastes commanded, "Fear God, and keep his commandments: for this is the whole duty of man." Beyond lust, there is true love, agape. When questioned by the Pharisees, Jesus responded, "Thou shalt love the Lord thy God with all thy heart, and with all thy soul, and with all thy mind. This is the first and great commandment. And the second is like unto it. Thou shalt love thy neighbor as thyself. On these two commandments hang all the law and the prophets."[23]

These principles are not peculiar to the Christian faith. The teachings of the Buddha coincide largely with the Christian message, as Babbitt pointed out. Freedom of the highest order, according to the Buddhist, can exist only by limiting one's desires. The Buddhist strives to renounce his expansive desires, that is to say, his needs for fulfilling appetites and sensual pleasures that keep him tied to the perishing sensate world of flux. By limiting one's desires, especially those of lust, ill will, and delusion, the individual escapes from the flux of existence to the eternal, that which is immortal and abiding in his existence. To achieve one's highest goals in life, the individual must "impose progressively his ethical will, affirmed as an immediate fact of consciousness, upon his outgoing desires." If he wants to be a carpenter, then he must do the work of a carpenter, just as a "king must do the work of a king," a saint must do a saint's work, and so forth. True liberty cannot be found in indolence. According to the Buddha, as Babbitt explained,

23. Kirk, *The Roots of American Order*, 162, 160, 167; Ecclesiastes 12:13; Matthew 22:37–40.

the greatest sin is the "lazy yielding to the impulses of temperament *(pamada);* the greatest virtue *(appamada)* is the opposite of this, the awakening from sloth and lethargy of the sense, the constant exercise of the active will." Liberty, then, as various philosophical and religious traditions aver, can be found neither in individual self-gratification (as the utilitarian would hold) nor in flowing with one's spontaneous impulses (as the Rousseauist would affirm), but resides instead in the individual's "ethical self; and the ethical self is experienced not as expansive emotion, but as an inner control." Ethical work establishes order. By working ethically in the manner of Buddha, the individual "grows more at one with himself and at the same time tends to enter into communion, not indeed with mankind at large, but with those who are submitting to a similar ethical discipline" and so moves to the "universal centre." Liberty, then, involves a struggle, not primarily to gain control over others, but to gain control over one's own expansive appetites.[24]

The principal threat to ordered freedom in the West comes from the advance of ideological doctrines urging the throwing off of the traditional restraints on the expansive will. In his analysis of this threat, Kirk invoked the arguments of philosopher and historian Eric Voegelin (1901–1985) who saw modern ideological movements as Gnostic heresies that substitute "a dream of a perfect mundane society for the City of God." The dream's two main manifestations in contemporary politics are communism and liberalism. Marxist egalitarianism challenges the foundation of the traditional sources of order. The Marxist holds that men should "be treated as identical units, and compulsory equality of condition enforced." Liberalism, a milder, right wing version of the avowedly collectivist Marxist heresy, also eventually brings about the totalitarian state. Inspired by Rousseauistic and Benthamite suppositions, liberalism unleashes awesome state power. It often arrives at the behest of the Gnostic activist who sees as his mission the furthering of merely man's material needs while ignoring his spiritual needs. Progress is defined as providing creature comforts and a life of ease for citizens of the state. "The Gnostic passion to alter society and human nature

24. Babbitt, *The Dhammapada,* 96; Babbitt, *Democracy and Leadership,* 194, 222; Babbitt, *Literature and the American College,* 36n1. Paul Elmer More once declared that this sentence was the teaching of all of Babbitt's work. See Frederick Manchester and Odell Shepard, eds., *Irving Babbitt: Man and Teacher,* 328.

endures no opposition, and, when it can, destroys all the traditional political and economic institutions which impede its consolidatory progress." If it is assumed, as liberals do, that the sole purpose for earthly existence is material and terrestrial success, then, Kirk asked, "why should reactionaries be allowed to delay the advent of Utopia?"[25]

Kirk depicted the diabolical imagination that inspires the Gnostic mind in an elaborate allegorical novel, *Lord of the Hollow Dark*. The evil protagonist of this gothic tale, Mr. Apollinax (an occultist with diabolical ambitions and a character who closely resembles the scientist-reformers in C. S. Lewis's fantasy novel, *That Hideous Strength*) has assembled a group of disciples, mostly damned souls. He has promised them "The Timeless Moment"—when they will experience ecstasy and, through a diabolical ceremony, escape time itself to experience pleasures eternally. In a "sermon" to his disciples, Mr. Apollinax outlines the substance of his Gnostic religion, "'[T]he first truth,' Apollinax began, 'is that there is but one Lord, and but one world. That Lord is not the unjust Demiurge. He is kind, and all impulses in his world are natural. It has been the repression of natural impulses that has worked ferocious mischief upon mankind almost from the beginning. Now modern science teaches us that universal happiness may be secured through the removal of repression and inhibition.'"

Christian symbols are inverted here. Mr. Apollinax has to use a Voegelinian phrase, "immanentized the eschaton"; in other words, he has expressed the belief that the world can be turned into a terrestrial paradise. He has preached a "New Morality" in which all the disciplining restraints provided by Christianity and universal moral norms are to be extinguished. Mr. Apollinax is a moralist in the Rousseauistic sense of that word. His is a hedonistic faith: all pleasure-giving impulses are by definition good. Appealing insidiously to his disciples' base urges, Mr. Apollinax promises his followers a terrestrial paradise in which all their Promethean desires can be fulfilled, "'... not in some fancied 'other world,' is to be found our immortality. Here and now, you and I can be in eternity. What we hear now, see now, feel now, do now can be our seeing, hearing, feeling, acting when the dream-realm

25. Kirk, *Enemies of the Permanent Things,* 254, 287; Kirk, *Beyond the Dreams of Avarice,* 24–25.

of material things has passed away altogether. Our passionate pleasures need know no termination: they may outlast the great globe itself.
You and I may dwell unchanged, at what [T. S.] Eliot calls 'the still
point of the turning world,' quite freed from past and future, quite unalterable. You and I may be as gods." Mr. Apollinax's faith, like twisted
ideologies of our age, panders wholly to the lower inclinations—which
explains its enormous attraction. Every longing or urge, no matter how
diabolical or evil, is left unchecked. Furthermore, these pleasures can
be experienced utterly without guilt. Without transcendent norms to
check the lower impulses, nothing is impermissible, "Our Lord is not
the lord of prohibitions and shackles. We are too liberated . . . liberated
from guilt, from shame, from memory, from expectation. We shall be
immersed in the true reality, the eternal present. Our ceremony of inno-
cence shall purge us of lesser fears and longings. In an experience that
fulfills and satisfies every dream and desire, an experience attainable
nowhere but here on Ash Wednesday night, you shall know such pleasure as the ordinary senses cannot afford. And again I promise you
that this pleasure shall have no end."[26]

Symbolically, Kirk intended his complicated and highly allusive
philosophical novel to depict modern society fearfully threatened by
Gnostic ideologies that tempt us to throw off all religious and moral
sanctions. The old myths and symbols "through which truths about
order are conveyed grow dim with the passage of world-time and many
disrupting events." The Gnostic heresies erect new symbols, promise
the perfection of man and society, and invite people to expect eternal
bliss and a life without restraint. Such powerful doctrines have severed
man from the divine ground of being and from the moral prerequisites
of social order.[27] Order is impossible when the diabolic or idyllic imagination of Gnostic ideologues gains sway over the minds of men. As
peoples' egos go unchecked, they come into remorseless conflict with
one another. Moral anarchy engenders social anarchy, only to be in turn
succeeded by the grim order of the totalitarian state. Consistent with
his dualistic view of human nature, Kirk insisted that the measure of a

26. Kirk, *Lord of the Hollow Dark,* 93–95.
27. Russell Kirk, "Voegelin on History as Consciousness of Reality" (paper
delivered at Indiana University, Bloomington, as part of the Patten Lecture Series,
January–March 1980), 21.

man's liberty is determined by the extent to which his selfish appetites are brought into conformity with enduring norms.

THE CHALLENGE OF TECHNOLOGY

Although Kirk understood that time cannot be halted, his attitude toward even those changes that materially benefit society was always tinged with ambivalence. He feared the socially and morally disruptive consequences of innovation and progress. He frequently commented on the adverse effects of certain modern inventions, such as the automobile and television, upon the stability of society, community, and home. Unlike the libertarians and most neoconservatives who uncritically praise economic efficiency, productivity, and competition, Kirk stressed the disruptive effects of modern capitalism on traditional mores, habits, and well-ordered communities. He abhorred the internal combustion engine, for example, even more passionately than does Al Gore. But while Gore worries about its environmentally destructive consequences, Kirk feared its socially destructive effects. He assailed the internal combustion engine as "a mechanical Jacobin" that "rivaled the dynamo" (that is, the modern industrial system) in terms of its "power to alter national character and morality more thoroughly than could the most absolute of tyrants." The mass production of automobiles destroyed the old patterns of community and order, creating a mass proletariat.[28] Materially well-compensated workers now rush about, thoroughly isolated in their automobiles, with little opportunity and less desire to foster the mutual dependence and fellowship found in preindustrial societies. Another innovation, television, in spite of its power to communicate and entertain, is similarly pernicious, not only because of the decadent quality of its programming (which Kirk presumed), but also, and more significantly, because it draws people away from serious reading, reflection, and fellowship with family members and neighbors. Spouses and children become strangers to one another as the flickering light of the television box becomes the dominant presence in the household. The vast Hollywood culture industry, which controls the content of most television programming, has usurped the traditional role of parents as the primary transmitters of culture and moral values to their

---

28. Kirk, *The Conservative Mind,* 325–26; Kirk, *Enemies of the Permanent Things,* 98.

progeny. The anonymous programmers for the television networks often exert more influence over the formation of children's moral character and their views than does anyone else, including parents.[29]

The passion for altering our physical environment likewise disrupts the order of community. The sweeping away of the beauty, charm, and historical association of many fine old buildings and their replacement by the standardized ugliness of modern steel and glass office structures or rows of identical suburban houses is a trend that must be resisted, Kirk believed. The eagerness to tear down the old, often merely because it is old, in order to build the new, may be "one of the great errors of our age." When urban planners "destroy a neighborhood landmark, they efface one more bond of community and leave men and women rootless and vaguely dissatisfied." In Kirk's judgment, we have done more damage to our nation's "artificial and natural beauty since the Second World War than we were able to accomplish in the hundred years preceding. Our obsession with fast cars and our longing for the prestige of the suburban home have driven freeways remorselessly through a thousand living communities, destroying everything in their path. These appetites have drained leadership and money out of our cities, at the same time devouring the countryside through subdivisions, so that capitalistic America fulfills the prophecy of Marx that countryside and town merge in one blur."[30]

29. Kirk, *The Conservative Mind*, 325–26; Kirk, *Enemies of the Permanent Things*, 98; see Kirk, "Battle of the Boob-Tube," *National Review*, January 4, 1980, 38. Kirk was not any more enamored of the personal computer (what he called the "electronic computer") than he was of automobiles and television. While he was primarily troubled by the destructive consequences of these two later contraptions on the fabric of traditional society, his criticism of the emergence of the computer technology involved a different concern. He viewed computers as mere computation machines. Their use dulls the imagination and displaces real learning in schools and institutions of higher learning. Computer technology, in the mid-1980s when he wrote this essay, was in a relatively primitive stage of development compared to what was commonly available by the late 1990s. He did not envision the possibilities of the personal computer as a powerful tool for research, communication, and creativity. Kirk, "Humane Learning in the Age of Computer," in *Redeeming the Time*, 115–27.

30. Kirk, *The Intemperate Professor: And Other Cultural Splenetics*, 144–47. See John R. E. Bliese, "Richard M. Weaver, Russell Kirk, and the Environment," 148–58, for a discussion of Kirk's views on the environment. Bliese's analysis is marred by his tendency to indulge in "Club of Rome" apocalyptic scenarios of impending environmental disaster.

Kirk's longing for traditional order and his hostility to the advance of technology parallels closely the reaction of such nineteenth-century English conservatives as Sir Walter Scott, Samuel Taylor Coleridge, and Robert Southey, who were profoundly disturbed by the radical changes wrought by the Industrial Revolution on England's traditional rural society. Mass industrialism in Britain, America, and most of Europe, coupled with the emerging of egalitarian, democratic institutions, was effacing much of the old conservative order. With accelerating speed, Kirk wrote, "the control of wealth was passing from rural proprietors to industrialists and financiers, from commercial interests of the old sort to great new manufacturing enterprises." The population was migrating from the countryside to the industrial towns in pursuit of work in the emerging factories. The growth of industry brought about a changing social structure that spawned the emergence of two new sorts of people: the rising entrepreneur, who despised tradition and the old social order because his "immediate advantage lay in alteration, aggrandizement, consolidation..." and the proletarian, "rootless and ignorant, sporadically hungry," who "knew almost nothing of the old values; also he was bored, and change is a show; and his appetites were material." While the commercial classes were gravitating toward radical individualist doctrines, the working classes, impatient for material gains, were making egalitarian collectivist demands.

The old aristocratic order suffered displacement by these powerful forces. In traditional England and "even in America," Kirk pointed out, "the structure of society had consisted of a hierarchy of personal and local allegiances—man to master, apprentice to preceptor, householder to parish or town, constituent to representative, son to father, communicant to church." This old "network of personal relationships and local decencies," the loyalty to persons that Cardinal Newman had called Toryism, however, was "brushed aside by steam, coal, the spinning jenny, the cotton gin, speedy transportation, and the other items in that catalogue of progress which school-children memorize." Thereafter, personal loyalties "gave way to financial relationships." Coinciding with this phenomenon was the triumph of democracy. By the end of the century, the franchise was extended to include nearly all classes. Many of the newly enfranchised citizens were afflicted with a naive confidence in the power of elected officials to legislate universal happiness. As a consequence of rising popular demands for public services, governmental benefits, and protections from life's hardships, power and authority became alarmingly centralized in the state.

Conservatives did not, and could not, check this flood of social change, which left them "nearly impotent" and reduced "to the function of trimmers." By "trimmers," Kirk meant politicians who habitually seek expedient solutions to issues. The "intensification of industrial production and the decline of the old patterns of life in town and country" and the "triumph of the masses," which reduced the power of the old classes to maintain and preserve high standards of taste and decorum in the arts, resulted as well in the decay of taste and beauty in architecture and all the other artistic endeavors in both England and America. For Kirk, these events formed a catastrophic combination. Social order demands the support of multiple examples of beauty to elevate the mind. Today, instead, numerous distressing examples exist of the degradation of beauty brought about by the rise of the mass mind.[31]

As a social and cultural critic rather than a policy analyst, Kirk seldom offered specific detailed corrective policies for the social and cultural ills he perceived. His recommendations for controlling the alarming rapid progress of the modern forces of urbanization and industrialization were neither precise nor extensive. He never seriously proposed that we escape from the present into an idealized preindustrial past. "The conservative, knowing that radical backward-looking alteration is quite as perilous as radical forward-looking alteration, accepts certain things as givens in history, and reconciles irrevocable change to certain unchanging values" is Kirk's realistic judgment. Hence, even in his most nostalgic moments, he realized that the pastoral world of sturdy yeoman farmers and the landed gentry of Jane Austen's England or the antebellum South had vanished forever. The task of the conservative, rather, is to strive to achieve a tolerable balance between the preservation of traditional patterns of life and the forces of modernization. This principle is central to Kirk's discussion of British statesman George Canning's abortive Corn Bill of 1827. As noted in chapter 4, he considered the failure of this bill to be a lost opportunity for British

31. Kirk, *The Conservative Mind,* 226–30; Kirk, *The Intemperate Professor,* 156–57.

conservatism to preserve "a tolerant and far-seeing balance between the land and the mills." If Canning's bill had been enacted, "British rural life might have suffered only minor dislocations," he speculated.[32] Yet, ironically, his defense of protective tariffs instead vividly illustrates the daunting task facing even the most imaginative conservative who labors to balance in the real world the competing demands of change and permanence.

Kirk endorsed the arguments made by the original defenders of the Corn Laws in the early 1800s that protective tariffs were necessary to maintain the nation's natural aristocracy and preserve the balanced economy of farming and industry. But, even if additional economic protectionism could have prevented the proletarianization and industrialization of England, as Kirk believed, this goal would have been attained probably only at a prohibitively high political price. The earlier British Corn Laws, by raising the tariffs on the importation of grains, had driven up the prices for all grain products in England, causing considerable deprivation and suffering. The protective duties imposed by the Corn Laws provoked numerous, sometimes violent, public protests, including the famous Peterloo Massacre of 1819, which could have led, if the laws had not eventually been repealed, to a general popular rebellion. The laws constituted a classical example of how bad legislation can divide a population into two warring groups: landowners and their tenant farmers who benefited from protectionism, and the wage earners who found their breadstuffs rapidly becoming unaffordable. In the post-Napoleonic War depression, wages fell and many members of the British working classes were thrown into the ranks of the unemployed. The flames of political radicalism were consequently stoked by the economically depressed conditions in which the least privileged classes found themselves.[33] Conservatives are at their best, as Kirk had acknowledged, when they prudently accede to necessary change for the sake of order. Arguably, then, the free trade legislation that ended the anti–Corn Laws protests, despite Kirk's misgivings, were a necessary conservative measure that put these widespread public protests to an end.

32. Kirk, *The Prospects for Conservatives,* 204; Kirk, *A Program for Conservatives,* 247; Kirk, *The Conservative Mind,* 130–33, 390. See chap. 4 for a more extensive discussion of George Canning's abortive Corn Bill.
33. R. R. Palmer, *A History of the Modern World,* 446–47, 462–63.

In any event, Kirk's critique of industrialism and democratism reveals the extent to which he was troubled by the moral and cultural consequences of these social and economic forces. In his depiction of the baneful influence of industrialization on nineteenth-century British society and morals, Kirk stressed the influence of economic factors more than is usual in his work. His argument that industrialization was largely responsible for the breakdown of the traditional order of Great Britain seems to contradict his usually strong abhorrence of deterministic economic theories. To largely blame the prevailing market system for the rise of rationalism, the egalitarian spirit of the age, and the decline of old social institutions may be getting the cart before the horse or, at least, may be oversimplifying causal relationships. In this interpretation, ideas and culture are given a secondary importance as causal factors in history. Kirk did not, unfortunately, adequately examine the interplay of economic, intellectual, and social forces in the eighteenth and nineteenth centuries that made possible the burst of technological energy we know as the Industrial Revolution.

Although misguided or ill-conceived governmental or economic programs can weaken or destroy a social order, they cannot by themselves create or maintain true order. Typically in the West, social reformers have tended to unduly trust either the power of scientific or technological innovation or political or economic reform to ease such symptoms of social disorder as crime, drug abuse, poverty, class conflict, divorce, sexual promiscuity, etc. Scientific advances in health care will enable us all to live happier and longer lives, and the spread of democracy and the free markets will ease class warfare, it is commonly believed.[34] Kirk dismissed such panaceas as delusions. He recognized that the problem of order is not easily susceptible to technological, economic, or political fixes. Order, he affirmed, is ultimately a moral and cultural problem. If a society fails to nurture a class of leaders who possess what

34. Regarding this point, I am reminded of an expert on conflict resolution who spoke at my college recently about the troubles in Northern Ireland. He argued that the tensions between Catholics and Protestants were caused mainly by the disparity of wealth and opportunity between these two warring factions. The solution to the conflict would be for the British government to redistribute the wealth more equitably and expand the social welfare safety net. One of my colleagues commented sarcastically to me later that the speaker "imagines that all the problems of Northern Ireland could be resolved if only they had an adequate dental care program."

Kirk called "the unbought grace of life" (that is, a spirit of class, duty, honor, and responsibility) or a people who willingly adjust their conduct to accord with universal standards of right and wrong, then a true social order will always elude it. The spread of democracy or material wealth cannot by themselves reduce the self-absorption or belligerence of human beings.

6 COMMUNITY AND FREEDOM

To be attached to the subdivision, to love
the little platoon we belong to in society, is
the first principle (the germ as it were) of
public affections. It is the first link in the
series by which we proceed toward a love
to our country, and to mankind.
—Edmund Burke, *Reflections on the Revolution in France*

[H]e who is unable to live in society, or who
has no need because he is sufficient for him-
self, must be either a beast or god; he is no
part of a state. A social instinct is implanted
in all men by nature . . .
—Aristotle, *Politics*

ONE OF THE EFFECTS that Russell Kirk sought in his writings and lectures during the 1950s and 1960s was to draw the then nascent American conservative intellectual movement away from its flirtation with the doctrinaire individualism of the libertarians toward a genuine conservative individualism. Although libertarians and traditionalists were united in their opposition to prevailing liberal dogmas, their fragile alliance was frequently disrupted by angry mutual denunciations. Libertarians, troubled by the growth of the modern Leviathan state and its concomitant threat to individual liberty, bemoaned Kirk's reverence for prescriptive institutions and rights, organic society, and inherited wisdom. Given their natural suspicion of any constraints on freedom, libertarians sensed a statist bias in Kirk's thought. Typically, libertarians such as the late Edith Efron, author of the widely read *The News Twisters,* dismissed traditionalists such as Kirk as "collectivists and statists" who deny "the individual's right to think, value, and act freely, save in one realm:

economic production." The traditionalists' position is little more, she claimed, than a "blueprint for fascism."[1]

At worst, Kirk replied, such individualistic doctrines are destructive to civilized social existence. At best, they reflect a naive view of the individual's potential to act morally and rationally outside the confines of community. The genuine conservative, Kirk explained, has "always stood for true community, the union of men, through love and common interest, for the common welfare." When emancipated from the traditional ties that bind them to family, kinship groups, church, voluntary associations, and all those other social groups that give meaning and purpose to their lives, people typically become anxious, frustrated, lonely, and bored. Our age is haunted, as the noted American sociologist Robert Nisbet (1913–1996) proclaimed, by the "specter of insecurity." Nisbet (whose community conserving principles were greatly admired by Kirk) graphically depicted the disastrous consequences of the loss of community for the modern world:

> Surely, the outstanding characteristic of contemporary thought on man and society is the preoccupation with personal alienation and cultural disintegration. The fears of the nineteenth-century conservatives in Western Europe, expressed against a background of social dislocation, have become, to an extraordinary degree, the insights and hypotheses of present-day students of man in society. The widening concern with insecurity and disintegration is accompanied by a profound regard for the values of status, membership and community.[2]

Libertarians, blinded by their narrow dogmatic individualism, are oblivious to these concerns. The "towering moral problem" of our times, the loss of community, was to them no problem at all.

We are thus brought to Kirk's central argument concerning the modern problem of community lost and community regained. The necessary preconditions for community are, he held, order, tradition, authority, diversity, localism, and hierarchy. Beginning in the later part of the eighteenth century, a series of social and ideological disruptions afflicted traditional communities. The drive toward collectivism, foreshadowed

1. Edith Efron, "Conservatism: A Libertarian Challenge," 12.
2. Kirk, *A Program for Conservatives,* 140–41; Robert A. Nisbet, *The Quest for Community,* 3. See Brad Lowell Stone's *Robert Nisbet: Communitarian Traditionist* for a perceptive exegesis of Nisbet's social theory.

by the Jacobin ideology of the French Revolution, loosened the old ties that once bound people to family units, local neighborhoods, and numerous autonomous groups. This emancipation from group memberships paved the way for widespread anomie and the desperate and often careless quest for new community. An ineluctable slide toward a totalist state, brought about by the progressive atomization of American society, could only be halted, Kirk believed, if the requisite social and moral foundations of community are restored.

We begin by looking at the body of social and moral principles and the tradition to which they are attached that inform Kirk's understanding of community. His diagnosis of the causes for the present loss of community and his remedies for its restoration are discussed in the following section. The last three sections deal with an issue central to the definition of conservatism. As previously noted, he and his libertarian adversaries struggled over the theoretical content of the postwar American conservative intellectual movement. In respect to his view on the nature of man, the transcendent nature of morality, and the role of the state, Kirk differed sharply with libertarian thinkers. The issues at stake in these debates over the nature and ends of community are described here. In the last section, I examine Kirk's prescription for reconciling laissez-faire doctrines with sound social and moral principles.

THE SOCIAL AND MORAL FOUNDATIONS OF COMMUNITY

Aristotle and Cicero first grasped the normative principles that bind men into genuine community in a manner most relevant to contemporary concerns. They were later absorbed and transmitted by Burke, Alexis de Tocqueville, and finally the American sociologist Robert Nisbet. These thinkers, among others, form within Western political thought an intellectual tradition in which community in its moral and social dimensions is valued as indispensable to civilized existence. The conservative thought of Kirk is, in fact, a summary and development of this tradition applied to the contemporary problem of community.

Aristotle famously described man as a social animal. We desire the company of others for both survival and fellowship. A creature "who is unable to share in the benefits of political association, or has no need to share because he is already self-sufficient" could not be a man, but would have to "be either a beast or a god." An omnipotent god does not need others to survive, and nonhuman creatures rely largely on their instincts for survival. By contrast, man depends on others of his species to help clothe, feed, house, and protect him. Moreover, cut off from the fellowship of others of our kind, we would be unable to rise above the level of savagery to develop our full potential as humans.[3] The notion, then, that man once existed outside society in a prepolitical state of nature would have struck Aristotle as inconceivable.

Genuine community, though, serves higher purposes beyond passing fellowship and convenience. Among its ends, as Aristotle taught, is character formation achieved by inculcating moral habits. We become habituated to moral self-discipline by conforming to the laws and customs of society.[4] Community, in its highest form, is an association of people united by common agreement on ethical norms. It is a "human association under the guidance of ethical conscience," Claes Ryn explains. "Man's true humanity is realized by being shared. It should be understood that community is experienced between those who order their lives with reference to the same universal moral authority."[5] Insofar as we obey the directives of our higher will, we are in spiritual unity with others.

For obvious practical reasons, the members of a community must agree upon a basic code of right and wrong. Otherwise, they would be living in continual fear of injury from others. Even among a band of thieves, to use Cicero's famous example, justice must be observed. While robbers will practice their villainy and wickedness on others, they would never "steal from another that belonged to the same confederacy" lest they would be "immediately expelled as unfit to be members of even a society of robbers; and should the leader himself not distribute their booty according to the measures of justice and honesty, he would either be murdered or deserted by his company."[6] A community, then, can be defined as an association of persons united by justice.

Necessity forces a band of thieves to deal honestly and truthfully with each other. If they are to succeed in their enterprises, then they cannot rob or cheat their associates. But such an association would amount to no more than an "uneasy peace" between its morally corrupt members. Criminal conspiracies are notoriously short-lived. Mutual suspi-

3. Aristotle, *Politics,* book 1, 1253a, 1–35.
4. Aristotle, *Nicomachean Ethics,* book 2, 1.1103a–1103b, 1–25.
5. Ryn, *Democracy and the Ethical Life,* 83.
6. Cicero, *Offices,* book 2, 11.

cion and betrayal typically cause a breakup. A true community endures because its members are under the guidance of norms that transcend mere enlightened self-interest. For these norms to have enduring value and universal validity, Kirk understood, they must exist in their own right independently of any other justification and transcending all immediate self-interest. Genuine community cannot be sustained by a group of men "who lead ethically undisciplined lives," Ryn explains. It "can emerge only in a society where the forces of egotistical interests are tempered by concern for the common good." Voracious and sanguinary impulses erupt with ferocious intensity if not properly checked by the disciplinary power of transcendent norms. "Lacking an apprehension of norms, there is no living in society or out of it," Kirk observed. "Lacking sound conventions, the civil social order dissolves."[7]

As embodied in the fundamental laws of the society, norms represent the unchanging element in social existence—that which unifies people into community. But social differentiation, both Aristotle and Cicero agreed, is also desirable. Aristotle defined the polis, the Greek political community, as an entity composed "of different kinds of men, for similars cannot bring it into existence." No single person is either omniscient or omnicompetent, hence no one can claim total self-sufficiency. Given this basic fact of human nature, it follows that the polis "is composed of different elements, mutually exchanging different services in virtue of different capacities." This exchange of goods and services among the various elements of the polis enables the collective to attain a higher level of self-sufficiency than would be possible for any individual or family.

A polis, then, "by its nature is some sort of aggregation." Imposing uniformity on a people by making them too similar would destroy the polis and transform it into a kind of household. Aristotle denounced Plato's proposal for communizing wives, children, and property as a solution to the problems caused by divisive class animosities within the polis. "None of those evils ... is due to the absence of communism. They all arise from the wickedness of human nature."[8] To control the destructive consequences of social conflict, instead, the constitution of the polis

7. Ryn, *Democracy and the Ethical Life,* 83; Kirk, *Enemies of the Permanent Things,* 27.
8. Aristotle, *Politics,* book 2.2 and 2.5.12.

must be constructed to check the inclination toward partisan and arbitrary behavior while enhancing the possibilities for social cooperation. Aristotle proposed a mixed government, the polity, based on principles as old as Solon's reforms of the sixth century BC Athenian constitution. The polity had as its final aim the reconciliation of the diverse interests composing the polis. Ideally, in such a state, none of the legitimate interests of any class, wealthy or poor, would be violated because each class would have sufficient power and resources to protect its vital interests.

Similarly, Kirk praised the rich diversity, found in contemporary American society, as a guarantor of freedom and individuality. He strongly opposed pressures to supplant the federal structure of government, what Orestes Brownson called "territorial democracy," with a centralized "plebiscitary democracy." He valued the proliferation of local autonomous groups as barriers against governmental intrusions into local liberties and personal affairs. The "Federal Constitution deliberately erected barriers against direct popular control of the national political apparatus. But in their townships and counties, and to some extent even in their state governments, the mass of people enjoyed strong powers and rights—'territorial democracy.'" Kirk contrasted this "territorial democracy" with "plebiscitary democracy," which he defined as "the infatuation with an abstract, infallible People, and the concentration of 'popular' power in an absolute, centralized government."[9]

Group memberships were not seen by Kirk as a problem to be overcome by public administration but as indispensable aids to a vital community and to human moral development. First, we love, as Burke pointed out, that "little platoon we belong to in society," the family and the local community. From these primary associations we move upward along a hierarchy of relationships that finally bring us to "a love of country, and to mankind."[10] The principle that our attachment to what is near and dear to us, our immediate relationships, must take precedence over any affections that we may feel for the larger social whole is a fundamental principle in Kirk's conservative position.

The modern collectivist, on the other hand, strongly objects to the formation of group memberships. These attachments dilute the power of centralized authority and induce people to adopt the perspective of

9. Kirk, *Enemies of the Permanent Things*, 235–36.
10. Burke, *Reflections on the Revolution*, 136–37.

the group to which they are attached rather than that of the collective whole. Group associations are condemned, therefore, as barriers to collective cooperation and unity. Once stripped of their local and group associations, the political collectivists predict, the people, as an undifferentiated mass, will become wholly responsive to the collective interests of society. The community of voluntary associations and strong neighborhoods "is detested by the radical social reformer, in our century," Kirk asserted, "who would like to see society forced into a single rigid mold, characterized by central administration, ruled through executive decree, uniformity of life, and eradication of all personal and local distinctions." People find their identity and purpose in life through membership in groups. Remove these associations and the possibilities for community are not enhanced but extinguished. Recent historical experience has not been encouraging to radical reformers who had eagerly anticipated the beneficial consequences of detaching people from group memberships. The modern release of the individual "from traditional ties of class, religion, and kinship," while it has made him free, explained Nisbet, it has not given him the anticipated "sense of creative release" predicted and hoped for by the humanitarian enthusiasts, but rather has resulted in a growing "sense of disenchantment and alienation. The alienation of man from historic moral certitudes has been followed by the sense of man's alienation from fellow man." As a consequence, such terms as frustration, anxiety, and insecurity, descriptive of social disintegration, "have achieved a degree of importance in present-day thought and writing that is astonishing."[11]

Kirk admired Aristotle's "best practicable regime," the polity, in which power is vested in a large middle class. The polity is "founded upon common affections as well as upon common interests." The "community of friendship advocated by Aristotle became an American ideal; the reconciling of interests and classes was a conscious objective" of the American Founding Fathers. "And Aristotle's praise of the middle class was a kind of endorsement of American society, for from the beginning America was predominantly a middle-class society, in the sense that small independent farmers made up the bulk of the population.... The middle was almost all encompassing in America." The idea of

11. Ibid., 136–37; Kirk, *The Intelligent Woman's Guide to Conservatism,* 52; Nisbet, *Conservatism,* 10, 52.

political and social balance, "expressed by Aristotle and Polybius and Plutarch, was incorporated directly into the American constitution."[12]

Aristotle's concept of distributive justice adds a further support to community. According to this principle, those citizens who contribute the most to the good of the polis will receive a proportionally greater share of its rewards and honors. Personal merit and contribution to the well-being of the community are held at a premium. Community, as has been pointed out, requires a special orientation of will that brings one into harmony with others similarly motivated. Distributive justice rewards those who exercise their humanistic self-control while punishing those who would pursue purely selfish advantage for themselves or their group to the detriment of others.[13]

The Decay of Community

If a genuine community is an association of persons voluntarily united by affections and interests, then self-indulgent, partisan, and selfish impulses will bring about its destruction. Such, Kirk believed, is precisely the present situation. Community has been terribly afflicted in our times by social and ideological disruptions. Consequently, for Kirk, like Nisbet, the "towering moral problem" of our time is the loss of community. He attributes this decay to three interconnected causes: industrialization, urbanization, and social boredom.

Mass industrialization, Kirk admitted, has given the modern world a degree of material comfort and wealth previously unknown. But, it has also contributed to the "revolutionary destruction of traditional society." Invoking rhetoric similar to the nineteenth-century Tory critics of the Industrial Revolution, Kirk blamed rapid technological innovation for uprooting people from inherited community. With the triumph of technology, the "veneration of humane learning began to diminish among men of business, especially in America. Applied science seemed the key to power, possibly the cure to all the ills of humanity; the social theories grouped under the label of 'positivism' provided a convenient

12. Kirk, *The Roots of American Order,* 91, 94.
13. Aristotle, *Politics,* book 3, 9. My analysis of Aristotle on community has been aided by Sir Ernest Barker's introductory essay and chapter notes in his translation of Aristotle's *Politics.* See Sir Ernest Barker, Introduction to *The Politics of Aristotle.*

apology for the deification of technology." In addition, mass industrialization draws people from rural communities, where the sense of continuity and purpose flourish best, to more urbanized areas where they become deracinated members of the proletariat. Shorn of tradition and roots, they join the "Lonely Crowd" of the late David Riesman— "a mass of individuals without real community, aware that they matter to no one, and often convinced that nothing else matters."[14]

To counter the spread of industrialization and urbanization, Kirk recommended that conservatives embrace agrarianism:

> The conservative will do everything in his power to prevent the further diminution of our rural population, he will recommend the decentralization of industry and the deconcentration of population, he will seek to keep as many men and women as possible close to the natural and customary world in which tradition flourishes. This will not be an artificial reaction against a natural process of consolidation, for our intensive industrialization and urbanization, from the days of Hamilton to the Korean War, have been deliberate policies, encouraged by state and national governments and by great corporate bodies. If we were to apply half as much energy and thought to the preservation of rural life and the old structure of community as we have put to consolidation, we might be as well balanced in these relationships as is Switzerland.[15]

The "Lonely Crowd" of the modern urbanized, industrialized society is also the bored crowd. Boredom, as a social phenomenon, occurs when the ultimate objects of existence are lost. When people lose sight of their ultimate spiritual purposes (their obligations to God, family, community), they turn to the pursuit of material and sensual gratifications. "Boredom, sloth of spirit, is a vice and the most deadly boredom brings on the appetite for the most forbidden diversions." Social boredom is a powerful destructive social force. As Dean Inge noted, the effect of social ennui upon social upheavals has been largely underestimated: "It is a main cause of revolutions, and would soon bring to an end all the static Utopias and the farmyard civilization of the Fabians. Boredom often generates wars, the supreme exhibition of human folly and wickedness.

---

14. Kirk, *The Conservative Mind,* 483; Kirk, *The Intemperate Professor,* 115; Kirk, *A Program for Conservatives,* 308.

15. Kirk, *A Program for Conservatives,* 308–9.

The criminals who arrange them have studied the minds of the masses who vote for them and of the young men who will joyfully and gallantly die in them. Wars are not boring."[16]

Kirk considered industrialization and certain revolutionary notions to be the two chief causes of social boredom. While admittedly not "the sole cause of this weariness of mind and heart among us, nevertheless, the triumph of the machine is intimately linked with the decay of variety and individuality among the modern masses." As societies became more industrialized, the traditional patterns of life and the ties to family, church, and community from which people derive meaning and purpose in their lives are subsequently undermined and disrupted. Mass production and the machine culture have imposed upon "the human mind a boredom and lassitude probably unequalled in any previous age of decadence." Modern man has become, as a result of the triumph of the machine, "intoxicated with motion." While neglecting his responsibilities to family, church, and community, he "seeks insatiably after new sensations." Mere hedonism, the insatiable lust for novel sensual pleasures, becomes the norm. The pleasures of the contemplative life are unknown in this environment. Since thinking involves pain, the individual abandons "himself to the flux of novelty and speed."[17]

The "ideas men hold about themselves" also contribute to mass stupefaction. These ideas do not rise up from the mass of men, but filter down to them from the men of ideas who prevail in any age: "The ordinary man takes his ideas from the leading minds of his time or the time just preceding." If social boredom "oppresses the great mass of men, the blame . . . lies with the shapers of national destinies and the philosophers in the Academy. Nature does indeed imitate art. The realm of letters is not a reflection of the mood of society: it is a principal cause of the mood of society."[18] It is in the realm of the imagination, especially great literature, that the recovery of norms has to take place. "Good literature and bad literature exert powerful influences upon private character and upon the policy of the commonwealth." If our age is an age of literary decadence that neglects normative consciousness, he pre-

16. Ibid., 102–3; William Ralph Inge, *The End of an Age,* 216.
17. Kirk, *A Program for Conservatives,* 105; Kirk, *Beyond the Dreams of Avarice,* 308.
18. Kirk, *Beyond the Dreams of Avarice,* 299.

dicted that we will be "left at the mercy of consuming private appetite and oppressive political power. We end in Darkness."[19] When the literature of the age becomes diabolical and perverse, the prevailing norms reflect a similar orientation. An imaginative literature grounded in enduring norms, on the other hand, can lift a society from sloth or material diversions to a life of high purpose and moral self-discipline. Ideas, Kirk maintained, not impersonal socioeconomic forces, as the Marxist would argue, determine the behavior of men.

One of the chief ideas that Kirk combated is the Benthamite notion that economic production is inherently beneficial: "The real end of economic production is to raise man above the savage level, to make possible the leisure which sustains civilization and to free man from the condition of being a simple drudge." Because the regular improvement of one's material condition is not the sole purpose of life, the economic system should aim at things other than the mere gratification of desires. In this respect, socialists and Manchesterian individualists represent two sides of utilitarianism. Each holds as the final goal of the political-economic system the maximization of pleasure for the greatest number of citizens. "Both are founded upon the presumption that the real end of man," wrote Kirk, "after all, is the production-consumption equation." They suppose that the criterion for civilization and the good life is the guarantee of even higher standards of material existence. Their idea of work, as Babbitt pointed out, "tends to reduce work to the lowest terms and to identify it with manual labor." This one-sided definition of work contributes to a deterioration of that inner spiritual life of the individual on which the utilitarians place no value. Confidence in organization and the efficiency of the machine results in the neglect of any consideration of the inner struggle for the attainment of ethical ends. Further, this purely quantitative definition of work, which assumes that all work must result in some good or service maximizing the immediate pleasure of a consumer, if generally accepted, would bring about the collapse of civilization. Civilization depends on the mental effort and self-discipline of a few persons relieved from the drudgery of physical labor. It "is of the highest moment," Babbitt wrote, "that certain individuals should in every community be relieved from the necessity

19. Kirk, *Enemies of the Permanent Things,* 15.

of working with their hands in order that they may engage in the higher forms of working and so qualify for leadership." A genuine civilization "must have men of leisure in the full Aristotelian sense."[20]

The value of true leisure has suffered as a consequence of the quantitative definition of work. The teachings of Karl Marx and Thorstein Veblen's *The Theory of the Leisure Class* have had an enormous impact upon the modern conceptions of work and leisure. For them, Kirk observed, "leisure is simply ostentation, the arrogant luxury and display of privileged classes; it is sought simply out of a longing for selfish superiority, and indulged in as a conspicuous waste." In other words, leisure "meant idleness." The "highest kind of leisure," Kirk retorted, "is at the same time the highest kind of work: that strenuous contemplation which demands the utmost in human powers." Its chief practical object is "self-improvement, or emulation of the highest types of humanity." The Benthamite and the Marxist, on the other hand, "detest the whole realm of contemplation, for contemplation refutes, by its very existence, their system of materialism." True leisure escapes them "because they do not admit the transcendent importance, in this life of ours, of belief in an order that is more than human and more than natural." All forms of leisure have additionally come to be viewed as "equally desirable." The higher forms of leisure, such as "the leisure of contemplation, of artistic achievement, of literary endeavor, of moral reflection, of all the elements which make up the unbought grace of life, are shamefully neglected in favor of a leveling 'leisure' which is mere amusement or idleness." The quality of culture and the higher forms of thinking, by necessity, must suffer. Those who are to carry on "the spiritual and cultural instruction of the people" find that their work is no longer valued because they do not produce anything that gives immediate pleasure. The moral and intellectual tone of a civilization decays since those of superior intellect are not permitted the leisure to think. They must instead serve Mammon or whatever powers that prevail. The true ends of knowledge, truth, and the sources of reason, which need no further justification, are replaced by a Baconian insistence that the object of knowledge is power. This idea "has been embraced by innumerable students of the natural and physical sciences," Kirk noted;

20. Kirk, "Ideology and Political Economy," 389–90; Babbitt, *Democracy and Leadership,* 192, 213, 215, 203.

"power over nature and power over man gratify the *libido dominandi* of man." However, there exists "something within us, for all that" which "cries out for knowledge that is not mere control over nature, a knowledge which is its own justification, a knowledge which reaches upward toward the source of reason." The loss of such knowledge results in a spiritual and social decay. No ends beyond material gratification can be perceived, and the forces of unchecked will and appetite prevail. When the scientist abandons the pursuit of knowledge, he is likely, argued Kirk, to be attracted to the pursuit of power. "What better relief from boredom could there be than demolition of the moral codes of the ages?" asked Kirk. "What work more gratifying to the ego?"[21]

If modern man is to be redeemed from the morally debilitating and socially disintegrative consequences of social boredom, they must be made aware once more of the ends or objects of existence. The will atrophies when man cannot perceive any end or object to existence. Sloth overtakes us as we become "obsessed by means and trifles." A bored people cannot manage the effort required to form a community. They lack the will to form social relationships sustained by love and to sacrifice their immediate personal advantages for the sake of others. Rather, they pull from one another to dwell upon their own personal amusements and diversions or to become candidates for fanatical political causes or religious cults. To escape from this "spiritual malady," which in Kirk's eyes has become a kind of modern purgatory, modern society must restore "certain ends, or purposes in life, which have acted as motives to integrity" since "civil social existence began." He listed seven: the most powerful of these is religious faith. Other motives include "emulation, or the desire for the approbation of the people who set the tone of society," "the desire to provide for the welfare of one's family and heirs," "the desire for worldly prosperity and improved station," the "desire for personal liberty," the "longing for continuity, the assurance that things might be with a man as they had been with his father before him, and so might continue with his son after him." If society discards all these ends, or "motives to integrity," Kirk concluded:

> [T]hen truly men are but flies of a summer, left with no reason for existence except flirtation with paltry amusements. The ancient yearning of strong men to fight the battle of life manfully, to contend against

21. Kirk, *A Program for Conservatives,* 124, 133, 138, 129, 131, 135, 118.

adversity and evil, is dethroned in favor of a feeble infatuation with creature-comforts. Frustration brings lassitude and boredom; and out of boredom grows vice, crime, and the destructive compulsions of the mass-mind. The unbought grace of life is traded at Vanity Fair for a toy and a snigger; but the trinkets of Vanity Fair lose their glitter before morning; and there descends upon the purchasers a satiety more oppressive than the most grinding physical poverty.[22]

The Challenge of the False Individualism

Kirk warned that despite "the potential strength of the conservative instinct in America, American conservatives in this century have had a way of undoing themselves." Their principal error, in his estimation, was "their neglect of the need for true community." The preoccupation "in conservatively-inclined circles [is] with economic doctrines and the dry vocabulary of Efficiency and Success." Having emphasized "economic abstractions at the expense of nearly everything else in society," he predicted that they "will fail to rouse the imagination and sympathy of the best men and women in the rising generation unless they take a different track."[23] He was referring, of course, to the libertarians then gaining influence in conservative circles—a prospect that he viewed with dread. The conservatives could commit no greater folly, he felt, than to abandon their traditional defense of community to pursue the false god of laissez-faire individualism.

The American conservative intellectual movement during the 1950s and 1960s was split basically into two competing camps: traditionalists concerned with the preservation of traditional moral values and rooted communities, and libertarians troubled by the growth of the omnipotent state. Perceiving that this division within the conservative ranks endangered the chances of conservatism becoming a potent intellectual and political force, some conservatives under the leadership of Frank S. Meyer sought to develop a consensus position that would unify these adversaries. It was Meyer's opinion that despite sharp differences of opinion between these "two streams of thought," they "can in reality be united within a single broad conservative political theory, since they have their roots in a common tradition and are arrayed against a com-

22. Ibid., 106–7.
23. Ibid., 140–41.

mon enemy."[24] Meyer proposed that libertarians and traditionalists overcome their "differences of emphasis" and develop a conservative consensus position, "fusionism," "comprehending both emphases." Both camps should keep in mind that their primary common enemy is the "Liberal collectivist body of dogma that has pervaded the consciousness and shaped the actions of the decisive and articulate sections of society over the past half century or more." Because the liberals desecrate the image of man, attack his freedom and transcendent dignity, libertarians and traditionalists have reason to make "a common front and a common struggle." By comparison, Meyer could find no comparable issues of "underlying opposition" between the libertarians and traditionalists. The advantages of a united front are twofold: both positions would find their beliefs deepened as a result of their struggle to work out a common conservative doctrine. A "hard-fought dialectic" will permit them to better understand not only their differences but also their common heritage. In addition, the common-front idea has the immediate tactical advantage of uniting diverse and often conflicting elements of the conservative movement under a common conservative body of ideas. Such an alliance would be a formidable intellectual and political force.[25]

Kirk's reaction to Meyer's proposal was immediate and unequivocal. He adamantly opposed any effort to form for the sake of an opportunistic political advantage a "common front" of traditionalists and libertarians. He saw no advantage in allying himself with libertarians, whom he denounced as a modern ideological variation of utilitarianism. The philosophical canyon separating the Benthamite doctrinaire individualism espoused by libertarians from the community-conserving principles of genuine conservatism was just too great for him to bridge. "A real conservative . . . cannot be a real individualist," maintained Kirk. "The thoroughgoing individualist, in the strict sense of that term, is

24. Frank S. Meyer, "Freedom, Tradition, Conservatism," in *What Is Conservatism?* 8. The intention of this collection of essays written by intellectuals widely considered at the time to be the chief exponents of conservative ideas was to forge a "fusionist" synthesis position so that the libertarian and traditionalist wings of American conservatism would be united.

25. Ibid., 18–19. Meyer, a former Communist, apparently thought that the conservatives would be more politically successful if they formed something like the United Front forged by the Communist party with the Socialists in the 1940s.

hostile toward religion, toward patriotism, toward the inheritance of property, and toward the past," which are all essential to the preservation of genuine community. "A conservative, on the contrary," he continued, "is a friend to religious belief, to national loyalty, to established rights in society, and to the wisdom of our ancestors."[26] Therefore, true conservatism must be "uninfected by Benthamite or Spencerian ideas. . . . Individualism is social atomism; conservatism is community of spirit. Men cannot exist without proper community, as Aristotle knew, and when they have been denied community of spirit, they turn unreasoningly to community of goods."[27] Without community to channel their impulses and give purpose to lives, they become dissipated and purposeless. The Benthamite individualists are oblivious to the true end of social existence—love. Hence, Kirk predicted that if their principles were to gain a hold on the popular imagination, social order would be imperiled. Without love, a community decays into a warring camp of competing individuals.

Kirk's animosity toward the libertarians and their radical individualistic doctrines in the mid-1950s nearly erupted into a permanent break between him and the newly founded *National Review,* soon to become the principal vehicle of conservative opinion in America. During its first year of publication, William F. Buckley, Jr., its young editor, wanted to place Kirk's name on the masthead as a member of the magazine's staff. Having just written *The Conservative Mind, A Program for Conservatives,* and several other books, Kirk was rapidly winning wide critical acclaim as one of America's foremost conservative thinkers. It was only natural that he be included in this new conservative publishing venture. To Buckley's surprise, Kirk objected to having his name appear on the magazine's masthead next to those of Frank Chodorov and Meyer, both strongly committed to libertarian individualism. To have his name placed next to theirs would imply, he wrote to Buckley, in the minds of many, that he was climbing into the same political and intellectual bed with these "ideologues," whose individualistic principles stood at antipodes to his own. He felt that any immediate practical advantage to be gained by an alliance with the libertarians could be attained only at the prohibitive cost of compromising the integrity of his

---

26. Kirk, *The Intelligent Woman's Guide to Conservatism,* 37.
27. Kirk, *A Program for Conservatives,* 211.

position. "I had much rather sacrifice the support of ten ossified Benthamites," he explained to Buckley, "than the support of one real conservative." Nevertheless, Buckley ignored Kirk's objections. Now infuriated, Kirk fired off a blistering rebuke. Although he would manage, he wrote in a strongly worded letter, "to endure appearing between the same covers with Chodorov and Meyer, I won't be cheek by jowl with them on the masthead." To Buckley, Kirk appeared to be indulging in tedious ideological quibbling. "So help me God, I cannot understand your obsessive preoccupation with Frank Meyer and the direction his work is taking," replied the now clearly exasperated Buckley. "Admittedly he disagrees with you on a number of points which are, he feels and a number of others feel, important at a point when the very nature of conservatism is being re-examined."[28]

Genuinely puzzled by Kirk's testy obduracy, Buckley was either unaware of the gravity of the issues at stake for the substance and direction of conservatism, or else he felt that these debates distracted from the more urgent task of building a united front against collectivist ideologies. In either case, he was tackling a more difficult task than he probably realized. Donald Atwell Zoll describes the formidable complications of such unifying efforts: "The crux of the Fusionists' position rests upon an attempt to merge the doctrines of classical nineteenth century liberalism with some elements of traditional conservatism. But it is an unhappy wedding; John Stuart Mill and James Fitzjames Stephen cannot be made to share a nuptial couch."[29]

Babbitt perceptively described the core issues distinguishing the libertarian from the traditionalist in his discussion of "true and false liberalism." These two types of liberal doctrines represented for Babbitt antithetical orientations competitively struggling to shape contemporary ethical thought. True liberalism, which Babbitt identified with the

---

28. Russell Kirk to William F. Buckley, Jr., September 1, 1955; Russell Kirk to William F. Buckley, Jr., November 29, 1955; William F. Buckley, Jr., to Russell Kirk, April 6, 1956. Kirk had perhaps additional personal reasons for wishing to disassociate himself completely from Chodorov and Meyer since he believed that both "were conducting a campaign to reduce his influence among conservatives." Nash, *The Conservative Intellectual Movement,* 151.

29. Donald Atwell Zoll, "Philosophical Foundations of the American Political Right," 125; reprinted in Zoll, *The American Political Condition,* 32. Zoll's essay is a useful introduction to the variety of positions that currently constitute the American intellectual Right.

thought of Burke, he praised for its recognition of the dualistic nature of man. As we have been developing this concept, the dualistic view of the nature of man holds that the true moral condition of man involves an ineradicable tension between man's higher moral potential, which is under the guidance of "the permanent things," man's intuitive perception of the ethical ultimate, and his lower, selfish ego with its destructive and separative impulses. Babbitt felt that the modern age was progressively plagued by an "unexemplary type of individualism" derived from the "utilitarian conception of life" and the "political economy of the school of Adam Smith." This "false individualism" ignored the higher will and its role as a veto power over man's expansive desires. It rejected the old outer controls on man's acquisitive self provided by community, traditional mores, family, religion, and a sound cultural tradition that serve to liberate man's higher nature from his lower impulses. Ultimately, the very idea of liberty itself is transformed. Liberty was coming to mean the emancipation of the individual from all inner and outer controls. By failing to recognize standards supplied by authority, imagination, and the intellect, man is left with only his feelings to guide his actions. With no universal standards to which to appeal beyond self-interest, morality becomes a kind of expansive emotion, a feeling, a sense of sympathy or pity that we have for others. Egoism and blatant self-interest are not checked by standards or authorities exterior to the individual will. Even enlightened self-interest (as defined in chapter 3) can be easily transformed into a ruthless self-interest. With the decline of the inner life and the veto power over individual wills, a weakening of self-control over the intemperate or excessive impulses follows. The *libido sciendi,* the lust of knowledge, *libido dominandi,* the lust of power, or *libido sentiendi,* the lust of feeling, can easily be disguised as enlightened self-interest. The social reformer, for example, may be motivated more by his lust for power or public recognition than by any genuine desire to improve the condition of the recipients of his reforming efforts.

Babbitt, moreover, accused the "false liberals" with fomenting a gross materialism that enervates civilization's old standards of morality and integrity. Inspired by a Baconian definition of work, the "false liberals" identify work with purely physical labor to the neglect of the mental and spiritual energies necessary to build and preserve civilization. Progress in society is measured not in terms of achieving the high moral demands placed on man by civilization, but simply in terms of his material accomplishments: bigger factories, greater Gross National Products, higher standards of living, new technological gadgetry, etc.[30]

Babbitt's "false liberalism" is what Kirk called the "conservatism of desolation." Its adherents are devotees "of spiritual and social isolation." By making utility the basis of their politics, they leave modern man "defenseless against the self-interest of the fierce egoist and the hard knot of special interests."[31] The weakening of the ethical control over the expansive will encourages blatant selfishness and enfeebles the social bonds. Everyone would tend to regard everyone else as a dangerous competitor.

The distinction between these two orientations is central to understanding what is at the heart of the controversy between Kirk and the libertarians. Kirk believed that they elevate individual reason as a guide to ethical judgment while assuming that laissez-faire economics would lead to the greatest possible happiness. They view human life in a way that is incompatible with Kirk's idea of community as a spiritual unity among men. The breadth of the philosophical gap between these two positions can be further illustrated by reviewing some of the arguments that have been exchanged between Kirk and two of his most influential libertarian adversaries: Frank S. Meyer and Ludwig von Mises, the Austrian economist.

Troubled by widening ideological divisions during the 1950s between two competing strands of conservatism, Meyer strove to articulate a philosophical position in which both the libertarian stress on individual autonomy and the traditionalist emphasis on tradition and organic community could be integrated. He anticipated that one happy consequence of this conservative consensus would be the formation of a united front against statist ideologies. Despite their many differences, Meyer was convinced that libertarians and traditionalists could unite in their opposition to the Leviathan state. Meyer betrayed his individualistic tendencies, though, in a particular attack on Kirk. On the first page of his *In Defense of Freedom,* Meyer stated that the book's purpose

30. Babbitt, *Democracy and Leadership,* 188–238 passim.
31. Kirk, *A Program for Conservatives,* 47; Kirk, "The Unbought Grace of Life," 19.

was "to vindicate freedom of the person as the central and primary end of political society." The core of his political theory was the primacy of the individual. While the ultimate purpose of politics is to preserve and enlarge man's freedom, the "true end of man's existence" is virtue. Freedom is merely a means for achieving virtue. However, the ethical basis of his thought was wholly voluntarist. Man can acquire virtue (which, by the way, he never explicitly defined) only if he has the absolute freedom to choose. While clearly not indifferent to the moral ends of society, he was so repelled by anything smacking of social or political coercion that he was unable to accept as legitimate any constraints on liberty. He was convinced that most men possess sufficient reason to enable them to choose virtue over vice. If man falls below this standard, however, he appeared unwilling to accept even then a minimal role for society in the moral development of the individual. The possession of power was so thoroughly corrupting, in his eyes, that the state (or society, in general, for that manner) cannot be "the proper organ for the enforcement of virtue." Given his individualistic ethics and the primacy he gives to freedom in his thought, it is not surprising that he defined community as merely a "voluntary association of individual human beings in the myriad of relationships that are available for each person to choose or to reject in a free society." While he admitted that the state, when "limited to its natural functions," is "necessary for the proper life of men as men," he tended to regard it as no more than one of many voluntary associations to which men may freely choose to belong. He denied explicitly Burke's concept of a contract of eternal society by which generations are linked by mutual moral obligation.[32]

From these individualistic premises, Meyer rejected Kirk's argument "that true freedom of the person . . . subsists in community." Rather, Meyer replied, "it subsists in the individual," who may "find freedom in communal participation, or he may find it in ignoring community, even in revolt against community." He denied, by implication, Aristotle's principle that man is a social being for whom existence outside com-

---

32. Meyer, *In Defense of Freedom,* 1, 66–68, 135, 140, 134. See Kevin J. Smant, *Principles and Heresies: Frank S. Meyer and the Shaping of the American Conservative Movement,* chap. 6, for a discussion of Meyer's "fusionism" and his criticism of Kirk's traditionalism.

munity would be an impossibility.[33] Instead, he appeared to be in essential agreement with the social contract theorists for whom community represents no more than an aggregation of individuals bound together by convenience and utility. When implemented, Kirk held that this radically individualistic doctrine exposes "that great spiritual continuity which we call society to the whim and egotism of present interests."[34]

Throughout his life, Kirk rarely responded to attacks on his work, preferring for the most part to ignore his critics. Yet, Meyer's barbs provoked Kirk to an uncharacteristic strong retort. In a sarcastic review of Meyer's *In Defense of Freedom,* Kirk accused Meyer of isolating "freedom from the other necessities of the good society. Order and justice lacking, man is left with the terrible 'freedom' of the Congo. The eccentric Mr. Meyer himself could not exist for a week under such conditions of absolute liberty as he demands."[35]

Ludwig von Mises (1881–1973) is perhaps the most powerful mind among the twentieth-century libertarian thinkers. Kirk paid considerable respect to his immense influence by devoting nearly a chapter in *A Program for Conservatives* to an analysis of von Mises's economic and social thought.[36] He praised his book, *Human Action,* as "the work of a man of powerful intellect, much read in various fields; and in closeness and clarity of argument von Mises is much accomplished." Even

33. Smant, *Principles and Heresies,* 59. Meyer declared that he did accept Aristotle's principle regarding man's social nature, but to him it only meant that on an empirical level "each man has a multifarious set of relationships with other men." This interpretation so vitiates the original meaning of Aristotle that it serves more to substantiate rather than disprove my point. See Meyer, *In Defense of Freedom,* 27–28.

34. Kirk, "John Locke Reconsidered," 297.

35. Kirk, "An Ideologue of Liberty," 350. For a less critical view of Meyer, see Paul Gottfried, "Toward a New Fusion? The Old Right Makes New Alliances," *Policy Review* (Fall 1987): 64–70. "Perhaps thoughtful libertarian Old Rightist critics of the welfare state will come together in building a true conservative counter establishment," he writes hopefully. "In the end, conservatives may even find themselves returning to Frank Meyer's blend of traditional social values and resistance to managerial collectivism, whether they call it fusionism or not" (70). Like Meyer, Gottfried believes that the persistent infighting between the traditionalists and libertarians weakens their capacity to successfully combat their real enemy— the proponents of the modern managerial state.

36. See chap. 6. See his "The New Humanism of Political Economy," 180–96 for an earlier version of this chapter.

so and despite Mises's shrewd and perceptive analysis of the fallacies of the Marxists, psychologists, and social engineers, Kirk charged that Mises's defense of the free enterprise system, while impressive, was flawed by utilitarian social principles. Early in his monumental study, Mises, Kirk pointed out, "makes clear his stern confidence in scientific law and in the reasonableness of humanity."[37] Further, Mises's description of the origins of society illustrates how powerfully the social contract theories and utilitarian doctrines dominated his thought. Society is, he writes, simply "concerted action, cooperation." The social bonds tying people together into community develop after each individual rationally weighs the benefits of social cooperation as opposed to pursuing in isolation his own advantage:

> Every step by which an individual substitutes concerted action for isolated action results in an immediate and recognizable improvement in his conditions. The advantages derived from peaceful cooperation and division of labor are universal. They immediately benefit every generation, and not only late descendants. For what the individual must sacrifice for the sake of society he is amply compensated by greater advantages. His sacrifice is only apparent and temporary; he foregoes a smaller gain in order to reap a greater one later. *No reasonable being can fail to see this obvious fact.* When social cooperation is intensified by enlarging the field in which there is division of labor or when legal protection and the safeguarding of peace are strengthened, the incentive is the desire of all those concerned to improve their own conditions. In striving after his own—rightly understood—interests the individual works toward an intensification of social cooperation and peaceful intercourse. Society is a product of human action, i.e., the human urge to remove uneasiness as far as possible.[38]

Individual rational choice and voluntary consent form the basis of society. A rational decision maximizes the pleasure of the individual while diminishing his pain. Social cooperation, because it results in utilitarian advantages, enhances the prospects of individual pleasure. Here, the rational man freely chooses to do those things, such as obey laws and follow rules of moral conduct, which will enhance rather than diminish social cooperation.

37. Kirk, *A Program for Conservatives,* 144.
38. Ludwig von Mises, *Human Action: A Treatise on Economics,* 143, 146 (emphasis added).

Responding to Mises's restatement of the social contract, Kirk questioned whether reason alone would suffice to restrain men from socially disruptive acts. Mises himself admitted that man fails frequently to use his reason. Although he declared emphatically that man "has only one tool to fight error: reason," he acknowledged that the "characteristic mental attitude of our age" is the "revolt against reason." By the middle of the nineteenth century, economists "had entirely demolished the fantastic delusions of the socialist utopians." But, unable to withstand the devastating critique of the economists, the socialists then attacked "logic and reason," for which they substituted "mystical intuition." Also, they ignore the facts of history. What "is wrong with our age is precisely the widespread ignorance of the role which these policies of economic freedom played in the technological evolution of the last two hundred years." He pointed, in support of this argument, to the "Marxian myths" which hold that not classical economics, but "the operation of mysterious 'productive forces' that do not depend in any way on ideological factors," were responsible for the development of modern industrialism. "Classical economics, they believe, was not a factor in the rise of capitalism, but rather its product, its 'ideological superstructure,' i.e., a doctrine designed to defend the unfair claims of the capitalistic exploiters." Therefore, the abolition of capitalism, as the Marxists assert, would not hinder technological development. On the contrary, under socialism, the material well-being of everyone would improve because all the "obstacles which the selfish interests of the capitalists" have placed in the way of producing wealth would be removed.[39]

The difficulty with Mises, in Kirk's judgment, is that he is not "free from that liberal delusion concerning active reason among the mass of men. If so much territory already has been lost to the violence, cupidity, and envy stimulated by Marxist propaganda, just what will more doses of 'reason' accomplish? How much effect will *Human Action* or a dozen books like it have upon popular opinion?" Will and appetite cannot be restrained by reason alone. The source of social order must be located in something more than one's rational self-interest. Men respect "property, private rights, and order in society out of deference," Kirk maintained, to what Mises had dismissed as mere "myths." These "myths" include divine social intent, tradition, and natural law. "Capi-

39. Ibid., 73–74, 187, 9.

talism has been imperiled directly in proportion to decay of these principles among men." Extensive public deference to these noneconomic
and nonrational "myths" strengthens the free market system and is
indispensable to its preservation:

> Hardly anyone but Dr. Ludwig von Mises and his intellectual ancestors
> of Manchester ever pursued beneficent social conduct upon the grounds
> of pure reason and pure utility. Theirs is a doctrine which destroys itself
> in proportion as it is generally promulgated: once supernatural and tradi-
> tional sanctions are dissolved, economic self-interest is ridiculously
> inadequate to hold an economic system together, and even less adequate
> to preserve order. Prescription and prejudice are the defenses of justice
> and peace. Laugh them away, and in come those forces of delusion and
> unrest which Marxism exemplifies today; men refuse to live by economic
> reasonableness alone.

In addition, because capitalism has improved the material well-being
of most people, Mises succumbed, Kirk contended, to the fallacious
notion that "capitalism" is an absolute good. Yet, despite the fact that
capitalism has brought human progress unheard of in the annals of
mankind, many are still dissatisfied. Why are they so willing to be "de-
luded by false prophets?" Can it be, asked Kirk, "that the classical assumption concerning the reasonableness of humanity is inadequate for
a man who presumes to analyze human action? Can it be that humanity
needs something more than reason—love?"[40] Mises could not answer
this question because he failed to consider "the enormous destructive
power of social boredom which threatens the continued supremacy of
the capitalism he praises." These workers (Kirk is writing here about
laboring conditions in the 1950s) have "lost their community; they are
atoms in a loveless desolation; they are desperately bored." They eagerly
join unions and follow the union organizers because at least through
activities they can recover some semblance of community "which any
true human being loves a great deal more than an abstract standard of
living."

The effects of Mises's works or ideas do not adequately explain
why so few American workers have been radicalized. Neither has persuaded workers of the rational advantage of defending the capitalist
system responsible for improving their material well-being. Rather,

---

40. Kirk, *A Program for Conservatives,* 145.

the weakness of the radical movement among American laboring man, Kirk believed, is the result of his deep roots "in religion and in political prescription and in an old dislike of the doctrinaire." Yet, Kirk cautioned, if "the sense of community is steadily weakened among" the working classes, then their continued conservatism cannot be guaranteed. "A great part of the industrial workers of America were brought up in very different surroundings, and knew true community once, and therefore are not easily moved by revolutionaries. Their children, however, may be another kettle of fish." The prime problem for conservatives, then, Kirk concluded, is "to bring back to the industrial laborer the reality of community, and the taste for things beyond the paycheck."[41]

Of course, if Kirk were alive today, he would have to update this analysis. The industrial working class and union membership during the past thirty years has shrunk considerably. Although working conditions and wages have vastly improved in recent decades, the issues of deracination and social boredom persist. In fact, the old working-class neighborhoods of the past came closer to being true communities where neighbors knew and interacted with each other than do today's middle-class suburbs. Civic and church participation has declined in modern suburbia, while the rates of social pathologies such as divorce, drug addiction, and abortion have climbed. The loss of community, it may be argued, is felt more keenly today than when Kirk began discussing this topic nearly fifty years ago.

TRUE INDIVIDUALISM AND MORAL SELF-RESTRAINT

Mises was convinced that the vast majority of people could be persuaded, through an appeal to reason, "that peaceful cooperation within the framework of society better serves their rightly understood interests than mutual battling and social disintegration." This assumption fails, Kirk replied, because of its inherent utopianism. It overestimates man's capacity for reason and underestimates his proclivity for pure

41. Ibid., 146–49. The children of this generation of workers are the "baby boomers," many of whom became student radicals during the 1960s and 1970s and in their mature years became self-indulgent, acquisitive yuppies. They are, as Kirk predicted, less rooted in traditional community and more inclined toward hedonistic pursuits than their parents. Not unexpectedly, government in recent years has expanded into areas that were traditionally the responsibilities of family, church, and neighborhoods.

self-indulgence. "Man does not exist by pure rationality," but "is governed, much more commonly, by immediate appetite, and he cannot be expected to perceive even his own remote self-interest." Against avarice, lust, selfishness, and all the other passions that afflict the soul and the commonwealth, libertarians such as Mises offer no safeguards, no checks, other than an optimistic hope that the mass can be persuaded to obey their sense of reason rather than their impulses and that they will be disciplined by the competitive operations of the marketplace. The first aim of this sort of individualism is the pursuit of wealth rather than the striving to achieve mastery over one's acquisitive impulses. Leave the acquisitive self without any controls, and, Babbitt predicted, "the right kind of competition will degenerate into the wrong kind which was actually encouraged by the Manchester School of economics and in which mill operatives become mere 'cannon-fodder' in the industrial welfare." This sort of laissez-faire individualism "without moral restraints or just laws," claimed Kirk, "often has led to selfish excess; there are many such instances in the history of our country."[42]

Real community, on the other hand, is not experienced "between skillfully calculating egotists," as Ryn explains, but between persons striving to overcome "whatever is separative and disruptive in their characters to what is highest in each of them." The libertarian, however, is unable to acknowledge genuine community because he denies the existence of an ethical ultimate beyond that of the discipline of the marketplace. The individual, though he may be guided by what he perceives as his own enlightened self-interest, is thus left to rely upon his own subjective considerations to provide the ethical norms by which to order his existence. Ultimately, the libertarian must depend upon the utilitarian calculus of pleasure and pain as the standard by which to judge the moral worth of any human act. As Mises put it, "the ultimate goal of human action is always the satisfaction of the acting man's desires. There is no standard or lesser satisfaction other than individual judgments of value, different for various people and for the same people at various times. What makes a man feel uneasy and less uneasy is established by him from the standard of his own will and judgment,

42. Mises, *Human Action,* 56, 157; Kirk, *A Program for Conservatives,* 191; Babbitt, *Democracy and Leadership,* 213–14; Kirk, *Intelligent Woman's Guide to Conservatism,* 41.

from his personal and subjective valuation. Nobody is in a position to decree what should make a fellow man happier." Mises further observed that some men live solely on what Plato called the appetitive level, while others prefer a virtuous existence. "There are individuals eager to adjust their actions to the requirements of social cooperation; there are, on the other hand, refractory people who defy the rules of social life." Mises, however, is careful not to make moral judgments about which orientation is preferable. His sole task, as he saw it, was to demonstrate the means by which a rational man might achieve maximum satisfaction.[43]

The consequence of the individualism that Mises espoused, Kirk declared, is that the private and personal self becomes the measure of all things. But community is only experienced between men who rise above their own personal desires. To escape the tyranny of self, with its socially disruptive dimension, the individual must recognize the existence of a self that transcends his momentary, personal whims and even Mises's enlightened egotism. Libertarians, though, have a pronounced reductionist tendency in their thought. Man's behavior in their scheme of explanation can be wholly treated in terms of economic motives. They possess little sense of the individual's inner life described by Babbitt as a "recognition in some form or other of a force in man that moves in an opposite direction from the outer impressions and expansive desires that together make up his ordinary or temperamental self." Rather, the libertarians are concerned solely with the outer workings of human behavior. According to them, the cure for the social and political problems of our time is found not in moral self-reform but through improvements in the efficiency and productivity of the economic system. The loss of the truths of the inner life of which libertarians and all naturalistic political doctrines are guilty had brought about, further, as Babbitt argued, "a profound alteration in the idea of liberty. Liberty has come more and more to be conceived expansively, not as a process of concentration, as a submission or adjustment to a higher will." By worshipping abstract individual liberty, the libertarians fail to realize that not all individuals are equally qualified for liberty. The greater the degree of his self-control, the greater is the range of freedom that should be granted. At the extreme, liberty for a psychopath, for example, would

43. Ryn, *Democracy and the Ethical Life,* 85; Mises, *Human Action,* 14–15.

be destructive to any standard of civilized social order. By controlling his appetitive self, the individual exerts, further, a will to community. Civilization itself is possible only if many thwart their lower inclinations. By forgoing immediate desires, they enjoy the pleasures brought by a superior, enduring happiness found in the spiritual satisfaction of true labor and communal fellowship. The enjoyment of genuine liberty always entails, according to Kirk, the imposition of some restraints on will and appetite: A "coherent and beneficial freedom" 1) "must have the sanction of moral order: it must accord with principles, religious in origin, that establish a hierarchy of values and set bounds to the ego"; 2) it "must have the check of social order: it must accord with a rule of law, regular in its operation, that recognizes and enforces prescriptive rights, protects minorities against majorities and majorities against minorities, and gives some meaning to the idea of human dignity. Freedom as an abstraction is the liberty in whose name crimes are committed."[44] Without these moral and social sanctions, liberty would have socially centrifugal consequences.

Upon what basis are libertarians able to choose liberty as the paramount value in their system of ideas? Their defense of liberty depends on an appeal ultimately to utilitarian premises. Liberty, the libertarians argue, provides the most convenient and efficient means for achieving one's happiness without imposing arbitrary preferences on others. Further, they seem to value liberty only because it promotes technological progress and growth in the standard of living. Implicit in this argument is the assumption that the primary end of human existence is economic production. Freedom is desirable because it serves that end. As Erik von Kuehnelt-Leddihn (1909–1999) tellingly observed in his review of Friedrich Hayek's *Constitution of Liberty,* if "freedom were not pragmatically productive" to the libertarian, then "there would be no reason for freedom."[45] Economic production, Kirk responded, is not an end, but only a means to an end. "The real end of economic production," he insisted, "is to raise man above the savage level to make possible the leisure which sustains civilization and to free man from the conditions of being a simple drudge. When efficiency of production becomes an

---

44. Babbitt, *Democracy and Leadership,* 52, 236; Kirk, *Beyond the Dreams of Avarice,* 170.
45. Quoted in Nash, *The Conservative Intellectual Movement,* 170.

end in itself, then truly technology has triumphed over humanity." By making material well-being the whole of human existence, Kirk insisted, the moral worth of men decays. Men become in the libertarian system "no better than units of production and consumption. Divorced from religion, morals, the imagination, and ordinary human longings, economics becomes thoroughly inhumane—indeed, hostile to high human achievement."[46]

LOCALISM AND COMMUNITY

While Kirk held that the greatest threat to true liberty is the breakdown of community, the libertarians, by contrast, are convinced that historically the most formidable threats to individual freedom come from the state. A sure safeguard against the possibility of the continued growth of state power and the concomitant contraction of individual freedom is to prohibit any functions or powers to the state beyond the minimum necessary for defense and the maintenance of internal order. Yet, in their eagerness to expand individual liberty, the libertarians unwittingly prepare the way for a totalist state. The atomistic individualism they espouse undermines the mediating institutions (family, local associations, churches, etc.) that play a vital role as barriers against the encroachments of state power. Abolish "the traditional concept of community and substitute a doctrinaire individualism" and the natural reaction is a growing proclivity in society toward collectivism. Doctrinaire individualism emancipates the person from not only state controls but also restraints placed on him by custom, tradition, and membership in local associations.[47]

Economic and personal freedoms depend upon the existence of these autonomous groups. As Nisbet pointed out, there has never been "a time when a successful economic system has rested upon purely

46. Kirk, "Ideology and the Political Economy," 390; Kirk, "Humane Political Economy," 226.

47. Kirk, *A Program for Conservatives*, 140; "To dissolve local and voluntary association," even Hayek, a leading libertarian economist, recognized, "would leave the individual open to the brute force of the state." See his *Individualism and Economic Order*, 23. Nisbet in addition argued that if local associations are extinguished, then the way is prepared for the triumph of total community, a totalitarian ideology fueled by the boredom and hysteria of the rootless masses anxious to be "rescued" from "their intolerable individualism." See his *The Quest for Community*, 245.

individualistic drives or upon the impersonal relationships so prized by the rationalists. There are always, in fact, associations and incentives nourished by the non-economic processes of kinship, religion, and various other forms of social relationships." A humane free economic system cannot exist while disregarding the needs of genuine communities. Wilhelm Röpke (1899–1966), a German economist whose Burkean insights Kirk frequently praised, recognized this condition. He rejected the moral isolation inherent in Mises's social philosophy: "Self-discipline, a sense of justice, honesty, fairness, chivalry, moderation, public spirit, respect for human dignity, firm ethical norms—all of these are things which people must possess before they go to market and compete with each other. These are the indispensable supports which preserve both market and competition from degeneration. Family, church, genuine communities, and tradition are their sources." Moreover, the "highest interests of the community and the indispensable things of life have no exchange value and are neglected if supply and demand are allowed to dominate the field."[48]

Likewise, Kirk held that the individualists' "assault on institutional religion, on old-fashioned economic methods, on family authority, on small political communities has set the individual free from nearly everything, but that freedom is a terrifying thing, the freedom of a baby deserted by his parents to do as he pleases." The result is the enfeeblement of all those group memberships that traditionally fulfilled men's need for certitude and membership. Stripped of their local association by social atomism and large-scale economic impersonalities, the resulting detached individuals would become, as the historian Rowland Berthoff predicts, "fearful, embittered, and unable to look beyond material success to any higher purpose in life." What is needed is a higher freedom, solidly grounded in a stable community, that would liberate people to achieve their ultimate spiritual and cultural goals.[49]

48. Nisbet, *The Quest for Community,* 238. See also "Capitalism, Socialism and Nihilism," in Irving Kristol, *Two Cheers for Capitalism,* 51–65. Kristol argues that if capitalism is to survive it must be sustained by old moral values and religion. The greatest enemy of capitalism is not socialism, but nihilism. Wilhelm Röpke, *A Humane Economy,* 125, 137.

49. Kirk, *The Conservative Mind,* 421; Rowland Berthoff, *An Unsettled People: Social Order and Disorder in American History,* 478–79.

In conclusion, Kirk affirmed that genuine conservatism must strongly oppose the social atomism preached by contemporary libertarians. However, this does not involve giving up, he acknowledged, the advantages of the free market system. The task for conservative leaders is to reconcile individualism "—which sustained nineteenth century life even while it starved the soul of the nineteenth century—with the sense of community that ran strong in Burke and Adams." What is needed is a new philosophy that combines freedom and tradition. Its object would not be to "liberate" the abstract individual. Instead, it would "recognize" as the basic unit the group: the family, the local community, the trade union, the church, the college, the profession. It will seek not unity, not centralization, not power over masses of people, but rather diversity of culture, plurality of association, and division of responsibilities. Repudiating the error of the total state, it will restore the sort of State through which, as Burke said, Providence designed that men should seek their perfection as persons. In such a state, the primacy of ethics is recognized, and the true freedom of the person, which subsists in community, will be guarded jealously.[50] A conservatism devoted to valuing the individual person within a traditional social context would be, in Kirk's view, a substantial step toward the restoration of genuine community.

---

50. Kirk, *The Conservative Mind*, 460, 489–90. For Kirk's defense of family against the reformers who would seek to replace it with the "universal orphanage" see his "The Little Platoon We Belong to in Society," 1–6. Also see Russell Kirk, "The Enfeebled American Family."

7 Leadership and Education

*More than ever, we should look to education
today to preserve us from the error of pure
contemporaneity.*

—T. S. Eliot, *To Criticize the Critic*

*Our colleges and universities could render no
greater service than to oppose to the worship
of energy and the frantic eagerness for action
an atmosphere of leisure and reflection.*

—Irving Babbitt, *Literature and the American College*

IF THERE IS ANY ISSUE on which Russell Kirk could justly be called an inno-
vating radical, it is education. The enfeeblement of primary and secondary schooling and the higher learning had become so severe and alarming that slow, cautious, and incremental reform seemed inadequate. In
his fulminations against the American education establishment, Kirk
became, in his own words, a "reactionary radical." Immediate and radical reform was demanded to reverse the precipitous decline in standards and rigor. Taking up their cudgels against these trends in American education, conservatives must, Kirk declared passionately, "echo
the Jacobin cry of Danton, 'Audacity, and again audacity, and always
audacity.'"[1]

Although Kirk wrote on a wide variety of contemporary social and
political topics in his various works, no issue so engaged his attention
as the state of instruction in America's schools and colleges. He wrote
three books specifically on educational issues: *Academic Freedom: An
Essay in Definition* (1955), *The Intemperate Professor, and Other Cultural Splenetics* (1965), and lastly his most comprehensive critique,
Decadence and Renewal in the Higher Learning (1978). In addition,
several of his other books, *A Program for Conservatives, The Intelligent*

1. Kirk, *A Program for Conservatives,* 63.

Woman's Guide to Conservatism, Beyond the Dreams of Avarice, and
The Wise Men Know What Wicked Things Are Written on the Sky, contain chapters about education. He published innumerable articles on
the topic in magazines, learned journals, and anthologies. His monthly
column, "From the Academy," which appeared for nearly twenty-five
years in *National Review,* dealt primarily with issues in higher education. Lastly, he contributed nearly a score of textbook reports to the
Textbook Evaluation Committee of America's Future, Inc., and during
the 1980s was the director of the Educational Research Committee of
Cleveland, Ohio. Without question, education amounted to a subject of
considerable interest and passion for him.

"Every educational system has a moral goal that it tries to attain
and inform its curriculum," the late Allan Bloom observed in *The Closing of the American Mind,* his best-selling critique of the American
system of higher education. "It wants to produce a certain kind of human
being."[2] Plato, Aristotle, Locke, and Rousseau, for example, devoted a
considerable portion of their work describing a scheme of education
for the citizenry of their ideal regimes. Their efforts to elucidate a complete program of education were not digressions from the central purposes of their political philosophy. Each understood that their preferred regime could not be realized unless its citizens are educated into
its ethos. Kirk's educational philosophy also augments and supports his
vision of a moral and political order. The political and moral disorders
of the time that he sought to remedy originate ultimately not in inex-
orable laws of economics or history but in the ideas people hold about
themselves and reality. As with Coleridge, Newman, T. S. Eliot, and
the others within the cultural conservative tradition with which he is
allied, Kirk's thought is not devoted primarily to the explication and
analysis of the orthodox issues of political philosophy: for example,
the obligation of the citizen to the state, the definition of sovereignty,
the origin of the state, and so forth. Rather, for him, the fundamental
problems of society are ethical and cultural in nature. Therefore, the battle for a civilized social order begins for the conservative in the home,
the church, and, lastly, the schools.

Order in the soul and commonwealth, as he stated often, are inter-
woven and mutually dependent upon each other: "if the order of the

2. Allan Bloom, *The Closing of the American Mind,* 26.

soul suffers, the order of the commonwealth decays; or if the order of the commonwealth falls into confusion, the order of the soul is maintained with difficulty." A stable and just society cannot endure unless the bulk of the people are disciplined by the promptings of their higher wills. Second only to religion and family, education serves as the chief means by which society transmits its moral and cultural patrimony to the rising generation. The issues of education, then, are inseparably bound up with contemporary cultural, moral, and social problems. The neglect or decay of sound standards in public instruction, he believed, exacerbated the present social, political, and ethical confusion. A renewal of sound educational doctrines, grounded in the realization that the proper end of instruction is the formation of good character and moral imagination, then, is key to restoring a genuinely humane social order. As Babbitt put it, "The necessary basis . . . of an ethical type of state is an ethical type of education." "The natural function of formal education is conservative," Kirk added, "in the best sense of that word, that is, formal education conserves the best of what has been thought and written and discovered in the past, and by a regular discipline teaches us to guide ourselves by the light of the wisdom of our ancestors."[3]

Few well-informed observers today of the educational establishment are satisfied with its performance. Not only are schools and colleges dismally failing to transmit cultural and moral knowledge to students, but they are also performing a wretched job of instructing them in the practical skills. The production of books and articles bewailing the deplorable condition of the American system of education and offering recommendations for substantial reform has become a major cottage industry. Bloom's *Closing of the American Mind* soared to the top of the best-seller lists (almost inexplicably, given its pedantic prose). The American public was beginning to notice that something was rotten in the state of education.[4]

"We have succeeded in sending a great many people to college and university," Kirk noted nine years before Bloom's work, but "we have

3. Kirk, "Traditions of Thought and the Core Curriculum," 14; Babbitt, *Democracy and Leadership,* 198; Kirk, *Intelligent Woman's Guide to Conservatism,* 91.
4. In addition to the books cited in this chapter, E. D. Hirsch, Jr., *Cultural Literacy* and Diane Ravitch and Chester E. Finn, Jr., *What Do Our 17-Year Olds Know?* are among some of the most recent significant contributions to this discussion.

not succeeded in educating most of them."[5] In this chapter, the underlying principles of his philosophy of education and diagnosis of and prescription for the ills presently afflicting American schools and colleges are examined. In the first section, his statements on the objects or ends of education are summarized. The second section discusses his analysis of the causes for the decline of American schooling. Section three is devoted to an examination of his proposals for reform and the model college he offered as an alternative to the present institutions of higher learning. Finally, I look at Kirk's response to the advocates of civil education who contend that the fundamental focus of schooling should be to adapt students to the ideals and practices of a democratic society.

EDUCATION FOR LEADERSHIP

Standards in contemporary education have been gravely battered, in Kirk's estimation, by rash innovators promoting collectivist and egalitarian social agendas. Given its long-reaching impact on society, education represented for him a first line of battle against the corruption of the intellectual and moral norms on which a civilized humane social order depends. Both Kirk and his adversaries (largely inspired by utilitarian doctrines or the pragmatist theories of John Dewey), hence, agree that the control of the agenda of education has enormous political and social implications. The norms that a system of education promotes will determine ultimately not only the shape of the social order but also one of the most basic questions of politics: who governs? If the system serves basically utilitarian values, then the result will be the creation of a technocracy—rule by a narrowly technically trained elite of experts. Rule by technocrats lacking in humane liberal learning, in Kirk's opinion, would represent an appalling prospect. A genuine humane social order requires leadership from persons of elevated learning, in other words, those possessing good character, moral imagination, and right reason.

"When a society decides to quarrel over education," Thomas Fleming, editor of *Chronicles of Culture,* perceptively points out, "it may be that the parties to the dispute are really talking not so much about books

5. Kirk, *Decadence and Renewal in the Higher Learning,* 342.

or disciplines as they are advocating rival visions of human life."[6] Kirk accused the radical reformers of using schooling as a vehicle for promoting their social and political programs and, hence, perverting the ends of education. The institutions of learning hence exist in their minds not to develop the character and talents of individuals, but as vehicles for "improving, or at least changing society" through political indoctrination.[7] In his attack on their program, Kirk presented the following summary of those doctrines and attitudes most responsible for the degradation of education standards:

1. The "wisdom of our ancestors is deliberately discouraged."
2. An "impossible future of universal beneficence" is "taken for granted."
3. All "the wealth of myth and fable, the symbolic study of human nature, is cast aside as so much rubbish."
4. Religion "is treated, at least covertly, as nothing better than exploded superstition, or at best a vague collection of moral observations."
5. The "splendor and drama of history is discarded in favor of amorphous 'social studies.'"
6. "Imaginative literature of twenty-five centuries is relegated to a tiny corner of the curriculum, in favor of 'adjustment.'"
7. The "physical and natural sciences are huddled incoherently together, as if they formed a single discipline, and then are taught as a means to power over nature and man, not as a means of wisdom."
8. The "very tools of any sort of apprehension of systematic knowledge, spelling and grammar, mathematics and geography, are despised as boring impediments to 'socialization.'"[8]

The radical hence conceives of education primarily as training for service in a society that will be vastly different, and deliberately so, from the past.

Looming large in Kirk's educational thought are the principles of old-fashioned liberal learning found in the works of Sir Thomas Elyot, Cardinal Newman, T. S. Eliot, C. S. Lewis, Bernard Iddings Bell, and especially the humanists, Babbitt and More. With these defenders of the humane studies he shared the conviction that the ultimate aim of education is wisdom—the "apprehension of enduring reality" and

6. Thomas Fleming, "The Roots of American Culture: Reforming the Curriculum," *Content, Character and Choice in Schooling,* 30.
7. Kirk, *Intelligent Woman's Guide to Conservatism,* 86.
8. Kirk, *A Program for Conservatives,* 64.

virtue—"the development of strong moral principles and habits." At
the heart of his criticism is the principle, as Babbitt expressed it, that
"men need to be disciplined to some ethical centre." Education must
conserve and transmit "the permanent things," those enduring norms
without which social order cannot endure. Humane learning restores,
then, what Burke had called the "unbought grace of life." Kirk explained
that "Burke employs this idea . . . to describe the great civilizing and
ordering influence of a liberal mind, in the old and true sense of the
word 'liberal'—that is, the disciplined reason and imagination of free
men, which were the product of the education of a gentleman." Persons
of unbought grace possess the "habit of acting upon principles which
rise superior to immediate advantage and private interest." These persons who exhibit "the spirit of a gentleman" have "what the later Roman
writers called *humanitas,* that ethical discipline acquired through knowledge of great literature and great lives which teaches men the meaning
of duty and of continuity."[9]

Egalitarian reformers sharply dissent from Kirk's views on the importance of educating a class of "gentlemen," characterizing such notions
as "elitist" and "undemocratic." Indeed, given his premise that talents
and abilities are unequally distributed among persons and that society
as a whole benefits from the contributions of persons of elevated intellect and good character—the natural aristocracy—it follows that he
saw education as a process by which those possessing superior qualities are selected and prepared for moral and social leadership. Education is necessarily aristocratic because it strives "to awaken the highest
talents of the best persons among us." Even a democratic society needs
a natural aristocracy "of opinion and taste and serious thought." Schools
and colleges, then, must "resuscitate that liberal learning which teaches
men the meaning of time and duty, and which nurtures the idea of the
gentleman," and "impart that intellectual discipline to as many persons as can possibly benefit from it, so that we will possess a considerable class of truly educated men and women, able to be moulders of
thought and arbiters of taste each in his little circle." By lowering educational standards in the name of equality, educational reformers both
debase education and lose an indispensable means for nurturing the

9. Kirk, *Decadence and Renewal in the Higher Learning,* 294–95, 37; Babbitt, *Democracy and Leadership,* 303; Kirk, *A Program for Conservatives,* 51–52.

growth of true leadership. Fundamental to Kirk's position, consequently, is his belief that an educational system that fails to cultivate the imaginative ethical faculties of the individual through the study of literature, history, philosophy, and the arts and sciences is seriously flawed. He recommended that Paul Elmer More's brief description of the essence of a humane education be the "manifesto" of the educator: "The scheme of the humanist might be described in a word as a disciplining of the higher faculty of the imagination to the end that the student may behold, as it were in one sublime vision, the whole scale of being in its range from the lowest to the highest under the divine decree of order and subordination, without losing sight of the immutable veracity at the heart of all development, which 'is the only praise and surname of virtue.'"[10] Kirk's educational scheme for leadership is rooted firmly in the humanities and expressly abjures the intellectual straitjacket of mere vocationalism, narrow fact accumulation or practical skill training. It goes without saying that among its purposes would not be the notion, now popular in the education establishment, that education should promote the self-esteem of whose who perceive themselves marginalized by society, or assist in the eradication of sexism, racism, homophobia, or other perceived societal ills.

Decadence in the Higher Learning

For nearly four decades, Kirk described and deplored the movement of American education away from its traditional purposes and standards. Confessing his utter exasperation with the apparent irreversibility of this trend, he admitted in a 1980 article for *National Review* that he felt thoroughly "beaten down, horse, foot, and dragoons" by the educational reformers responsible for the degradation of academic standards. "From kindergarten through graduate school, American education is an extravagant failure." There had been no improvement "at any level" since he began his *National Review* column on education in the mid-1950s; "on the contrary, standards have been abandoned, average performance has declined conspicuously, and the rising generation will have to pay the penalty."[11]

10. Kirk, *A Program for Conservatives,* 74, 76, 59; Paul Elmer More, *Shelburne Essays,* vol. 9, *Aristocracy and Justice,* 56.
11. Kirk, "Imagination against Ideology," 1576.

Higher learning in America, on which Kirk focused most of his attention, seemed to be damaged beyond repair. His proposal for a model college (discussed later in this chapter) established outside the framework of any extant institution of education and his absence of praise for any of the major institutions of higher learning graphically revealed the depth of his dissatisfaction with all existing colleges and universities.

His convictions on the true purposes of education were formed early and remained remarkably unaltered. While still a young sergeant in the U.S. Army during the last days of World War II, he launched in a *South Atlantic Quarterly* article his first salvo against the materialistic and utilitarian forces obliterating the old purposes of education. During the height of America's war effort, some well-intentioned people were in the name of patriotism urging colleges and universities to discard liberal education to train people instead in science and technology. Educating the mind was deemed to be a nonessential activity when there was a war to be won. Kirk denounced this suggestion as short-sighted and an ultimate betrayal of the purposes of education and the interests and well-being of students, who were regarded here as mere wards or the property of the state. If such notions gained wide acceptance, he predicted, genuine education would not long endure. If "we warriors are to shape the globe anew and are to be taught global architecture," he proclaimed, "a conscript sergeant, a military speck in the mass of our armies may venture to inquire concerning the type of intellect with which he should equip himself for the purpose—and, more important, to inquire if anyone has remembered that intelligence, benevolent or malign, has far more to do with making new worlds than have dreams and machines." We need, then, he continued, to reexamine the fundamentals in learning when many appear "heroically willing to sacrifice other men's educations upon the altar of Mars."[12]

The American system of education, he continued, was suffering from four principal sins. It exalts the gratification of sensate desires over the acquisition of true wisdom because it reflects "equalitarianism, technicalism, progressivism, and egotism." Given the leveling spirit dominating all aspects of contemporary social existence, we educate for mediocrity rather than leadership. For the ostensible purpose of providing useful "practical" knowledge and skills, we give up teaching

12. Kirk, "A Conscript on Education," 82.

history, literature, and philosophy. The pursuit of knowledge and virtue is forgotten as educators, animated by a materialistic spirit, assume that persons can be improved not by liberal learning, but by training in the skills needed to swell America's economic and military capability. The "progressive" movement in education led by John Dewey taught further that education should be pleasant and free of compulsion. But, this notion amounts to a delusion. The fruits of learning never come easily or pleasantly, but must be striven for. The strenuous self-discipline and self-denial necessary to master a difficult or complicated body of knowledge at least initially involves pain. To teach that things which bring lasting happiness to the individual can be acquired effortlessly and enjoyably is to ill-prepare one for the real hardships of life. The last affliction, egotism, "lies in the unjustifiable conceit of a great many teachers. A preference for transient educational fads as opposed to true learning typifies many teachers." The combined effects of these "sins," he predicted, would do irreparable damage to the emerging generation's understanding of education. "Are we teaching ourselves to govern the world? Are we teaching ourselves to govern ourselves?" Kirk asked. If Americans are to win no more from the war effort "than another piece of pie and another pat of butter, and at the same time lose much of what remains of our intellectual birthright, our ecstasy over the restoration of the four freedoms will have been as sorry a show as the salvation and subsequent backsliding of a street-corner sot. A physical victory by ourselves and our allies now has become inevitable; but our intellectual victory still is in doubt. It may prove more difficult for us to think clearly and loftily than it is for us to strike lustily and often; but without one triumph, the other is worth little."[13]

Thirty years later, Kirk concluded that all he had predicted had come to pass. Scant evidence existed of much improvement in America's system of education. "For a quarter of a century," began *Decadence and Renewal in the Higher Learning,* "higher education in America has been sinking lower." The antecedents of the present rot began shaping thought on schooling, as Kirk had perceptively recognized during his service in the Armed Forces, long before 1953. Indeed, the "old pattern

13. Ibid., 88–90, 83.

was beginning to fall apart at Harvard College seven decades ago" (a reference to President Charles W. Eliot's "elective system" that had reduced the number of prescribed courses and increased electives in the undergraduate core curriculum). But the year 1953 represented for Kirk a "watershed year" in which the practical consequences of decadence in American education had been felt following the enormous swelling of the ranks of students at universities and colleges. With this influx of students that commenced that year, a substantial, rapid decline in standards ensued.[14]

America's colleges and universities can only be described, he affirmed, as "decadent." As C. E. M. Joad explained in his book, *Decadence: A Philosophical Inquiry* (1948), decadence occurs "when people have 'dropped the object'—that is, when they have abandoned the pursuit of real objects, aims, or ends—and have settled instead for the gratifications of mere 'experience.'" Kirk elaborated, "[T]he characteristics of decadence are luxury, scepticism, weariness, superstition, also, in Joad's words, 'a preoccupation with the self and its experiences, promoted by and promoting the subjectivist analysis of moral, aesthetic, metaphysical, and theological judgments.'"

The fundamental object of education is ethical discipline. Higher learning "is meant to develop order in the soul for the human person's own sake" and "order in the commonwealth, for the republic's sake." Any system of education that neglects these aims, Kirk concluded, is decadent. He was not suggesting, though, that education could instill "moral values" directly. It is impossible to make men and women better, "simply by compelling them to enroll in Moral Worth 101. A college, however diligent, cannot turn a young man of bad inclinations and habits into a child of light." Moral virtue cannot be taught didactically in school, but instead is acquired primarily from the family, neighborhood, peer groups, etc. The moral habits formed in youth determine far more significantly one's moral beliefs than those taught by formal schooling. On the other hand, it also "remains true that college and university cannot remain indifferent upon grave ethical questions, or to the consequences of study upon the lives of students. College training ought to be intellectual in character, not moralistic; yet it dare not ignore

14. Kirk, *Decadence and Renewal in the Higher Learning,* ix–xi.

its ultimate ethical end. And one reason why some American colleges may seem morally didactic in their methods is that ethical instruction had been neglected by parents, church, and school, where such moral precepts more properly belong."[15] A hostile or skeptical attitude in schooling toward morality, moreover, by instilling in the minds of young people the notion that determining right from wrong is merely a question of personal preference, diminishes the disciplining authority of traditional norms and leaves students morally rudderless.

American education tends to oscillate between the extremes of moral didacticism and relativism. The "principal achievement of liberal education in America," he pointed out, "had been the imparting of a sense of moral worth among the more intelligent of the rising generation." But this achievement has been steadily losing ground to "utilitarian and pragmatic theories and practices, which tend to regard moral worth— so far as they regard it at all—as merely the product of private rationality and social utility." Ordinarily, the typical college offers "no first principles of morality, no ethical direction, no aspiration toward enduring truth." Instead it provides only what Kirk called "defecated rationality," "a narrow rationalism or logicalism, purged of theology, moral philosophy, symbol and allegory, tradition, reverence, and the wisdom of our ancestors." Private judgment and hedonism are exalted "at the expense of the inner order of the soul and the outer order of the republic." This "altered view of the ends of American education" has effaced higher education's "old sustaining principle" of inculcating "a sense of moral worth, achieved Socratically, through right reason." The purpose of the American college then becomes either that of "the sophist, to teach success at any cost," or "of the utilitarian, to teach pure facts." As a consequence, the American college has lost its capacity to impart "to the better minds and hearts of the rising generation a union of reason and moral worth," thereby developing "better human beings and a better society."[16]

Four major causes are responsible for the present decline in American higher education. The first involves a sense of purposelessness generated by the loss of "the old ends of formal education"—wisdom

15. Ibid., ix–x, xvii–xviii, 3, 73; Kirk, "Virtue: Can It Be Taught," 346.
16. Kirk, *Decadence and Renewal in the Higher Learning,* 191–93.

and virtue.[17] The college has instead become a place of job certification, "socialization and sociability," a center for the aimless and neurotic, and for public entertainment. In addition, it is increasingly viewed as a vehicle for elevating various underprivileged groups to higher socio-economic classes. Having lost sight of its higher ends, education understandably becomes afflicted with intellectual disorder. All "integration and order of knowledge" is in flux. Lacking broadly accepted standards of what is to be considered as knowledge, the higher learning has suffered from an inability to agree upon a body of wisdom to be transmitted to students. Professors specialize in narrow fields, the degrees in many subjects have grown soft and shallow, and ideas not "relevant" to the events of the moment are dismissed. "Ideological infatuation," secondly, is substituted for "the old philosophical habit of mind," and a "preoccupation with the self and its experience" has replaced "the old concern of the higher learning for order in the soul and order in the commonwealth." Thirdly, there is the affliction of gigantism in scale on the campus, the emergence of the enormous state university, which Kirk dubbed "Behemoth U." Its population cannot be described as a community of scholars, but only as a bored, restless mob. Its crowdedness alone fosters an atmosphere inimical to the things of the mind. "A crowd readily becomes a mob. Culturally rootless, anonymous, bewildered, bored, badly prepared for higher studies, other-directed, prey to fad and foible, presently duped by almost any unscrupulous or self-deceived ideologue, a great many of the students at Behemoth U. came to feel defrauded and lost; only the more stupid did not suspect that anything was wrong with their condition." After the early 1970s, this unrestrained growth that Kirk deplored came to a virtual halt. Because of declining student enrollments and tight state and local governmental budgets, the empire building of vast college or university campuses ended. The day when state governors such as Nelson Rockefeller of New York could realize a dream of a vast archipelago

17. Ibid., xii. Bloom complained that modern education values openness to other points of view and ethical relativism to avoid teaching moral dogmatism. Hence, students have become unable to distinguish between right and wrong. To make a moral judgment would amount to an unjustified imposition of his/her values on someone else. This attitude in Bloom's estimation has stunted students' intellectual and moral growth. Bloom, *The Closing of the American Mind,* 26.

of state colleges scattered across their states may be permanently over. Lastly, Kirk pointed to a problem that every college instructor has experienced—the inadequacy of preparation for the higher learning in the primary and secondary schools.[18] The typical freshman enters "college wretchedly prepared for the abstractions with which college and university necessarily are concerned." Kirk blamed the progressive decline of functional literacy in the public schools on the triumph "of 'look-say' methods of reading-instruction over phonetic teaching, and the supplanting of books and periodicals by the boob-tube of television."

These proximate causes of the decay of undergraduate education result from "deep-seated misunderstandings of what the higher learning is all about." Kirk had two relevant fallacies in mind. The first is "the notion that the principal function of college and university—if not the only really justifiable function—is to promote utilitarian efficiency." The institutions of higher learning exist, so goes this Benthamite argument, to "serve society" or to "serve the people." Man is considered to be little more than a "producing and consuming animal." If society is beset with welfare cases, then colleges and universities should produce more masters and doctors of "social work"; if nuclear technicians are required to produce more nuclear weapons, then colleges and university should produce them. If there is a war to be won, whether a cold or hot one, then the educational institutions must be reconstructed to better serve the needs of the military establishment. But, Kirk countered, social utility should never be the prime motive for education. Utilitarian justifications for education deflect colleges from doing what they do best—preparing the rising generation for life rather than specific careers. Education for social utility fosters the narrow specialization of the half-educated. As Paul Elmer More wrote, remarking on the problem of overspecialization, courses in sociology and government "send men into the world skilled in the machinery of statecraft and with minds sharpened to the immediate demands of special groups, but with no

18. See Ernest L. Boyer, *College: The Undergraduate Experience in America,* 3, for a discussion of the discrepancy between student preparation and faculty expectations. This study, sponsored by the Carnegie Foundation for the Advancement of Teaching, strives to evaluate comprehensively the state of undergraduate studies on private and public campuses.

genuine training of the imagination and no understanding of the longer problems of humanity."[19]

The second fallacy is "the notion that everybody, or practically everybody, ought to attend college." This error involves what the late Ernest van den Haag described as "America's Pelagian heresy"—the illusion that everyone "will be redeemed soon, through formal schooling, without the operation of thought." Education is good for all, its proponents argue, and hence should be granted as a right to everyone willing to attend college. Consequently, hordes of bored and unqualified students are herded onto campuses, depressing the standards for admission and graduation. These poor unfortunates suffer from the delusion that a four-year "sentence" on a college campus will be sufficient to guarantee them "the good life." The ends of the democratic dogma are then carried to their ultimately absurd logical extreme. In the name of equality, no one, literally no one, no matter what the paucity of his or her intellectual qualifications is, will be denied the right to an academic degree.[20]

The painful consequences of these misguided policies were not long in coming. By the mid-1980s, complaints were coming from parents, educators, panels of experts, and even students themselves about the devaluation of the undergraduate degree and the failure of colleges and universities to educate. Finally, the "business community," noted an Association of Colleges report in 1985, "complains of difficulty in recruiting literate college students."[21] Students were shocked to discover that since their undergraduate degree did not represent any significant intellectual attainment, it was no longer a sure ticket to a job. Kirk and neoconservative scholar Allan Bloom were writing almost simultaneously about the problems of education. They agreed that the American system of education was in a deplorable state and in need of drastic

19. Kirk, *Decadence and Renewal in the Higher Learning,* xii–xiv; More, *Aristocracy and Justice,* 59. Preprofessional programs in business, law, or medicine, complained Bloom, have the effect of denying the undergraduate the benefits of a liberal education. "The effect of the MBA is to corral a horde of students who want to get into business school and put the blinders on them, to legislate an illiberal, officially approved undergraduate program for them at the outset, like pre-meds who usually disappear into their required courses and are never heard from again." Bloom, *The Closing of the American Mind,* 370.

20. Kirk, *Decadence and Renewal in the Higher Learning,* xv–xvi.

21. *Integrity in the College Curriculum: A Report to the Academic Community* (Washington: Association of American College, February 1985), 1.

radical reform. Although allied in their awareness of the crisis and of its consequences for society and the culture, they notably disagreed on the causes. Bloom argued that its failure was brought about by the importation of the historicist doctrines of Nietzsche and Heidegger by German immigrant intellectuals, constituting "the German connection." The "value revolution," precipitated by the spread of German historical relativism, corroded the traditional commitment of educators to reason and democracy. Defeated in two world wars, the resourceful Germans were now exacting their final revenge by deliberately infecting our universities and colleges with cultural barbarism. Now a dominant force on most campuses, deconstructionists, having absorbed the worse aspects of German philosophy, promote multiculturalism and treat humanistic education with dismissive contempt.[22]

As we have seen, Kirk's explanation for these failures is vastly different. He attributed the enfeeblement of academic standards to errors and misunderstandings emanating from the American educational establishment. While these misconceptions also have existed in Germany (as well as Britain and France) since World War II, the Germans cannot be blamed for the degradation of our standards. Several decades before these German immigrant intellectuals arrived in America, Irving Babbitt wrote a scathing critique of the tendency of colleges and universities to supplant training for wisdom and character with training for power and service.[23] Even before World War II, there were troubling signs of eroding academic standards.

My thirty years in the academic profession compels me to conclude that Kirk offered a more realistic appraisal than Bloom of the causes of the current troubles besetting America's universities and colleges. Never in my experience have I heard a college administrator invoke Heidegger's attack on rationalism or Nietzsche's will to power to explain why the traditional aims of education should be replaced with the latest educational fad. Rather, the concerns of administrators always struck me as far more mundane: an obsessive concern with student admission and retention rates coupled with a desire to appear nice. Like the managers of Wal-Mart department stores, administrators want students (or

22. Bloom, *The Closing of the American Mind,* 141–56.
23. See Babbitt, *Literature and the American College,* 1955.

"customers") to have "happy learning experiences." Happy students tend not to leave before completing their programs of study, nor do they make annoying complaints. The perks of the academic world (tenure, promotion, merit pay) go to those who make students the "happiest," as demonstrated by favorable student evaluations.[24] The problems of Academe today result not from intellectual errors promulgated by German intellectuals but from the fact that our campuses are peopled by too many individuals for whom C. S. Lewis's description of "men without chests" would aptly apply. In other words, too many academics and administrators possess neither the will nor the character to defend rigorous academic standards.

Bloom's analysis of the state of higher education is not only abstract and far removed from the actual situation found on most campuses but also offers little in the way of practical prescriptions for reform. By contrast, Kirk in his analysis of identical issues marshaled considerable anecdotal evidence in support of his arguments. He also, as we shall see below, provided specific, detailed proposals for educational reform. The publication of Bloom's work was greeted by widespread publicity and critical acclaim. Yet, I see little evidence that it inspired any efforts to correct the problems that he decried. In contrast, Kirk's book received far less notice and certainly was not widely distributed among academics or readers of the *Chronicle of Higher Education*. In the long run, though, the influence and importance of Kirk's work may grow as future generations come to terms with what has been lost by sinking academic standards.

REACTIONARY RADICALISM

As I have already noted, education represents the one area where Kirk can justly be called a radical reformer. But like Martin Luther, whose "reformation" movement amounted to a call for the Church to return to its founding vision, Kirk sought to correct the present flawed vision of education by appealing to an older tradition of learning. His calls for change in education are within the spirit of Burke's tradition of reform.

24. See for example Paul Trout, "Flunking the Test: The Dismal Record of Student Evaluations," *Academe: Bulletin of the American Association of University Professors* (July–August 2000). Professor Trout notes that many administrators refer to student evaluation forms as "consumer satisfaction surveys."

The task of the true educational reformer, he understood, was to both preserve and reform. Kirk's avowed purpose was to conserve the traditional objects of education from those who seek, in the name of "democracy," "adjustment to society," or some other abstract benefit to a future generation, to obliterate them. His description of his proposed program as "reactionary radicalism" is apt.

By the early 1970s, the process of decay within institutions of higher learning had reached such alarming proportions that a consensus was forming on the need for urgent reform. The better students had recognized that the "administrators' appetites for educational aggrandizement were working mischief—lowering intellectual standards and turning the grove of Academe into an unattractive educational factory." Kirk responded to this crisis with his program of "reactionary radicalism": "The reform of our higher learning must be radical: that is, it must go to the roots of culture. Also the reform of our higher learning must be reactionary: that is, it must react healthily against the intellectual diseases which have brought college and university to their present decadence." To accomplish these ends, Kirk proposed some general plans for the recovery of order, the integration of knowledge, and the renewal of the moral imagination.[25]

He began with an assessment of the state of public school education. The lower learning in primary and high schools must be restored before the restoration of the higher learning is possible:

> The performance of nearly all college students had been diminished by their inadequate preparation in the public-school apparatus. Their very ability to read, write, and understand mathematics has been unsatisfactory, this past quarter of a century and more, and the college had tried to enable them to compensate for their basic deficiencies—a task for which the college was not intended. In many other ways, elementary and secondary schooling have failed to prepare the rising generation for intelligent application to those abstractions which are the rightful concern of college and university.

In spite of the myriad of social problems besetting public schools today, such as racial turmoil, school busing, the decay of American inner cities, and rampant crime and drug abuse, Kirk submitted that they "could

25. Kirk, *Decadence and Renewal in the Higher Learning,* 153, 237.

have accomplished more toward preparing young people for higher education. Like colleges and universities, the schools had forgotten about wisdom and virtue."[26] They neglected to teach moral dogmas.

A tolerable social order requires widespread respect for and obedience to cross-cultural moral dogmas. Kirk defined dogmas as "formulated certainties," held on firm conviction and received on authority. When dogmas dissolve, the social bonds wither. People are then thrown back upon the resources of their meager experiences and intelligence, and the social order disintegrates. A society ignorant of dogmas does not learn to live without them but instead is afflicted with "strange new dogmas [which] rush in to fill the spiritual vacuum." Ideology or cultic enthusiasms are likely to gain sway. "For lack of a transcendent sanction, secular dogmas necessarily are harsher by far than religious dogmas."

Dogmatic teaching is principally, however, for primary and secondary schooling and only incidentally for the higher learning, wrote Kirk: "If the lower learning has been thorough, it should be unnecessary and indeed imprudent to teach dogmatically at college and university." If dogmas have not been taught by the sixth grade, then "no sure footing exists for the higher learning." The bewildered student "cannot even challenge first assumptions intelligently, for he does not know what the first assumptions are."[27] He attributed the present failure to inculcate dogmatic knowledge in the rising generation to five primary causes: John Dewey and his disciples who struck hard blows against dogmas, certain decisions of the Supreme Court, a general loss of the order and the integration of knowledge, vocationalism, and appeasement of the counterculture (popular in the late 1960s and early 1970s), which had "left little time for the imparting of truths not invented yesterday."

"Yet all success in schooling depends upon the acceptance of necessary dogmas," wrote Kirk. Without these first principles, "nothing can be achieved intellectually or morally, even by brilliant teachers." Lacking dogmas by which to govern their intellects, the student is left vulnerable to faddish opinions. Further, without dogmas, "there is no reason why we should behave in community as spiritual brothers, or even as thirty-second cousins in spirit. Sound dogmata liberate us from

26. Ibid., 247–48.
27. Ibid., 257.

enticement by fad and foible, from intellectual servility, from a society that is nothing better than a congeries of competing selfish interests."

These dogmas represent a body of beliefs that are not the product of personal preference but have been generally considered valid since time immemorial. They are found in "every culture, because without them there can be no culture." In his description of these necessary dogmas, Kirk borrowed from C. S. Lewis's book *The Abolition of Man.* One of England's most powerful Christian thinkers, Lewis distinguished "eight large laws of universal validity": "the law of special beneficence, duties to parents, elders, ancestors; duties to children and posterity; the law of justice; the law of good faith and veracity; the law of mercy; the law of magnanimity." The "principle instrument of this teaching of ethical truth" has been humane letters, "yet in some degree this understanding of how we are to live with ourselves and with our neighbors used to run through every school discipline." In addition, Kirk suggested instruction in political dogmata, "in moderation." "Among these are the affirmation of the dignity of man; adherence to the benefits of representative government; knowledge that the tolerable society requires a tension between the claims of order and the claims of freedom; assertion that a humane and free economy is better than a servile economy."[28]

More than any other discipline, literature nurtures the moral imagination from which is derived our knowledge of these dogmata. Yet, today, it is badly taught in the high schools. Students come to college with insufficient background and preparation in culture, and even after arriving may acquire no more than what "can be extracted from a survey-course in 'communications skills,' perhaps." The "voice of true poetry," he observed, "is nearly extinguished in our schools." The imagination, our intuitive perception of reality and life, more than reason, governs our will and appetite. The mind, Kirk repeatedly argued, is primarily moved by images. "By imagery our minds are moved, our emotions are directed, our characters are formed; and if that imagery is base, a society degrades itself. By this word 'imagery' I mean the formation of images of art, a type of general likeness; a descriptive representation, and exhibition of ideal images to the mind; figurative illustration. 'Imagery' is mental representation."[29] Kirk warned that a people denied an acquaintance

28. Ibid., 253–56.
29. Ibid., 258, 260–61.

with the source of these enduring images of their culture, classical liter-ature, "presently find themselves in personal and social difficulties: for their moral imagination is parched. Immersed in the ephemeral moment, and reading (if they read at all) at best the selections of the Book of the Month Club, such a people fail to apprehend adequately the human condition in the twentieth century, or in any other century."

Kirk distinguished between three different types of imagination: the moral, the idyllic, and the diabolic. The moral imagination, defined in chapter 3, "is informed by the great ethical poets. The idyllic imagina-tion responds to primitivistic fantasies—to the notions of Rousseau . . . The diabolic imagination loves the violent and the perverse." If we are "deprived of the imagery of virtue, we will seek out the imagery of vice. The triumph of the diabolic imagination, however, soon terminates in per-sonal and social extinction," Kirk warned. "Therefore, when the corrupt-ing of imagination has proceeded to intolerable lengths, there emerges some grim new morality, very unlike the 'New Morality' of license and irresponsibility so much talked about in recent years; and the pun-ishments of the total state substitute, after a fashion, for that control over will and appetite previously exercised by the moral imagination."

These poetic images are not to be regarded as "mere Corinthian or-naments of a culture." The teaching of great literature in our elementary and secondary schools is necessary for two reasons: first, a "principal object of the schools is the seeking of truth through images." Through the moral imagination awakened in students by the poetic imagery of great authors, students come to apprehend the human condition and the life of the spirit. Second, the study of literature gives "us all a common culture, ethical and intellectual, so that a people may share a general heritage and be united through the works of the mind."

The teaching of literature in courses from the ninth through the twelfth grades presently "suffers from two chief afflictions. The first of these is a misplaced eagerness for 'relevance.' The second of these is a kind of sullen purposelessness—a notion that literature, if it had any end at all, meant either to stir up discontents, or else merely to amuse." He strongly objected to the idea that the literature taught in the schools should be relevant to "the latest political troubles, the fads and foibles of the era, the concerns of commercial television or the daily news-paper." Such notions of relevance "leave young people prisoners to what has been called the provinciality of time." "Genuine relevance in literature, on the contrary, is relatedness to the permanent things: to the splendor and tragedy of the human condition, to constant moral insights, to the spectacle of human history, to love of community and country, to the achievements of right reason. Such a literary relevance confers upon the rising generation a sense of what it is to be fully human, and a knowledge of what great men and women of imagination have imparted to our civilization over the centuries." The second affliction, purposelessness, is a consequence of our having forgotten that great literature "was and is intended to persuade people of the truth of certain standards or norms." Literature is supposed "to wake us to truth through imagination, rather than through the discursive reason" in order to form our "normative consciousness."

To remedy these problems, Kirk proposed an alternative program of reading for the concluding years of secondary schooling. His proposal emphasized the literature of fantasy for the ninth grade, history and biography for the following year, books requiring serious interpretation and discussion for grade eleven, and for the senior year, works of humane letters to develop the critical imagination and an intuitive moral sense. Shakespeare, Robert Louis Stevenson, Ray Bradbury, Melville, T. S. Eliot, Samuel Johnson, and Samuel Taylor Coleridge are among the authors found in Kirk's list of suggested reading.[30] "College freshmen who had studied literature in high school on some such plan as I have suggested above," concluded Kirk, "would be competent to enter upon the serious study of literature, in English or some other language, at an advanced level. Also they would have been taught how to think and to write by such a program, and thus generally [be] prepared for an active part in higher learning."[31]

Improving academic standards on such a vast scale at the secondary level would require imaginative and well-trained and educated teachers. Given the current state of college preparation for secondary-school teachers, the present pool of persons capable of the level of instruction urged by Kirk would hardly meet the demand. According to the controversial and influential 1983 report of the National Commission on Excellence in Education on the state of America's elementary and secondary schools, *A Nation at Risk,* "Too many teachers are being drawn

30. Ibid., 270–77.
31. Ibid., 279.

from the bottom quarter of graduating high school and college students."[32] If the teaching profession cannot attract better-qualified candidates, then the prospects for improving the quality of schooling subsequently suffer. Poor teachers send poorly prepared students on to college, where they contribute to the further degradation of academic standards. The question, then, is how to end this vicious cycle of mediocrity. One possible remedy, adopted in some states, would be to require all teachers to return to college for an additional year of instruction or periodic competency testing. Another option would be for the local school authorities to dismiss or encourage early retirement of the least-qualified faculty (determined perhaps by teacher testing) and replace them with better-qualified instructors. Many currently unemployed or underemployed Ph.D.s would be exceptionally well qualified to teach on the secondary level. The commission report recommends even the use of "substantial nonschool personnel resources ... to help solve the immediate problem of the shortage of mathematics and science teachers" and "other areas of critical teacher need, such as English." This idea could be implemented more broadly to bring many uncertified but otherwise competent and motivated persons into the teaching profession. But, the adoption of such proposals for reform faces nearly insurmountable obstacles. First, powerful teachers' unions, especially the National Education Association, for which the primary issue in education has always been job security and pay, adamantly oppose teacher testing and the hiring of uncertified instructors. Kirk's proposals would violate in many school districts the rights of teachers as stipulated in union contracts. Further, most states require all public school teachers to be certified. Teacher certification requires the candidate to take specified teacher education courses. The prospect of sitting through a battery of these courses, many of which emphasize trivia over substance, would discourage many a bright mind from considering teaching as a career.[33]

32. *The National Commission on Excellence in Education, A Nation at Risk: The Imperative for Educational Reform* (Washington, D.C.: U.S. Department of Education, 1983), 22, 31. College and university departments of education still have a reputation on most campuses for attracting academically weak students.
33. A recent National Endowment for the Humanities report on the state of public education addresses itself to many of the problems with teacher preparation courses. Its authors note that many teachers "have come through teacher preparation programs in which they have taken courses of dubious intellectual quality." Many regard "education courses as a waste of time." The report criticizes teacher

The commission also recommends higher educational standards for teachers, more competitive salaries to attract more qualified teachers (although it has never been proven that a positive correlation exists between teacher salary and student performance), and grants and loans to attract the better students to the teaching profession.

Of course, the alternative to public schooling, where reform is always difficult, is private education. Private educational institutions, because they are less subject to outside interference from government bureaucracies, entrenched special interest groups, and teachers unions, generally are better equipped to fend off the pressures to degrade academic standards. But private schooling is not affordable to all. The "voucher plan" could be a large step toward remedying this hurdle for many families. According to this proposal (although touted by the Reagan and George W. Bush administrations, it has not been enacted, though some cities, notably Milwaukee and Cleveland, have implemented voucher plans), a student's education at a private school would be subsidized in part by general tax revenues. Kirk supported this plan as a means of encouraging the development of private education as an alternative to the generally academically moribund public school system. Although popular with the public, the education establishment strongly opposes vouchers.[34] Home schooling and charter schools are also increasingly popular alternatives to the public school system.

The "conceivable renewal" of American higher learning is possible, but once more, radical measures are required. Skeptical of the prospects

---

education programs for overemphasizing education courses and deemphasizing studying content areas. Studies have shown that prospective "teachers had a weaker general education curriculum than most arts and science graduates." As a consequence, "[t]eacher preparation requirements can leave teachers knowing less than they should about the subjects they teach." After they are hired, teachers are not encouraged to become more knowledgeable in their subjects. The report urges humanities faculties at colleges and universities to work to help "improve humanities teaching in our schools." See Lynne V. Cheney, *American Memory: A Report on the Humanities in the Nation's Public Schools,* 22–26. For further evidence concerning the academic deficiency of college teacher-training programs, see Martin L. Gross, *The Conspiracy of Ignorance: The Failure of American Public Schools* (New York: HarperCollins, 1999), especially chap. 3.

34. Kirk, "Diversity in Schooling," 542; "Free Choice: A Voucher Plan," 598. Kirk's ideas on primary and secondary education did influence, albeit somewhat indirectly, American public policy. In 1981, his wife, Annette Yvonne Kirk, was

for bringing about any fundamental reforms within an existing college or university, Kirk proposed beginning from scratch. For this purpose, he drew up "a model of a college which could be brought into being and could endure under favorable circumstances." Even though there is little practical hope that his model college could ever be established, he uses his proposal to depict an ideal of a humanistic college against which all existing academic institutions can be measured. To assure a degree of autonomy from governmental control, his model college would be private and probably church-related. Eschewing the objects of success, pleasure, or sociability characteristic of the bulk of colleges and universities, the college's chief object would be "the imparting of some measure of wisdom and virtue to the rising generation." It would be "an academic community, on a humane scale, in which a body of senior scholars (the professors) are united in seeking after the truth." While diversity of opinion among faculty and students will be valued, not all points of view will be tolerated. Doubts on first principles create confusion about what the aims of an educational institution should be and what should be considered as knowledge.[35]

Bypassing the immediate difficulties of financing this venture, Kirk suggested that the process of establishing his model college should begin by determining what the program of study would be, and only afterwards should the problems of staff, students, and "plant" be decided.

---

appointed as a member to the National Commission on Excellence in Education. The commission report gained immediate national attention as a direct consequence of having described the state of American education as "a rising tide of mediocrity." See *A Nation at Risk,* 5. Mrs. Kirk, a fervent supporter of her husband's educational principles and the representative for the interests of parents of elementary and secondary school children, took an active part in the commission's deliberations and the writing of its final report. While much of the report coincides with Kirk's arguments, its recommendations make no mention of the teaching of virtue and wisdom as one of the principal aims of education but instead stresses utilitarian objects—such as the importance of educating young people in technical skills in order to prepare them for the job market in an increasingly complex technological society. Gross, *The Conspiracy of Ignorance,* 158–67.

35. Kirk, *Decadence and Renewal in the Higher Learning,* 293–94, 302–7. While academic institutions nearly universally declare their commitment to academic freedom and diversity of opinion, they are often harshly intolerant of ideas that run counter to prevailing liberal dogmas. The regime of political correctness now prevalent on most American colleges and universities limits freedom of speech and thought far beyond anything Kirk had in mind here.

This sequence, he noted sardonically, is usually reversed in the United States.

The program of studies "ought to be designed to develop right reason and wake the moral imagination: to impart an apprehension of reality through disciplines which concern the nature of man and the condition in which we find ourselves in this world, it being understood that human beings are moral beings, in whose existence splendor and misery are blended." Although the mainstay of his curriculum would be the great works of literature and history, he significantly offered only a qualified endorsement of Bloom's "Great Books approach." The Great Books curriculum offers "a very good approach to the higher learning. But it is not the only very good approach, and I prefer a curriculum organized about a few subjects." One objection to this method is that historical continuity is neglected somewhat and "it does not include enough imaginative literature."[36] In Kirk's proposed curriculum, few subjects would be taught and survey courses would be generally avoided. The college year would last only six months ("after the Scottish fashion") to permit time for independent study, discussion, and travel. The typical student would have to possess a far greater degree of self-discipline and capacity for self-directed study than is presently expected at most American colleges. Quite clearly, only the exceptionally intellectually able, well-prepared, and motivated student could survive at Kirk's model college. No provisions are made for remedial instruction for the poorly prepared student or for activities to build student self-esteem.

The primary disciplines taught would be moral philosophy, humane letters, rhetoric, history, political economy, physics and higher mathematics, biological science, classical and modern languages and literature, and possibly music and visual arts. Noticeably absent from this curriculum are degree programs in business, computer science, education, social work, or other popular preprofessional fields. The purpose of his college is certainly not job certification or job training. Tests and examinations would be given only at the end of the academic year. The ordinary means of instruction would be the well-prepared formal lecture. A bachelor's degree would be conferred after only three years

---

36. Kirk, *Decadence and Renewal in the Higher Learning,* 334–35. See Bloom, *The Closing of the American Mind,* 334–47 for his defense of the Great Books approach.

of study, there being no reason to extend the period of education beyond that. Too much time, he believes, is wasted at most colleges and universities on worthless, needless courses.[37]

He further advised that the formal credentials requirements required for a faculty appointment be reconsidered. A candidate should be qualified by "learning and liveliness," rather than by attainment of formal degrees. "Experience of the world, or personal achievement in a particular field, often might be given preference over a doctoral degree, or over a list of specialized publications." The faculty members should be given the maximum amount of freedom in choosing their own method of instruction, with the proviso that it be understood that they are teaching an intellectual discipline and not merely a personal view of the world.

Likewise, formal admission requirements for prospective students would be largely abandoned. Students would be selected on the "basis of real intellectual interests and tolerable preparation," not solely on the basis of multiple-choice aptitude test scores, high school senior class ranking, or intelligence quotient. All of these measures he rejected as insufficient indicators of a student's capacity for higher learning. "What matters most is intellectual liveliness, application to studies, and literary competence."[38] Lacking standards that can be measured quantitatively for determining the best-qualified candidates for admission,

37. My own students yelp unless given weekly graded assignments. College instructors are now encouraged by administrators to abandon the lecture format in favor of group work. They are expected to play the role of facilitators of differing student learning styles rather than instructors of a body of information that students are expected to master.

Bloom agreed with Kirk that four years of college instruction is too long. A "well kept secret" of colleges, he maintained, is that they "do not have enough to teach their students, not enough to justify keeping them four years, probably not even three years." Bloom, *The Closing of the American Mind,* 350. There are of course examples of many college dropouts who have managed to be professionally successful in business and entertainment, including Rush Limbaugh, Peter Jennings, Bill Gates, and Matt Lauer.

38. The use of the Scholastic Aptitude Test by admissions officers as a measure of academic aptitude has long stirred controversy. In 1988, for example, some critics predicted "a coming revolution against" standardized admissions tests. Educators and even test makers themselves have expressed grave misgivings about the misuse of test scores. Critics question whether aptitude tests accurately measure students' reading and writing ability. See Fred M. Hechinger, "About Education,"

the director of admissions at Kirk's model college would not have an enviable job.

His suggestions for the design of the college's physical plant are offered as almost an afterthought. If a new college must be built, let it be "conspicuously handsome and permanent, but not luxurious." The administration building, however, Kirk added with an almost perverse delight reflecting his distaste for bureaucratic organizations, "should be as small and uncomfortable as possible, to discourage educational bureaucracy." An alternative to erecting new buildings would be to "acquire the premises of a defunct or dying college" or to restore a large building in the middle of the city. Lastly, the college should stick strictly to its main business of educating and refrain from entering the bookstore, housing, or cafeteria businesses.

Concluding his list of stipulations for the model college are a pot-pourri of final considerations. While beer and wine are allowed (local ordinances presumably permitting), members of the opposite sex are not to be enrolled. The availability of alcoholic beverages "takes the lure of the forbidden out of drink" and "discourages, rather than invites, heavy drinking." But, this same principle does not seem to apply where members of the opposite sex are concerned (is sex not a "lure"?). To avoid "the dating-and-mating pattern which obsesses the typical American campus," he maintained, flying obdurately in the face of the present movement for turning previously single-sex colleges into coeducational institutions, that his college would be segregated by gender.[39] A co-educational environment is too distracting and hence not conducive to learning. A near monastic isolation from the preoccupations of worldly concerns will be the lot of the students enrolled at his institution.

Unlike Thomas Jefferson, Kirk never realized his dream of founding a college. But, if such an opportunity had been available to him, he was convinced, like Jefferson's project, that his college would nurture

---

New York Times, December 7, 1988. Thirteen years later, Richard Atkinson, president of the University of California, proposed that the aptitude portion of the SATs no longer be required for admission to the University of California system. Many liberals have called for the elimination of SATs, condemning these tests as inherently biased against minority and poor students. See "The SAT Showdown," *Newsweek,* March 5, 2001, 48–50.

39. Kirk, *Decadence and Renewal in the Higher Learning,* 302–7.

future generations of the nation's natural aristocracy. From his college would emerge the "clerisy," the intellectual and moral leaders, responsible for elevating the nation's moral and social standards. Committed to character education and existing on a humane scale, his model college would attract "the better senior scholars, the better junior scholars, and the benefactions of private patrons, foundations, and business. The college can survive and prosper not by imitating the mass-schooling methods of Behemoth University, or the educational shams of Brummagem University, but by offering a discipline of intellect, ethical in aim, which mass-education and sham-education neglect."[40]

The closest that any existing institution of higher learning comes to approaching his ideal is the International College of California, founded in 1970 and established as an alternative to traditional higher education. The college has no campus and little staff. The students study under tutors, who are noted specialists in their field. Written evaluations by the tutors are the only means of evaluating the student's progress. The tutor-student model is patterned after the relationship that had existed between the student and sage during the age of Socrates. Endorsing this concept, Kirk admitted that its approach is only "for a Remnant," that is, for students genuinely seeking an education. Such notables as historian Page Smith, novelist Anaïs Nin, and men of letters Erik Ritter von Kuehnelt-Leddihn and Buckminster Fuller were among the college's tutors.[41] For more than a decade, Kirk also served as a tutor in the program. During those years, one or two students per year in the program would study political theory or literary criticism at his library/home in Mecosta.

EDUCATION FOR CITIZENSHIP OR FOR "THE THINGS OF APOLLO"?

Kirk believed that a society benefits from a system of education that fosters the development of souls who possess those qualities of mind and character without which a harmonious and just social order would be impossible. In other words, a sound educational system will be the breeding ground not for a bureaucratic or technocratic elite, but for the natural aristocracy, who would "leaven the lump of modern civiliza-

40. Ibid., 297.
41. Ibid., 330–33.

tion." Schooled in virtue and wisdom rather than mere fact accumulation or a narrow vocation, they will come to "possess some share of right reason and moral imagination."[42]

He strongly objected to the view that education's primary role should be to serve the ends of the state. "Civic education" distorts and corrupts the true purposes of education. Locke, Rousseau, and John Dewey, for example, argued that education should inculcate the civic virtues of duty and responsibility to ensure their obedience and loyalty to the regime. During the last half-century or more, most of the popular textbooks on American education have declared as a fundamental principle that schools should prepare students to become good "democratic" citizens. Students should be taught, they advised, the virtues of moderation, obedience to the laws, and patriotism, all of which were considered as necessary for American democratic order.[43] The interests of the state or the collective interests of society take precedence over the concerns and interests of the person.

Kirk's position on civic education has been unfortunately misrepresented and misunderstood. In one analysis, he was described as having advocated as an "important purpose" of education the imposition of "a uniform character upon the rising generation, rendering young people obedient to the state from habit and prejudice."[44] This interpretation of Kirk's point, however, is directly contrary to his intention. Later in the article from which this critic was quoting, Kirk stated emphatically that he "felt hostile" to this aim. Such proposals for a "civic education" distort the true aim of liberal education because they involve a dangerous confusion, Kirk would have agreed, between what Claes Ryn calls "The Things of Apollo," the "humanistic-artistic activities" of a culture, and "The Things of Caesar," those activities necessary for the maintenance of political order.[45] Genuine education is the imparting of truth unbiased by any appeals to political advantage. If education serves the

42. Ibid., xvii–xviii.

43. *The Purposes of Education in American Democracy* (Washington, D.C.: Educational Policies Commission, 1938), 2, 7, 26–27; John Dewey, *Democracy and Education: An Introduction to the Philosophy of Education,* 101.

44. Ridgely Hill Pate, "Russell Kirk, Friedrick Hayek and Peter Viereck: Three Positions in Contemporary Conservative Thought," 103. See also Kirk, *Confessions of a Bohemian Tory,* 16, from which Pate obtained this quotation.

45. See Claes G. Ryn, "The Things of Caesar: Notes toward the Delimitation of Politics," 440.

ends of the state instead, then truth itself will be abandoned to the shifting winds of political necessity. Kirk unequivocally affirmed his opposition to replacing the teaching of old dogmas with "the religion of democracy."

He likewise expressed the strongest possible revulsion for the doctrines of John Dewey that would supplant "the disciplining of the higher faculty of the imagination" with "adjustment-to-society." Attacking the disciples of Dewey, who "have put forceful emphasis upon the primacy of 'citizenship education,' 'political socialization,'" Kirk accused these "Progressive" educators of appearing to be "interested almost exclusively in training for democratic citizenship, to the exclusion of those disciplines which comfort the inner man." By "education," these Deweyite reformers mean, observed Kirk, "recreation, socialization, and a kind of custodial jurisdiction over young people." "Democracy" indicates no more to them than "all things that are kindly and just and good." It has become a "god-term," "a charismatic expression drained dry of any objective significance, but remaining an empty symbol intended to win unthinking applause."[46] The mission of the higher learning must be aimed at ends higher than this degradation of the democratic dogma. No educator should forget that his or her mission is to transmit wisdom and virtue to the rising generation. By nurturing the imagination through poetic images and great literature, schooling develops within us a self-awareness of our own defects and potentialities—in other words, it strengthens our sense of reality. By gaining insights into our own moral limits and weaknesses, we begin the process of moral self-reform that Kirk believed to be the only true reform. Immediate considerations of possible political benefits should not be permitted to deflect education from its primary aims.

Kirk's philosophy of education does have political consequences. His approach fosters the development of a reverence for the authority of tradition, long-established institutions, and dogmas. The habits of mind acquired by reading great works of imaginative literature and history will inoculate the minds of the rising generation against the dehumanizing and destructive visions of the radical innovators and social engineers. Liberally educated persons will prefer ordered change,

46. Kirk, *Academic Freedom: An Essay in Definition,* 44–45; Kirk, *Decadence and Renewal in the Higher Learning,* 255, 280.

feel an abiding sense of gratitude toward their ancestors and solicitude toward the interests of posterity, love what is loveable in their country and neighbors, and respect the just interests of others. Kirk's fundamental purpose, however, is not to shape persons into politically obedient or subservient citizens, but rather to cultivate their qualities of moral character and imagination. Training in the highest form of imagination and training in moral character are viewed as inseparable. The ideal product of this system of education would be a person fitted for moral and intellectual leadership, possessing what Burke once called the quality of "unbought grace." Order, freedom, and genuine community depend for their preservation on cultivating the minds and souls of citizens.

8 The Enduring Legacy

*[K]nowing the community of souls, he freed
others from captivity and lonely ego; in the
teeth of winds of doctrine, he attested the
permanent things.*

—Russell Kirk, *Eliot and His Age*

Although Kirk's work gives evidence of a wide range of concerns, it also forms a coherent whole. Whether writing about cultural, aesthetic, social, educational, or topical political issues, he brought to his thought consistently held principles. His literary and cultural concerns, far from being mere diversions, were inseparable from his social and political interests. He placed among his pantheon of teachers to be revered by conservatives a generous proportion of poets and literary thinkers who had not been previously honored for their political or social teachings. They included Samuel Taylor Coleridge, Charles Dickens, T. S. Eliot, C. S. Lewis, and Ray Bradbury. Kirk believed that these poets and novelists are conservative in the best sense of the term, because it is largely through the intuitive insights found in their works that the eternal truths of the soul, justice, and order are conserved. Great books and poetry teach us our place within the eternal order of things and about our ends and purposes as members of a human community; shape the normative consciousness of an age, thereby enhancing the prospects for a humane social order; and reveal our essence, both our magnificence as well as our baseness, through their imaginative visions. Kirk's own fictional work (about which little has been said in this work) was likewise an imaginative vehicle for depicting the tragic consequences that follow when man arrogantly defies "the permanent things."[1]

1. See Don Herron, "The Crepuscular Romantic: An Appreciation of the Fiction of Russell Kirk," 1–12 for a discussion and analysis of Kirk's fiction. As far as I can determine, this was the first extensive analysis of Kirk's supernatural

202 Russell Kirk and the Age of Ideology

We now come to another characteristic of Kirk's brand of conservative thought: its nonpolitical inspiration. While Kirk often wrote about contemporary political events and kept abreast of daily national and international news events (even though he famously did not own a television set), he rarely became involved in political advocacy (with the signal exception of the Pro-Life movement). Although Presidents Nixon and Reagan among other elected officials valued his counsel, he never actively sought political influence or power. Of primary concern for him instead was the discovery of and apprehension of the "permanent things," those eternal moral norms that give meaning to and enrich the quality of life. A conservatism identified with a mere laundry list of public policy issues, he believed, would not long endure. The battle for the future direction of America cannot be won by "conservative" political victories either in Congress or at the ballot box when the things of the heart and mind are neglected. Kirk also had no faith in the capacity of politics to cure the moral and spiritual failings of a society. One reason that Kirk was sometimes ignored within conservative political circles is that conservative activists have difficulty grasping the decisive importance he assigned to culture. Because he never offered specific programs on health care, tax cuts, foreign policy, market deregulation, or crime reduction, Kirk's work appeared irrelevant to those conservative activists who focused on political power. They dismiss his work as little more than a literary diversion, or even more disparagingly, call him a "beautiful loser" (more about that below). For Kirk, culture precedes politics, and unless a healthy, vibrant civilized culture exists, no amount of "conservative" political victories will have long-term significance. The breakup of the conservative movement following the Reagan administration and the short-lived "Republican Revolution" fol-

---

tales. While this article provides an excellent summary of Kirk's novels and short stories, Herron only briefly discusses the relationship between Kirk's political and social thought and his fiction. A far more extensive and thorough examination of Kirk's fiction can be found in James E. Person, Jr.'s excellent biography, *Russell Kirk: A Critical Biography of a Conservative Mind*. Person explains how Kirk used fiction to portray the truths of the human condition, man's flawed nature, spiritual destiny, and the character of good and evil that eludes the limitations of discursive reason. Person's study will undoubtedly inspire many to dip deeper into Kirk's often-neglected body of fiction.

lowing the 1994 congressional elections, Kirk would have agreed, can be explained by the failure of conservatives to pay sufficient attention to the moral ills afflicting contemporary culture.

Conservatives, of course, must have ideas and must profess principles, but principles, as we have noted earlier, are for Kirk the opposite of ideology. He strenuously opposed the argument made by neoconservatives such as Irving Kristol that conservatism, if it is to become a successful political force, must "develop a sharp ideological identity." Conservatives, advised Kristol, must forget their distaste for ideology since "you can't beat an ideology with no ideology." Politics is "governed by circumstances," explained Kristol, "not philosophy, and it has become clear that in our time, a nonideological politics cannot survive the relentless onslaught of ideological politics."[2]

Kirk was quick to challenge Kristol's notion of what the content of a genuine conservatism should be. In this time of troubles, roared Kirk in his last major article for *National Review,* what is needed is not the "politics of ideology," but "the politics of imagination." Reconstructing conservatism along rigid ideological lines would restrict rather than expand its appeal by ossifying this rich tradition of political principles "into a rigorous system of political dogmas, vulgarized for public consumption, narrow and intolerant as ideologies must be." Moreover, a "conservative" ideology "could not actually be conservative at all, the antipathy between conservatism and ideology being ineluctable." Rather than knitting a community together into a harmonious, humane order, ideological passions ferment strife and disorder. Order in the commonwealth and soul can be preserved only by "a general apprehension of enduring principles of order and justice and freedom," which "is a task for true education, not for ideological propaganda." In any case, a conservative ideology would not long endure, but would soon evaporate in the wake of some new faddish promise of a Terrestrial Paradise. An "imaginative conservatism is a different matter all together." Ideologues "readily dispense with men of imagination," believing them to be "dangerous." Conservatives, on the other hand, cherish them, knowing their poetic images "draw us toward a politics concerned with the actual

2. Irving Kristol, "The New Republican Party," *Wall Street Journal,* July 17, 1980.

circumstances of living men and women, as contrasted with the grisly abstractions of the ideologies."[3]

As an alternative to ideology, Kirk implored conservatives in 1980 to "aspire to what P. E. More calls the aim of Burke: 'to use the imagination as a force for order and self-restraint and political health.'" If conservatism "quickens the imagination" of this age, he predicted, we "may succeed in conserving far more than our goods and chattels." Yet, Kirk was not entirely confident that conservatives would heed his message. The sweeping conservative political victories on the national and state levels in 1980 would be the test of whether conservatives could match Kirk's expectations. Would conservatives use the power they had won at the polls to make decisive changes in the direction of American politics and culture, he wondered, or would trimmers and opportunists vitiate conservative principles? Liberals may be losing political support, but are conservatives making genuine, lasting gains? Kirk offered this cautious assessment of the prospects for conservatives at the dawn of the Reagan presidency: "In consequence of some thirty years of debate, it appears, American liberals are losing their ascendancy, and American conservatives are supplanting them in power. We conservatives have been better at *peitho* [eloquence or cogency] than have the liberals and the radicals. Whether this November's resounding triumph of conservatives at national and elections will bring to our governing counsels some measure of poetic imagination, however, we have yet to learn. If it does not, the ascendancy of conservatives may be brief."[4] His initial misgivings were far from misplaced, as subsequent events would bear out.

A MOVEMENT ADRIFT

After spending decades on the political fringe, conservatives by the late 1970s felt that history was moving decisively in their direction. Many of the most prominent voices within the American postwar con-

---

3. Kirk, "Imagination against Ideology," 1578, 1583. To be fair to Kristol, it must be noted that Kirk may have misrepresented Kristol's argument here. Kristol is employing the term "ideology" to mean a body of principles on which a group of like-minded persons could agree, not the "armed doctrine" of rigid abstractions that Kirk is suggesting. Because of the historical connotations associated with the term, though, its use alone was sufficient to arouse Kirk's suspicion.

4. Ibid., 1583, 1577.

servative intellectual movement hailed the 1980 landslide election of Ronald Reagan, the first self-described conservative, as evidence of conservative political success. No longer would conservatives be dismissed as merely a disgruntled, politically marginalized minority. History had handed them an opportunity to play a formidable role in America's political and cultural future. Never before had this embattled band of intellectuals, now basking in their good fortune, expressed their aspirations and purposes with such confidence. A clearly elated Kirk, just prior to the 1980 election, expressed the feelings of many conservatives. America is now "entering upon a period of conservative policies in the American Republic," he exalted. "In both the great political parties, I suggest, conservative views will tend to dominate. Men and women who profess conservative convictions will be elected to office. And what matters more, the conservative political imagination will set to work to allay our present discontents and to renew our order."[5] While liberalism seemed intellectually exhausted and moribund, conservatism was energized by fresh ideas and vigor. Conservatives presumed that their principles and programs would fill the void created by a weakened liberalism.

Within a few years, though, this confidence gave way to doubt as the unity of conservatives began to unravel. Kirk and his fellow conservatives were soon disappointed by the direction of the Reagan administration. Despite the impressive "conservative" electoral victories, they questioned whether anything of value had been achieved during Reagan's first term. The ideas of the Left continued to prevail in colleges and universities, the media, and the bureaucracy. The march toward what conservatives saw as leveling social policies and intrusive managerial politics had not been significantly reversed. Conservatism had not moved America to the Right, but rather the Right allowed itself to be pushed leftward. In a 1986 symposium on conservatism published in the *Intercollegiate Review,* several prominent conservatives, including Kirk, the late M. E. Bradford, Clyde Wilson, and Paul Gottfried, voiced misgivings about the future of "conservative" ideas.[6] The traditional commitments to an isolationist foreign policy, minimal government, rooted

5. Kirk, "The Conservative Movement: Then and Now," in *Reclaiming a Patrimony,* 1. This lecture was delivered at the Heritage Foundation, Washington, D.C., on June 4, 1980.

6. See *Intercollegiate Review* 21, no. 3 (Spring 1986).

communities, and social hierarchies, once the pillars of the conservative cause, were falling into disrepute even on the Right. Instead, conservative activists were stressing material opportunity and social improvement, and, in the name of global democracy, an interventionist foreign policy.

These expressions of concern about the coherence and direction of the conservative movement marked the beginning of the "conservative wars." By the mid-1980s, the Old Right began vigorously questioning whether neoconservatives, a group of predominantly Jewish intellectuals based in New York and connected with *Commentary* who had "broken ranks" with the Democratic party, could be rightfully called conservative. The neoconservatives retaliated by bitterly scolding Old Rightists, including Kirk, as racists, anti-Semites, or xenophobes.[7]

To the contributors to the 1986 symposium, the conservative movement was fragmented, "adrift," and "in trouble." Its character had changed for the worse. As a consequence of their prominence in government and the media, the neoconservatives had effectively redefined the meaning of conservatism and steered it in the direction of social democracy.[8] By the early 1990s, it was no longer startling to hear conservatives proclaim their support for U.S. sanctions against the pre–Nelson Mandela South African government, the social welfare state, affirmative action, the removal of Confederate flags from public buildings in the South, open borders immigration policies, and global democracy. The "politics of nostalgia" seemed all but dead on the respectable Right. Instead, Jack Kemp, William Bennett, Ben Wattenberg, Irving Kristol, Norman Podhoretz, Midge Decter, and George F. Will, to name just a few, praised the march toward greater equality and material improvement. This "conservatism" seemed to have little or nothing to do with Edmund Burke, John Adams, Henry Adams, and Irving Babbitt,

7. See, for example, Richard John Neuhaus, "Democratic Conservatism," in *First Things* 1, no. 1 (March 1990): 65–66. See also David Frum, "Cultural Clash on the Right," *Wall Street Journal,* June 2, 1989, in which the split between Pastor Neuhaus and the Rockford Institute, which publishes the paleoconservative magazine *Chronicles: A Magazine of American Culture,* is described. See the late M. E. Bradford's "Undone by Victory: Political Success and the Subversion of Conservative Politics," *Imprimis* 15, no. 6 (June 1986): 1–4, for the mordant observations of one Old Rightist on the failures of the so-called "Reagan Revolution."

8. Paul Gottfried and Thomas Fleming, *The Conservative Movement,* 62, 108.

or, for that matter, with the libertarian principles heard in the 1964 presidential campaign of Barry Goldwater.

THE ASSAULT ON THE POLITICS OF TRADITION

Despite popular and media-inspired impressions, the postwar American Right was never a single movement, but a series of movements emerging out of divergent philosophical traditions. The widening gap between Kirk and his modernist adversaries, far from being a dispute over transient public policy issues, involves profound differences over questions of principles.

Among the most strident critics of the historical past that Kirk invoked to vindicate his sociopolitical principles are the neoconservatives: Irving Kristol, Michael Novak, Norman Podhoretz, and the disciples of Leo Strauss. Together, they have helped reshape political conservatism in a way that treats most of the Western past as a prelude to the present generation of democratic values and human rights. The neoconservatives, declares Catholic theologian Novak in an essay praising the teachings of liberal theologian Reinhold Niebuhr, "are forward-looking, not backward-looking. We contest with the Left the direction in which true social progress lies."[9]

The neoconservatives have been frequently accused of being "children of the Enlightenment." Indeed, taken as a whole, their positions owe far more to Locke, Rousseau, Tom Paine, Jeremy Bentham, John Stuart Mill, and John Dewey than to the views of Burke, Adams, Calhoun, Disraeli, and Irving Babbitt. Michael Novak, for all his opposition to the Catholic Left, illustrates this difference. Once a self-proclaimed democratic socialist, he now extols democratic capitalism. The path that led him to repudiate his youthful convictions was for Novak a kind of spiritual conversion. "I discovered spiritual resources in democratic capitalism I had long repressed in myself," he writes.[10] Yet, this conversion amounts to less of a repudiation of democratic socialism than to an effort to pour new wine into old bottles. His vision of a democratic capitalist future bears a startling resemblance to many of views expressed by the revolutionary Left.

9. Michael Novak, "Father of Conservatives," 42.
10. Novak, *The Spirit of Democratic Capitalism,* 26.

Novak admires capitalism's enormous productive capability and its power to destroy traditional social institutions while creating new social arrangements. Capitalism prepares the way for establishing for the first time in history a society based on abundance and consumption. Novak applauds democracy as the engine of progress that will move the world toward a final stage of human fulfillment. "Democratic polities depend upon the reality of economic growth," he argues. "No traditional society, no socialist society—indeed, no society in history—has ever produced strict equality among individuals or classes." A democratic capitalist society, however, will produce such sustained economic growth that scarcity will eventually disappear. All will share in the economy's bounty. "A democratic system depends for its legitimacy... not upon equal results but upon a sense of equal opportunity," he observes. "Such legitimacy flows from the belief of all individuals that they can better their condition. This belief can be realized only under conditions of economic growth." History, according to Novak, cannot prepare us for what lies ahead because society "in its complexity... is unlike... the historical societies which preceded it."[11]

Critics of democratic capitalism are not just blocking the path to material progress but also hindering God's purpose. "It is the religious task of Jews and Christians to change the world as well as to purify their own souls," he contends, "to build up 'the Kingdom of God' in their own hearts and through the work of their hands." We have, therefore, a moral responsibility to get on the right side of history. Novak imagines that he has discovered the laws of history that are carrying us toward previously unimagined peace and plenty: "The world as Adam faced it after the Garden of Eden left mankind in misery and hungry for millennia. Now that the secrets of sustained material progress have been decoded, the responsibility for reducing misery and hunger is no longer God's but ours."[12] Novak, a self-identified "Catholic Whig," appears to be suggesting that, contrary to Catholic teaching, the effects of original sin can be largely eradicated once the productive forces of the marketplace have been unleashed. Implicitly, he denies a fixed human nature, presuming that economic progress will end not only hunger and misery but also human depravity.

11. Ibid., 15–16.
12. Ibid., 18, 28.

Other neoconservatives have denounced the Old Rightists and traditionalists for dangerously antediluvian positions. Richard John Neuhaus, editor-in-chief of *First Things,* for example, accused the traditionalist Right of being "at war with modernity." These "anti-democrats" have brought "back into the conservative movement a list of uglies that had long been consigned to the fever swamps.... This list includes nativism, racism, anti-Semitism, xenophobia, a penchant for authoritarian politics, and related diseases of the *ressentiment* that flourishes on the marginalia of American life." While these discredited positions typified the thinking of conservatives (read the Old Right) thirty years ago, Neuhaus contends, conservatives have grown under neoconservative direction, embraced democratic pluralism, and cleansed themselves of embarrassing reactionary views.[13]

Neoconservatives, furthermore, openly disparage the Old Right, which they view as marginal at best. John B. Judis, Jr., senior editor for the *New Republic,* observes that the neoconservatives regard the traditionalists as "a dying breed who are without significant influence either within the academy or the government." The intellectual tradition of which they are a part, noted neoconservative Norman Podhoretz claims, "has pretty much lost its vitality." Burton Yale Pines, the former vice-president of the Heritage Foundation, a Washington-based conservative think tank, "compares the traditionalists to the Old Bolsheviks who were passed by during the revolution."[14]

Though a harsh critic of the libertarians throughout his career, Kirk only aroused himself to respond to the neoconservatives in 1988, long after they had become a dominant force within the conservative movement. His prolonged silence on the neoconservative challenge was curious. Other than sharing the label "conservative," he and they had nothing in common. Further, the neoconservatives constituted a more formidable adversary than any he had faced within the conservative movement. Unlike the libertarians, they would energetically and ruthlessly redefine conservatism, leaving no place for Kirk. They did not share Kirk's appreciation of literature and art—save as something that might be instrumentalized for political value. Their primary interests were

13. Neuhaus, "Democratic Conservatism," 65–66.
14. John B. Judis, "The Conservative Wars," *New Republic,* August 12 and 18, 1986, 18.

policy studies and social statistics, and their admiration for democratic capitalism can be traced to a quasi-Marxist appreciation of its transformative power. Rooted communities, traditions, and prescriptive rights did not appeal to Kirk's new opponents because they are viewed as barriers to personal power and political change. In their new democratic order, neoconservatives were striving to become an integral part of the managerial elite. In addition, as Gottfried maintains, they "proclaim the world-historical need to transform all societies into democracies patterned on the present American model: political and sexual equality, limited capitalism together with well-organized labor unions, and cultural modernization." The past before the New Deal, the civil rights revolution, and other democratizing events represented for neoconservatives the "bad old days" from which they, like the Left, hoped to liberate mankind. Only an America "redeemed by Martin Luther King, Jr., Bayard Rustin and other civil rights leaders" is "a fit model for universal imitation in the speeches of Neuhaus and the neoconservatives' favorite politicians, William Bennett and Jack Kemp," observes Gottfried.[15]

Acknowledging these differences, Kirk complained:

> I had expected the Neoconservatives to address themselves to the great social difficulties of the U.S. today, especially to the swelling growth of a dismal urban proletariat, and the decay of the moral order. Instead, with some exceptions, their concern has been mainly with the gross national product and with "global wealth." They offer few alternatives to the alleged benefits of the Welfare State, shrugging their shoulders and the creed of most of them is no better than a latter-day Utilitarianism.
>
> I had thought that the Neoconservatives might become the champions of diversity in the world, instead they aspire to bring about a world of uniformity and dull standardization, Americanized, industrialized, democratized, logicalized, boring. They are cultural and economic imperialists, many of them.[16]

Kirk was convinced the neoconservatives would not long remain a powerful force. In this instance his predictive powers failed him com-

15. Gottfried, "The War on the Right," *Rothbard-Rockwell Report* 11, no. 2 (February 1991): 13.

16. Kirk, "The Neoconservatives," 8–9.

pletely. They were not an "endangered species," about which "within a very few years we will hear no more." Today, as Gottfried points out, they dominate the conservative movement because of their "money, journalistic clout, and administrative connections." As a result, they have "weakened and defunded whatever rightist challenge to the status quo had existed." Indeed, what is left of the Old Right "run[s] the risk of being swallowed up in the alliance that they initiated and sustained."[17]

Gottfried further contends that the neoconservatives have contributed to the present "cultural narrowing" of conservatism. Indifferent to a historical understanding of society, they focus on transitory public policy issues and "abstract universals" that typically arise out of the radical wing of the Enlightenment. When they do find useful quotations from Thomas Jefferson and other Founding Fathers, they frequently pull them out of context, turning these figures into modern welfare state egalitarians and advocates of open border immigration. Historical conservatives such as Kirk may have lost ground hence within the conservative movement irrevocably. "The passing of the historicist tradition from the postwar conservative movement has left a theoretical void that may eventually embarrass American conservatives," Gottfried cogently warns. "Having by now largely lost a shared vision of the past, conservatives may soon find themselves without any vision except that of dehistoricized persons who seek to enrich themselves and the gross national product through the tireless pursuit of self-interest."[18]

Despite the influence of Kirk's historically minded conservatism on segments of the intellectual Right, differences should be noted between his use of the historical past and the theorizing of other historically oriented conservatives. Two such conservatives, Paul Gottfried and Claes Ryn, are the subjects of a book by the Italian scholar Germana Paraboschi on the historicism of the American Right. While both of these self-identified historicists view themselves as men of the Old Right and speak respectfully of Kirk, their historical thinking differs from his. Gottfried and Ryn have been marked by the tradition of German idealism; also, neither denies that the dialectical philosophy modified by the Italian philosopher Benedetto Croce (1866–1952) and other twentieth-century Hegelians has left a strong imprint on their work.

17. Ibid., 4; Gottfried and Fleming, *The Conservative Movement,* 108, 70.
18. Gottfried, *The Search for Historical Meaning,* 125.

Ryn has frequently complained that the invocation of history on the postwar American Right lacks philosophical reflection and rarely rises above hortatory rhetoric. Gottfried has come to equate historical consciousness with "contextualizing" political ideas. He presents history as a series of concrete situations in which values have become instantiated and raises critical objections to a conservatism based on "abstract universals." Like Ryn, he ridicules the appeals to disembodied values in neoconservative and Straussian discourse.[19] Clearly, Kirk stressed another kind of historical understanding, and, although allied with Ryn and Gottfried, he insisted on the non-German and nonidealist character of his own historical conservatism.

CONCLUSION

Despite these differences and criticisms from segments on the American Right, Kirk is assured a place of prominence as one of the foremost thinkers who anchored conservatism in moral norms and culture. Unlike the neoconservatives and members of the New Right, Kirk recognized that the key to the recovery of order lies in the discovery or rediscovery of those permanent norms that give meaning to and enrich the quality of life and community. The central principles and insights of his work have a perennial significance because they address the eternal dilemmas of the human condition. Consequently, his essays and books will continue to be studied by generations of thinkers long after the works of some of his critics have been relegated to commentaries on late-twentieth-century cultural history.

Aside from his published work, Kirk's legacy lives on through his disciples. From the early 1950s, a continuous stream of young persons found their way to Piety Hill to work with Kirk as literary interns. Most, like me, were apprenticed to him for periods lasting from several months to several years, assisting with his research, correspondence,

19. Germana Paraboschi, *Leo Strauss e la Destra Americana.* See Randall Auxier, "Straussianism Descendant? The Historicist Renewal," 64–72, for a review of Paraboschi's book in which the author describes and classifies the varieties of contemporary conservative thought. The essay is particularly relevant for the historicist thinking of Gottfried and Ryn. See Claes G. Ryn, "How Conservatives Have Failed 'The Culture,'" 117–27. See Gottfried, "Panajotis Kondylis and the Obsoleteness of Conservatism," especially page 406, and his review of *The Conservative Intellectual Movement in America* by George Nash (October–December 1997), 11.

and other library chores. Some who admired his work simply arrived unannounced at his door and were nearly always welcomed. During his tenure as the Marguerite Eyer Wilbur Foundation's president (1979–1994), Kirk through its Fellowship Program mentored another legion of young people. The program enabled graduate students to receive university credit while working on research projects under Kirk's direction. The network of Kirk scholars and students solidified and expanded in the 1970s and 1980s through seminars held in his old library under the auspices of the Intercollegiate Studies Institute (ISI). Kirk, the focus of these gatherings, would engage the participants in discussions about a variety of literary, historical, and political topics.[20]

Kirk nurtured the minds of the young people who worked and studied under him as assiduously as he did the innumerable trees he planted around Piety Hill. His mentoring as well as his enthusiasm for tree planting was commemorated in a carving commissioned in the 1980s by some of his appreciative assistants. The wooden carving consists of a family crest designed by John Quincy Adams. The inscription, taken from Cæcilius Slatius as quoted by Cicero in the First Tusculan Disputation, reads: *Serit arbores quae alteri seculo prosint* ("He plants trees for the benefit of later generations"). The carving now hangs in the family home at Piety Hill and is a continuous reminder of Kirk's investment in the future. Kirk's trees would grow and thrive, as Burke wrote in another context, "after the grave has heaped its mould upon our presumption, and the silent tomb shall have imposed its law on our pert loquacity." Likewise, many of the minds first cultivated by Kirk at Piety Hill would become the bearers and purveyors of "the permanent things" long after he had passed from this vale. "By the Nineties, there were dispersed throughout the United States a great many people in their middle years or their careers who had read" his works "and had been moved thereby," he wrote near the end of his days, "Of the disciples who at one time or another had beaten a pathway to Piety Hill,

20. Frank Chodorov founded ISI (originally named the Intercollegiate Society of Individualists) in 1953. The purpose of ISI is to expose college students to libertarian and conservative ideas through its summer schools, symposia, and speakers bureau. ISI also publishes inexpensive editions of classic conservative books. The *Intercollegiate Review,* a journal of scholarship and opinion, is made available without cost to college students and faculty. In addition, it offers graduate school fellowships to conservatively oriented college graduates.

some had become lawyers, and some teachers, some journalists, some professors; some were in the book trade, others had been ordained, yet others obtained posts in government. They might leaven the lump of American society."[21]

After his death, his widow, Annette Kirk, and their son-in-law, Jeffrey Nelson, founded the Russell Kirk Center for Cultural Renewal (http://www.kirkcenter.org), to preserve and perpetuate the legacy of Kirk. Its headquarters is located at the Kirk residence and a branch office was established in 2003 in Grand Rapids, Michigan. Students continue to travel to the remote village of Mecosta to study and learn as they did during Kirk's lifetime. Although the books from Kirk's original library were removed to nearby Hillsdale College, many would later be replaced. His vast correspondence and other papers are now housed in the Kirk Library where they will someday, after they have been catalogued, become available to researchers. Scholars and students still do research in the library. The center hosts seminars, colloquia, and the Residential Fellows Programs for college students, scholars, or anyone with a serious interest in Kirk's work. Also, the center manages and edits *The University Bookman,* a quarterly review of books founded by Kirk in 1960 and now edited by Jeffrey Nelson.

There is evidence of Kirk's legacy elsewhere as well. ISI continues to publish the quarterly journal *Modern Age,* founded by Kirk in 1957. The Heritage Foundation maintains a "Hall of Fame" Web site in his honor where biographical information, transcripts of the major Heritage Foundation lectures he delivered between 1989 and 1993, and his "six canons of conservative thought" are posted.[22]

While Kirk's legacy may be assured, those trying to implement his ideas for the immediate future will face at least three major problems: first, the politics of tradition has only a limited appeal in a society in which change and progress are almost universally celebrated as unquestioned goods. Life in a mobile, technological, media-dominated, urban society has accustomed people to equate change with improvement. The past is deemed to have little value since the circumstances in which we find ourselves appear to be unprecedented. In any case, we feel little

21. Kirk, *The Sword of Imagination,* 467.
22. "Hall of Fame," Heritage Foundation, www.town.com/hall_of_fame/kirkirkhome.html (accessed July 3, 2002).

gratitude or reverence for the achievements of previous generations that we have come to identify with racism, sexism, and other politically incorrect attitudes. What is admired about the past is what can be shown to have prepared us for the present progressive age. Moreover, Kirk's notorious aversion to modern technology won him few converts among Americans who have grown attached to their technological contraptions and will only relinquish them when new and improved models are offered. His critical, and often hostile, attitude toward even some of the most beneficial achievements of modernity raise troubling questions concerning whether Kirk can be always taken seriously as a social critic and lends credence to the accusation that he frequently sought to escape from the uncertainties of the present into an idealized past. In one sense, traditionalists such as Kirk can be correctly accused of having failed to articulate a fully developed sense of historical consciousness. Although he never doubted the wisdom of Edmund Burke's famous observation that change is the means of a society's conservation and Irving Babbitt's insight that each new generation must creatively adjust to new circumstances, Kirk also experienced an ahistorical attachment to the past. History became for him almost a sacred garden in which no room could be made for new categories of thought. His instinctive aversion to technological change, for example, led him into deploring the spread of computers, automobiles, and modern communications technologies in society rather than considering ways in which these advances could be incorporated imaginatively into a living tradition.

Second, conservatives professing Kirk's historical consciousness run the risk of being displaced or defined out of existence by the neoconservatives who have maintained their visibility and strength, despite their lack of a significant popular following. As a consequence of their access to the establishment media and their control of influential Washington-based public policy institutions, neoconservatives continue to play a dominant role in shaping popular attitudes and perceptions. Hence, it may be generations before conservatives of Kirk's persuasion can regain lost ground.

Moreover, another faction on the intellectual Right has vigorously criticized Kirk's traditionalism. Emerging out of the internecine conservative wars of the 1980s, the paleoconservatives represent the latest oppositional response to the neoconservatives. Although they share Kirk's distaste for neoconservative ideology and his hostility to the

collectivist state, they sharply disagree with him on the value of cling-
ing to traditions in the modern era. Gottfried, who originally coined
the "paleoconservative" label, notes that this group is "mostly Protes-
tant, with a sprinkling of Central European Jews." Unlike traditional
conservatives such as Kirk, they have been strongly influenced by "modernist disciplines," basing their arguments on the work of sociologists
and political theorists from Machiavelli and Thomas Hobbes to Antonio
Gramsci and James Burnham. The primary threats to individual liberty
and civilization, in their eyes, are the leveling and collectivist tendencies
inherent in the "welfare-warfare" state. Because they perceive themselves to be a counterrevolutionary force against the modern "managerial state," they are defiantly indifferent to Kirk's "redundant" appeals
to tradition.[23] The managerial-therapeutic ideologies espoused by the
political class, they claim, have distorted and vitiated the traditions
that Kirk invoked. Appeals to these already weakened "traditions" present no threat to state managers and their media celebrants. Samuel
Francis, a widely published paleoconservative author, nationally syndicated columnist, and former adviser to Republican presidential primary
candidate Pat Buchanan, describes Kirk by implication as a "beautiful
loser," a fine writer whose work nevertheless has become historically
irrelevant.[24] Francis holds up the anti-Communist analyst of power

23. For a fuller discussion of the paleoconservatives, see Gottfried and Fleming, *The Conservative Movement,* 153–59.
24. See his *Beautiful Losers: Essays on the Failure of American Conservatism.* It should be obvious to anyone reading this work that I do not share Francis's characterization of Kirk's work. Francis holds that culture is merely a product
of the wills of the prevailing elites. The elite ruling class, which runs the managerial-
therapeutic state, manufactures and manipulates the culture for its immediate
political advantage. The use of power is the primary factor shaping all social and
political phenomena, and culture is secondary. Claes Ryn, in a lengthy review
essay of Gottfried's *After Liberalism: Mass Democracy in the Managerial State*
(Princeton, N.J.: Princeton University Press, 1999), cogently critiques the position
that moral, cultural, and intellectual phenomena are merely manifestations of
class interest. Because of their one-sided, narrow view of power, Ryn accuses
"realists" such as Gottfried and, by implication, Francis of being "insufficiently
realistic." "Narrowly political conceptions of power stand in the way of adequately
understanding political arrangements," writes Ryn. "Conceptions of that kind dis-
tract attention from what most fundamentally shapes human conduct. They obscure
the moral-intellectual-aesthetical dynamic behind social evolution." Kirk would
wholeheartedly agree. Ryn, "Dimensions of Power: The Transformation of Liberalism and the Limits of 'Politics,'" 4, 12.

politics and the managerial state, the late James Burnham, as a paradigm of clear-sighted counterrevolutionary thinking—in contrast to Kirk's mere aesthetic stances.

Lastly, because of their emphasis on the importance of practical political struggles and public policy issues, as noted above, conservatives are in danger of losing touch with their cultural and traditional intellectual roots. One reason why former Republican Speaker of the House Newt Gingrich, the Reaganites, and other movement conservatives were not particularly interested in Kirk is that they perceived him as not relevant to their policy goals. Kirk did not praise the free market uncritically. He supported tariffs to protect the small farmer against a capricious global market. He deplored the ruinous destruction of the environment wrought by corporate greed and commercial excess. Although historian Lee Edwards asserts that the Heritage Foundation "rests securely on the ideas of Kirk, Hayek and Weaver," one may be hard-pressed to name ideas of Kirk's to which their policy analysts consistently appeal.[25] Because conservative policy analysts typically ignore the teachings of Kirk and other defenders of civilization, Bruce Frohnen, author of several books on conservative political thought, asks pointedly whether the present generation of conservatives has "lost its mind."[26] By this, Frohnen means that conservatives have lost the power to expound and defend through reasoned discourse a coherent and morally compelling worldview.

Kirk's achievement cannot be measured by his influence on transient policy issues. Rather, he will—or should—be remembered because he championed those enduring norms of social interaction without which civilized existence is rendered impossible. Without the guidance of these "permanent things," order in the soul and commonwealth quickly evaporates. He reminds us that if conservatism is to survive in the twenty-first century as more than just a label, then conservatives must clearly rethink what it is they are trying to conserve. They cannot forget, without losing their reason for being, that sound political reform depends upon a healthy cultural environment.

25. Quoted in Person, Jr., *Russell Kirk: A Critical Biography of a Conservative Mind,* 217.
26. Bruce Frohnen, "Has Conservatism Lost Its Mind?: The Half-Remembered Legacy of Russell Kirk," 62. *Policy Review* is a quarterly journal published by the Heritage Foundation.

"Let no man consider himself happy until the hour of his death," said the ancient Athenian lawgiver Solon. If this be the measure of a happy life, Kirk by his own calculations considered his own life to have been happy. In his posthumously published memoirs, *The Sword of Imagination,* he wrote that he accomplished most of what he intended in his life. He had set for himself three goals: first, he "sought to conserve a patrimony of order, justice, and freedom; a tolerable social order and an inheritance of culture"—an aspiration in which "he had succeeded somewhat." Secondly, he had wanted "to lead a life of decent independence" as a man of letters. This goal, he believed, he had achieved as well. Lastly, he had "wanted to marry for love and to rear children," and with his wife, Annette, who bore him four daughters, he had accomplished this end. "Thus his three wishes had been granted; he was grateful. Power over others, and much money, he never had desired; he had been spared these responsibilities."[27]

His last wish was certainly granted. As for his other goals, his success was more problematic. He fought valiantly against the enemies of the "permanent things," that is, the forces of social disorder and cultural destruction, and he persuaded many to follow him. Yet, scant evidence exists that his efforts had much effect during his own lifetime. The destructive forces of egalitarianism and social engineering continue to eat at the vestiges of civilized existence. The world may have to sink further into decadence and disorder before it can begin the ascent back toward the civilized social order envisioned by Kirk. The "Reagan Revolution" of the 1980s and the "Republican Revolution," while slowing the growth of governmental power and expenditures, showed little interest in the cultural regeneration that was the main purpose of Kirk's crusading efforts.

If Kirk were still alive, he would entertain no illusions about conservative prospects for the short term. "Yet cheerfulness will keep breaking through," he always maintained. It was never his nature to succumb to despair, cynicism, or bitterness. When things appear at their worst, there is always reason for hope. While the fabric of social order seems today irreparably frayed, there are those (the "Remnant," as Kirk liked to call them) "doing their best to stitch together once more the fragments of that serviceable old suit we variously call 'Christian civiliza-

27. Kirk, *The Sword of Imagination,* 473–74.

tion' or 'Western civilization' or 'the North Atlantic community' or 'the free world.' Not by force of arms are civilizations held together, but by the subtle threads of moral and intellectual principle."[28]

Kirk, more than most, devoted his life to the long haul. As he frequently reminded his audiences, quoting his friend T. S. Eliot, "The communication of the dead is tongued with fire beyond the language of living."[29] Russell Kirk's books and essays, and his noble example of a life well spent, will outlast the work of his more famous contemporaries.

28. Kirk, "Cultural Debris: A Mordant Last Word," in *The Portable Conservative Reader,* 706.
29. This passage is inscribed on his tombstone in the cemetery of St. Michael's Catholic Church, Remus, Michigan.

BIBLIOGRAPHY

CITED WORKS BY RUSSELL KIRK

Only those works of Russell Kirk which have been either cited in this study or consulted are listed. For a more complete bibliography of his works published prior to 1981 see Charles Brown, *Russell Kirk: A Bibliography* (Mt. Pleasant, Michigan: Clarke Historical Library/Central Michigan University, 1981).

The Kirk Papers, including correspondence and manuscripts, are housed either at the Clarke Historical Library of Central Michigan University, Mt. Pleasant, Michigan, or the Russell Kirk Center for Cultural Renewal in Mecosta, Michigan. Shortly after his death, Kirk's vast personal collection of books was moved to Hillsdale College, Hillsdale, Michigan.

All the citations in this bibliography are listed in each category alphabetically.

Books

Academic Freedom: An Essay in Definition. Chicago: Henry Regnery Company, 1955.

The American Cause. Chicago: Henry Regnery Company, 1966.

Beyond the Dreams of Avarice: Essays of a Social Critic. Chicago: Henry Regnery Company, 1956.

Confessions of a Bohemian Tory: Episodes and Reflections of a Vagrant Career. New York: Fleet Publishing Corporation, 1963.

The Conservative Constitution. Washington, D.C.: Regnery Gateway, 1990.

The Conservative Mind: From Burke to Santayana. 1st ed. Chicago: Henry Regnery, 1953.

The Conservative Mind: From Burke to Eliot. 7th rev. ed. Chicago: Regnery Books Inc., 1986.

Decadence and Renewal in the Higher Learning: An Episodic History of American University and College since 1953. South Bend, Ind.: Gateway Editions, Ltd., 1978.

Edmund Burke: A Genius Reconsidered. New Rochelle, N.Y.: Arlington House, 1967.

Eliot and His Age: T. S. Eliot's Moral Imagination in the Twentieth Century. New York: Random House, 1971.

Enemies of the Permanent Things: Observations of Abnormity in Literature and Politics. New Rochelle, N.Y.: Arlington House, 1969.

The Intelligent Woman's Guide to Conservatism. New York: Devin-Addair Company, 1957.

The Intemperate Professor: And Other Cultural Splenetics. Baton Rouge: Louisiana State University Press, 1956.

John Randolph of Roanoke: A Study of American Politics. Indianapolis: Liberty Press, 1978.

Lord of the Hollow Dark. New York: St. Martin's Press, 1979.

The Politics of Prudence. Bryn Mawr, Pa.: Intercollegiate Studies Institute, 1993.

———, ed. *The Portable Conservative Reader* New York: Penguin Books, 1982.

A Program for Conservatives. Chicago: Henry Regnery Company, 1962.

The Prospects for Conservatives. Washington, D.C.: Regnery Gateway, 1989.

Reclaiming a Patrimony: A Collection of Lectures. Washington, D.C.: Heritage Foundation, 1982.

Redeeming the Time. Edited and with an introduction by Jeffrey O. Nelson. Wilmington, Del.: ISI Books, 1996.

Rights and Duties: Reflections on Our Conservative Constitution. Edited by Mitchell S. Muncy, with an introduction by Russell Hittinger. Dallas: Spence Publishing Company, 1997.

The Roots of American Order. LaSalle, Ill.: Open Court, 1974.

The Surly Sullen Bell. New York: Fleet Publishing Corporation, 1962.

The Sword of Imagination: Memoirs of a Half-Century of Literary Conflict. Grand Rapids, Mich.: William B. Eerdmans Publishing Company, 1995.

The Wise Men Know What Wicked Things Are Written on the Sky. Washington, D.C.: Regnery Gateway, Inc., 1987.

Articles

"The Age of Discussion." *Commonweal* 63 (November 11, 1955): 135–38.

"The American Conservative Character." *Georgia Review* 8 (Fall 1954): 249–60.

"The American Intellectual: A Conservative View." *Pacific Spectator: A Journal of Interpretation* 9 (Autumn 1955): 361–71.

"The American Political Tradition." *National Review,* February 8, 1958, 133–35.

"The Battle of the Boob-Tube." *National Review,* January 4, 1980, 38.

"Behind the Veil of History." *Yale Review* 46 (March 1957): 466–76.

"The Best Form of Government." *Catholic World* 192 (December 1960): 187–201.

"Books for Small Children." Textbook evaluation report prepared by the Textbook Evaluation Committee, Index no. 771. New Rochelle, N.Y.: America's Future, Inc., n.d.

"Burke and the Principle of Order." *Sewanee Review* 60 (Spring 1952): 187–201.

"Burke, Providence, and Archaism." *Sewanee Review* 69 (Winter 1961): 179–84.

"A Conscript on Education." *South Atlantic Quarterly* 44 (January 1945): 82–99.

"Conservatives and the Community." *U.S.A.: An American Bulletin of Fact and Opinion* 3 (October 12, 1956): 383–84.

"Diversity in Schooling." *National Review,* June 3, 1969, 541.

"The End of Learning." *Intercollegiate Review* 24 (Fall 1988): 23–28.

"The Enfeebled American Family." Grove City College, Public Policy Education Fund, Inc., Special Report No. 13 (June 1981).

"Ethical Labor." *Sewanee Review* 62 (Summer 1954): 485–503.

"Free Choice: A Voucher Plan." *National Review,* June 17, 1969, 598.

"History and the Moral Imagination." *Sewanee Review* 77 (April–June 1969): 349–56.

"Humane Letters and the Clutch of Ideology." *Political Science Reviewer* 3 (Fall 1973): 163–82.

"An Ideologue of Liberty." *Sewanee Review* 77 (Spring 1964): 349–50.

"Ideology and Political Economy." *America* 96 (January 5, 1957): 388–91.

"Imagination against Ideology." *National Review,* December 31, 1970, 1576–83.

"Is Capitalism Still Viable?" *Hillsdale Review* 3 (Winter 1981): 3–8.

"John Locke Reconsidered." *Month* 200 (November 1955): 294–303.

"The Little Platoon We Belong to in Society." *Imprimis* 6 (November 1977): 1–6.

"Momentoes." *Scholastic: The American High School Weekly* 28 (April 25, 1936): 5, 12.

"Mood of Conservatism." *Commonweal* 78 (June 7, 1963): 297–300.

"Obdurate Adversaries of Modernity." *Modern Age* 31 (Summer–Fall 1987): 203–6.

"The Poet as Conservative." *Critic* (February–March 1960): 19–20, 84–86.

"Popular Government and Intemperate Minds." *World and I* 11 (November 1988): 595–604.

"Prescription, Authority, and Ordered Freedom." In *What Is Conservatism?* edited by Frank S. Meyer (New York: Holt, Rinehart and Winston, 1964), 23–40.

"Returning Humanity to History: The Example of John Lukacs." *Intercollegiate Review* 16 (Fall/Winter 1980): 23–31.

"Small Books for Small Children." In *Textbook Evaluation Report,* prepared by the Textbook Evaluation Committee, Index no. 771. New Rochelle, N.Y.: America's Future, Inc., n.d.

"The Unbought Grace of Life." *Northern Review* 7 (October–November 1954): 9–22.

"What Are American Traditions?" *Georgia Review* 9 (Fall 1955): 283–89.

"York and Social Boredom." *Sewanee Review* 71 (Autumn 1953): 664–81.

Writings in Anthologies and Introductions to Books

"The Conservative Cast of American Society." In *Conservatism: Waxing or Waning,* edited by Dwynal B. Pettengill (Williamsburg, Va.: College of William and Mary, 1965), 27–39.

"The Enduring Influence of Irving Babbitt." In *Irving Babbitt in Our Time,* edited by George A. Panicheas and Claes G. Ryn (Washington, D.C.: Catholic University of America Press, 1986), 17–26.

"Influence of Religion in Contemporary Society." In *Great Issues: 1982* (Troy, Ala.: Troy University Press, 1982), 3–14.

Introduction to *An Enquiry Concerning Human Understanding,* by David Hume. Chicago: Henry Regnery Company/Gateway Editions, Incorporated, 1956.

Introduction to *On Liberty,* by John Stuart Mill. Chicago: Gateway Edition/Henry Regnery Company, 1955.

Preface to *An Essay Concerning Human Understanding,* by John Locke. Chicago: Gateway Editions/Henry Regnery Company, 1956.

"Traditions of Thought and the Core Curriculum." In *Content, Character and Choice in Schooling: Public Policy and Research Implications, Proceedings of a Symposium Sponsored by the National Council on Educational Research* (Washington, D.C.: n.p., April 24, 1986), 13–27.

"Vivas, Lawrence, Eliot and the Demon." In *Viva Vivas!* edited by Henry Regnery (Indianapolis: Liberty Press, 1976), 227–49.

Sᴇᴄᴏɴᴅᴀʀʏ Sᴏᴜʀᴄᴇs

Books

Adams, Brooks. *The Law of Civilization and Decay: An Essay on History.* New York: Alfred A. Knopf, 1963.

———, and Henry Adams. *The Degradation of the Democratic Dogma.* New York: Capricorn Books, 1958.

Adams, John. *The Works of John Adams.* Edited by Charles Francis Adams. Vol. 6. Boston: Charles C. Little and James Brown, 1851.

Allitt, Patrick. *Catholic Converts: British and American Intellectuals Turn to Rome.* Rev. ed. Ithaca, N.Y.: Cornell University Press, 1997.

———. *Catholic Intellectuals and Conservative Politics in America.* Ithaca, N.Y.: Cornell University Press, 1993.

Ames, Fisher. *Works.* Boston: T. B. Wait and Company, 1809.

Aquinas, St. Thomas. *Treatise on Law.* Chicago: Henry Regnery Company/Gateway Edition, n.d.

Auden, W. H. Introduction to *Tales of Grimm and Anderson.* New York: Modern Library, 1952.

Auerbach, M. Morton. *The Conservative Illusion.* New York: Columbia University Press, 1959.

Babbitt, Irving. *Democracy and Leadership.* Boston: Houghton Mifflin Company, 1925.

———. *The Dhammapada.* New York: New Directions Brooks, 1936.

————. *Literature and the American College.* Chicago: Henry Regnery, 1955.

————. *The New Laokoon: An Essay on the Confusion of the Arts.* Boston: Houghton Mifflin Company, 1940.

————. *On Being Creative and Other Essays.* New York: Biblo and Tannen, 1968.

————. *Rousseau and Romanticism.* Cleveland: World Publishing Company, 1966.

Baker, Sir Ernest. Introduction to *The Politics of Aristotle.* London: Oxford University Press, 1974.

————. *The Political Thought of Plato and Aristotle.* New York: Dover Publications, 1959.

Bantock, G. H. *T. S. Eliot and Education.* New York: Random House, 1969.

————. *Freedom and Authority in Education.* London: Faber and Faber, 1970.

Barth, Hans. *The Idea of Order: Contributions to a Philosophy of Politics.* Dordrect, Holland: D. Reidel, 1960.

Bernanos, Georges. *The Diary of a Country Priest.* New York: Macmillan Company, 1966.

Berthoff, Rowland. *An Unsettled People: Social Order and Disorder in American History.* New York: Harper and Row, 1971.

Biggs-Davison, John. *Tory Lives: From Falkland to Disraeli.* London: Putnam and Company, Ltd., 1952.

Birch, Nigel. *The Conservative Party.* London: Collins, 1949.

Birrell, Augustine. *Obiter Dicta.* 5th ed. London: Elliot Stock, 1894.

Bloom, Allan. *The Closing of the American Mind.* New York: Simon and Shuster, 1987.

Boswell, James. *The Life of Samuel Johnson.* New York: Harper Torchbooks, 1966.

Boyer, Ernest L. *College: The Undergraduate Experience in America.* New York: Harper and Row, 1987.

Bradford, M. E. *A Better Guide than Reason: Studies in the American Revolution.* La Salle, Ill.: Sherwood Sugden and Company, 1979.

Brevold, Louis. *The Brave New World of the Enlightenment.* Ann Arbor: University of Michigan Press, 1961.

Brightfield, Myron F. *John Wilson Croker.* London: George Allen and Unwin Ltd., 1940.

Brinton, Crane. *The Political Ideas of the English Romanticists.* New York: Russell, 1926.

Brown, Charles. *Russell Kirk: A Bibliography.* Mt. Pleasant, Mich.: Clarke Historical Library/Central Michigan University, 1981.

Brownson, Orestes A. *The American Republic: Its Constitution, Tendencies and Destiny.* Clifton, N.J.: Augustus M. Kelley, 1972.

Buckley, William F., ed. *American Conservative Thought in the Twentieth Century.* Indianapolis: Bobbs-Merrill Company, Inc., 1970.

Burke, Edmund. *The Correspondence of Edmund Burke.* Edited by Lucy S. Sutherland and Thomas W. Copeland, the latter as general editor. 9 vols. Chicago: University of Chicago Press, 1958–1970.

―――. *Reflections on the Revolution in France.* New York: E. P. Dutton and Company, Inc., 1960.

―――. *The Speeches of the Right Honourable Edmund Burke.* 4 vols. London: Ridgway, 1816.

―――. *The Works of the Right Honourable Edmund Burke.* 16 vols. London: C and J. Rivington, 1826.

Cheney, Lynne V. *American Memory: A Report on the Humanities in the Nation's Public Schools.* Washington, D.C.: National Endowment for the Humanities, 1987.

Chesteron, G. K. *Orthodoxy.* Garden City, N.J.: Image Books/Division of Doubleday and Company, Inc., 1959.

Chodorov, Frank. *The Rise and Fall of Society.* New York: Devin Adair Company, 1959.

Cicero, Marcus Tullius. *Offices, Essays, and Letters.* New York: E. P. Dutton and Company, Inc., 1937.

―――. *On the Commonwealth.* Translated by George H. Sabine and Stanley B. Smith. New York: Bobbs-Merrill Company, Inc., 1929.

Coleridge, Samuel Taylor. *The Table Talk and Omnians.* Edited by T. Ashe. London: George Bell and Sons, York Street, Covent Garden, 1884.

D'Entrèves, A. P. *Natural Law: An Historical Survey.* New York: Harper and Row Publishers/Harper Torchbooks, 1965.

Dewey, John. *Democracy and Education: An Introduction to the Philosophy of Education.* New York: MacMillan Company, 1929.

Dreyer, Frederick A. *Burke's Politics: A Study in Whig Orthodoxy.* Waterloo, Ontario: Wifrid Laurier University Press, 1979.

Dunbar, William Frederick. *Michigan: A History of the Wolverine State.* Grand Rapids, Mich.: William B. Eerdmans Publishing Co., 1965.

Eidelberg, Paul. *The Philosophy of the American Constitution.* New York: Free Press, 1968.

Eliot, T. S. *Christianity and Culture: The Idea of a Christian Society and Notes towards the Definition of Culture.* New York: Harcourt, Brace and World, Inc., 1949.

———. *On Poetry and Poets.* New York: Noonday Press, 1969.

Elyot, Sir Thomas. *The Bok Named the Governor.* New York: Dutton/ Everyman's Liberty, 1962.

Evans, M. Stanton. *Revolt on the Campus.* Chicago: Henry Regnery Company, 1961.

Francis, Samuel. *Beautiful Losers: Essays on the Failure of American Conservatism.* Columbia: University of Missouri Press, 1993.

Fryer, Russell G. *Recent Conservative Political Thought: American Perspectives.* Washington, D.C.: University Press of America, 1979.

Gottfried, Paul. *After Liberalism: Mass Democracy in the Managerial State.* Princeton, N.J.: Princeton University Press, 1999.

———. *The Conservative Intellectual Movement.* Rev. ed. New York: Twayne Publishers, 1993.

———. *The Search for Historical Meaning.* DeKalb: Northern Illinois University Press, 1986.

———, and Thomas Fleming. *The Conservative Movement.* Boston: Twayne Publishers, 1988.

Gough, J. W. *The Social Contract.* London: Oxford University Press, 1963.

Gross, Martin L. *The Conspiracy of Ignorance: The Failure of American Public Schools.* New York: HarperCollins, 1999.

Guttman, Allen. *The Conservative Tradition in America.* New York: Oxford University Press, 1967.

Halévy, Élie. *The Growth of Philosophic Radicalism.* London: Faber and Faber, 1928.

Harbour, William. *The Foundations of Conservative Thought: An Anglo-American Tradition in Perspective.* South Bend, Ind.: University of Notre Dame Press, 1982.

Harrison, Gordon. *Road to the Right: The Tradition and Hope of American Conservatism.* New York: William Morrow and Company, 1954.

Hartz, Louis. *The Liberal Tradition in America.* New York: Harcourt, Brace and World, Inc./A Harvest Book, 1955.

Hayek, Friedrich A. von. *The Constitution of Liberty.* South Bend, Ind.: Gateway Editions, Ltd., 1960.

———. *Individualism and Economic Order.* Chicago: Henry Regnery Company/A Gateway Edition, 1972.

———. *The Road to Serfdom.* Chicago: University of Chicago Press, 1962.

———, ed. *Capitalism and the Historians.* Chicago: University of Chicago Press, 1965.

Hearnshaw, F. J. C. *Conservatism in England.* London, 1933; reprt., New York: Howard Fertig, 1968.

Hirsch, E. D., Jr. *Cultural Literacy.* Boston: Houghton Mifflin Company, 1987.

Hogg, Quintin. *The Case for Conservatism.* London: Penguin Books, 1947.

Inge, William Ralph. *The End of An Age: And Other Essays.* New York: Macmillan Company, 1949.

Kendall, Willmore. *Willmore Kendall: Contra Mundum.* Edited by Nellie B. Kendall. New Rochelle, N.Y.: Arlington House, 1971.

Kristol, Irving. *Two Cheers for Capitalism.* New York: Basic Books Inc., 1979.

Kuehnelt-Leddihn, Erik von. *Leftism: From de Sade and Marx to Hitler and Marcuse.* New Rochelle, N.Y.: Arlington House Publishers, 1974.

Lamprecht, Sterling Power. *The Moral and Political Philosophy of John Locke.* New York: Russell and Russell, 1962.

Leander, Folke. *Humanism and Naturalism.* Göteberg, Sweden: Elanders Boktrycker, Akteibolag, 1937.

———. *The Inner Check.* London: Edward Wright, 1974.

———. *Irving Babbitt and Benedetto Croce: The Philosophical Basis of the New Humanism in American Criticism.* Göteberg, Sweden: Elanders Boktrycker, Akteibolag, 1954.

Lewis, C. S. *The Abolition of Man.* New York: Macmillan Company, 1947.

———. *An Experiment in Criticism.* London: Cambridge University Press, 1961.

Le Bon, Gustave. *The Crowd: A Study of the Popular Mind.* New York: Viking Press, 1972.

Lichtheim, George. *The Concept of Ideology and Other Essays.* New York: Random House, 1967.

Lippincott, Benjamin. *Victorian Critics of Democracy.* New York: Octagon Books, 1974.

Lippmann, Walter. *Essays in the Public Philosophy.* New York: Mentor Books, 1956.

Lora, Ronald. *Conservative Minds in America.* Rand McNally Series on the History of American Thought and Culture. Chicago: Rand McNally and Company, 1971.

Lukacs, John. *Historical Consciousness, or the Remembered Past.* New York: Harper and Row Publishers, 1968.

Macridis, Roy C. *Contemporary Political Ideologies: Movements and Regimes.* Cambridge, Mass.: Winthrop Publishers, Inc., 1980.

Magnus, Sir Philip. *Edmund Burke: A Life.* London: John Murray, 1939.

Maine, Sir Henry. *Popular Government.* Indianapolis: Liberty Classics, 1976.

Mallock, W. H. *A Critical Examination of Socialism.* London: John Murray, 1908.

————. *Social Equality.* New York: G. P. Putnam's Sons, 1882.

Manchester, Frederick, and Odell Shepard, eds. *Irving Babbitt: Man and Teacher.* New York: G. P. Putnam's Sons, 1941.

Manning, D. J. *Liberalism.* London: J. M. Dent and Sons, Ltd., 1976.

Mecosta Area History Book: 1879–1979. Mecosta, Mich.: Morton Township Library, 1979.

Meyer, Frank S. *In Defense of Freedom: A Conservative Credo.* Chicago: Henry Regnery, 1962.

————, ed. *What Is Conservatism?* New York: Holt, Rinehart and Winston, 1964.

Mill, John Stuart. *On Liberty.* With an Introduction by Russell Kirk. Chicago: Henry Regnery Company/A Gateway Edition, 1955.

————. *Utilitarianism, Liberty, and Representative Government.* New York: E. P. Dutton and Company, Inc., 1951.

Minogue, Kenneth R. *The Liberal Mind.* New York: Vintage Books, 1968.

Mises, Ludwig von. *Human Action: A Treatise on Economics.* 3rd ed. Chicago: Henry Regnery Company, 1966.

More, Paul Elmer. *On Being Human.* Princeton, N.J.: Princeton University Press, 1936.

———. *Platonism.* Princeton, N.J.: Princeton University Press, 1928; reprt., New York: AMS Press, 1969.

———. *Shelburne.* 11 vols. Boston, 1904–1921; reprt., New York: Phaeton Press, 1967.

Nash, George H. *The Conservative Intellectual Movement in America: Since 1945.* Wilmington, Del.: Intercollegiate Studies Institute, 1996.

Newman, William J. *The Futilitarian Society.* New York: G. Braziller, 1961.

Nisbet, Robert A. *Conservatism: Dream and Reality.* Minneapolis: University of Minnesota Press, 1986.

———. *The Quest for Community.* New York: Oxford University Press, 1969.

———. *Twilight of Authority.* New York: Oxford University Press, 1975.

Novak, Michael. *The Spirit of Democratic Capitalism.* New York: A Touchstone Book, 1982.

Paraboschi, Germana. *Leo Strauss e la Destra Americana.* Rome: Editori Riuniti, 1993.

Parkin, Charles. *The Moral Basis of Burke's Political Thought.* New York: Russell and Russell, 1968.

Phillips, Norman P. *The Quest for Excellence: The Neo-Conservative Critique of Educational Mediocrity.* New York: Philosophical Library, 1978.

Oakeshott, Michael. *Rationalism in Politics.* New York: Basic Books Publishing Company, Inc., 1962.

Orton, William A. *The Liberal Tradition.* New Haven, Conn.: Yale University Press, 1945.

O'Sullivan, Noel. *Conservatism.* New York: St. Martin's Press, 1976.

Panichas, George, and Claes G. Ryn, eds. *Irving Babbitt in Our Time.* Washington, D.C.: Catholic University of America Press, 1986.

Parrington, Vernon Louis. *Main Currents in American Thought.* 3 vols. New York: Harcourt, Brace and World, 1927.

Person, James E., Jr. *Russell Kirk: A Critical Biography of a Conservative Mind.* Lanham, Md.: Madison Books, 1999.

Patterson, Edwin W. *Jurisprudence: Men and Ideas of the Law.* Brooklyn: Foundation Press, Inc., 1953.

Plato. *The Republic of Plato.* Translated with notes and interpretive essay by Allan Bloom. New York: Basic Books, Inc., 1968.

Powers, Richard H. *The Dilemma of Education in a Democracy.* Chicago: Regnery Gateway, 1984.

The Purposes of Education in American Democracy. Washington, D.C.: Educational Policies Commission, 1938.

Regnery, Henry. *Memoirs of a Dissident Publisher.* New York: Harcourt, Brace, Jovanovich, 1979.

Richardson, Elliot. *The Creative Balance: Government, Politics, and the Individual in America's Third Century.* New York: Holt, Rinehart and Winston, 1972.

Ravitch, Diane, and Chester E. Finn, Jr. *What Do Our 17-Year Olds Know?* New York: Harper and Row, 1987.

Röpke, Wilhelm. *Civitas Humanas: A Humane Order of Society.* London: Hodge and Company, Ltd., 1948.

———. *A Humane Economy.* Indianapolis: Liberty Fund, 1971.

Rossiter, Clinton. *Conservatism in America: The Thankless Persuasion.* New York: Vintage Books, 1962.

Rousseau, Jean-Jacques. *Emile, or On Education.* Introduction, translation, and notes by Allan Bloom. New York: Basic Books, Incorporated, 1979.

———. *The Social Contract.* Translated and with introduction by Willmoore Kendall. Chicago: Henry Regnery Company/A Gateway Edition, 1954.

Ryn, Claes G. *Democracy and the Ethical Life: A Philosophy of Politics and Community.* Baton Rouge: Louisiana State University Press, 1978.

———. *Will, Imagination and Reason: Irving Babbitt and the Problem of Reality.* Chicago: Regnery, 1986.

Santayana, George. *Dominations and Power: Reflections on Liberty, Society and Government.* New York: Charles Scribner's Sons, 1951.

Santer, Richard A. *Michigan: Heart of the Great Lakes.* Dubuque, Iowa: Kendall/Hunt Publishing Co., 1977.

Schumpeter, Joseph A. *Capitalism, Socialism and Democracy.* New York: Harper Torchbooks, 1950.

Smant, Kevin J. *Principles and Heresies: Frank S. Meyer and the Shaping of the American Conservative Movement.* Wilmington, Del.: ISI Books, 2002.

Southey, Robert. *Colloquies on Society.* London: Cassell and Company, Ltd., 1887.

Squadrito, Kathleen N. *John Locke.* Boston: Twayne Publishers, 1979.

Stanlis, Peter J. *Edmund Burke and the Natural Law.* Ann Arbor: University of Michigan Press/Ann Arbor Papers, 1965.

Stephen, James Fitzjames. *Liberty, Equality, Fraternity.* London: Smith, Elder, and Company, 1873.

Stephen, Leslie. *The English Utilitarians.* 3 vols. London: Duckworth and Company, 1900.

Stone, Brad Lowell. *Robert Nisbet: Communitarian Traditionist.* Wilmington, Del.: Intercollegiate Studies Books, 2000.

Strauss, Leo. *Natural Right and History.* Chicago: University of Chicago Press, 1953.

Trilling, Lionel. *The Liberal Imagination: Essays on Literature and Society.* London: Secker and Warburg, 1951.

Twelve Southerners. *I'll Take My Stand.* New York: Peter Smith, 1951.

Viereck, Peter. *Conservatism: From John Adams to Churchill.* Princeton, N.J.: D. Van Nostrand Company, 1950.

———. *Conservatism Revisited: The Revolt against Revolt.* New York: Collier Books, 1962.

———. *Dream and Responsibility.* Washington, D.C.: University Press of Washington, D.C., 1953.

———. *Shame and Glory of the Intellectuals: Babbit Junior versus the Rediscovery of Values.* Boston: Beacon Press, 1953.

Vivas, Eliseo. *Creation and Discovery: Essays in Criticism and Aesthetics.* New York: Noonday Press, 1955.

———. *The Moral Life and the Ethical Life.* Chicago: Henry Regnery Company/A Gateway Edition, 1963.

Voegelin, Eric. *Science, Politics and Gnosticism.* Chicago: Henry Regnery Company, 1968.

Weaver, Richard M. *Ideas Have Consequences.* Chicago: University of Chicago Press/Phoenix Books, 1948.

———. *The Ethics of Rhetoric.* Chicago: Henry Regnery Company, 1965.

Weil, Simone. *The Need for Roots: Prelude to a Declaration of Duties toward Mankind.* Translated by A. F. Wills, with a preface by T. S. Eliot. New York: Routledge, 1997.

Wills, Garry. *Confessions of a Conservative.* New York: Penguin Books, 1979.

Zoll, Donald Atwell. *The American Political Condition.* Tempe, Ariz.: Beau Maris Books, 1973.

Articles and Essays

Aaron, Daniel. "Conservatism Old and New." *American Quarterly* 6 (Summer 1954): 99–110.

Auerbach, M. Morton. "Do-It-Yourself Conservatism." *National Review* 12 (January 30, 1962): 57–58.

Auxier, Randall. "Straussianism Descendant? The Historicist Renewal." *Humanitas* 9 (1996): 64–72.

Baldacchino, Joseph F., Jr. "The Value-Centered Historicism of Edmund Burke." *Modern Age* 27 (Spring 1983): 139–45.

Bliese, John R. E. "Richard M. Weaver, Russell Kirk, and the Environment." *Modern Age* 38 (Winter 1996): 148–58.

Brown, Stuart Gerry. "Democracy, the New Conservatism, and the Liberal Tradition in America." *Ethics* 66 (October 1955): 1–9.

Bush, George. "This President Not to Be Deterred." *New Guard* 21 (Spring 1981): 5–6.

Chalmers, Gordon. Review of *The Conservative Mind,* by Russell Kirk. *New York Times Book Review,* May 16, 1953, 7.

Coker, Francis W. "Some Present-Day Critics of Liberalism." *American Political Science Review* 47 (March 1953): 1–27.

Crick, Bernard. "The Strange Quest for an American Conservatism." *Review of Politics* 17 (July 1953): 361–63.

Edwards, Bruce L., Jr. "C. S. Lewis and the Deconstructionalists." *This World* 10 (Winter 1985): 88–98.

Efron, Edith. "Conservatism: A Libertarian Challenge." *The Alternative: An American Spectator* (October 1975): 9–13.

Eliot, T. S. "Tradition and Orthodoxy." *American Review* 2 (March 1934): 513–28.

English, Raymond. "Conservatism: The Forbidden Faith." *American Scholar* 21 (October 1952): 399–401.

Eulau, Heinz. "Liberalism versus Conservatism." *Antioch Review* 9 (December 1951): 397–404.

Feiling, Keith. "Principles of Conservatism." *Political Quarterly* 24 (April–June 1953): 129–38.

Fleming, Thomas. "The Roots of American Culture: Reforming the Curriculum." In *Content, Character and Choice in Schooling, Proceedings of a Symposium Sponsored by the National Council on Educational Research* (Washington, D.C., April 24, 1986).

————. "Thunder on the Right." *Chronicles of Culture* 9 (June 1985): 40–43.

Freund, Ludwig. "The New American Conservatism and European Conservatism." *Ethics* 66 (October 1955): 10–17.

Frohnen, Bruce. "Has Conservatism Lost Its Mind?: The Half-Remembered Legacy of Russell Kirk." *Policy Review* 64 (Winter 1994): 62–66.

Frisch, Morton J. "Burke vs. the New Conservatives." *New Republic,* April 23, 1956, 17.

Gay, Peter. Review of *The Conservative Mind,* by Russell Kirk. *Political Science Quarterly* (December 1953): 586–88.

Gottfried, Paul. "Panajotis Kondylis and the Obsoleteness of Conservatism." *Modern Age* (Fall 1997): 403–10.

Guroian, Vigen. "Awakening the Moral Imagination: Teaching Virtues through Fairy Tales." *Intercollegiate Review* 32, no. 1 (Fall 1996): 3–13.

————. "Natural Law and Historicity: Burke and Niebuhr." *Modern Age* 25 (Spring 1981): 164.

Haiman, Franklyn S. "A New Look of the New Conservatism." *Bulletin of American Association of University Professors* 41 (Autumn 1955): 444–53.

Hall, Chadwick. "America's Conservative Revolution." *Antioch Review* 15 (June 1955): 204–16.

Harris, Michael R. "Irving Babbit: Civilized Standards and Humanistic Education." In *Five Counterrevolutionists in Higher Education* (Corvallis: Oregon State University Press, 1970), 49–79.

Herron, Don. "The Crepuscular Romantic: An Appreciation of the Fiction of Russell Kirk." *Romanticist* (1979): 1–12.

Hechinger, Fred M. "About Education." *New York Times,* December 7, 1988.

Heckscher, August. "Where Are the American Conservatives?" *Confluence* 2 (September 1953): 54–59.

Hofstadter, Richard. "The Pseudo Conservative Revolt." *American Scholar* 24 (Winter 1954–1955): 9.

Hughes, Thomas. "Conservatives and Social Welfare." *South Atlantic Quarterly* 70 (Autumn 1971): 560–74.

Huntington, Samuel P. "Conservatism as an Ideology." *American Political Science Review* 51 (June 1957): 454–73.

Kopff, E. Christian. "Russell Kirk—A Bohemian Tory." *Southern Partisan* (Spring/Summer 1981): 11–13.

Kristol, Irving. "The New Republican Party." *Wall Street Journal,* July 17, 1980.

Kronick, Bernard L. "Conservatism: A Definition." *Southwestern Social Science Quarterly* 28 (December 1953): 731–32.

Lewis, Gordon K. "The Metaphysics of Conservatism." *Western Political Quarterly* 22 (Summer 1958): 231–39.

MacPherson, C. B. "Edmund Burke and the New Conservatism." *Science and Society* 22 (Summer 1958): 231–39.

MacDonald, H. Malcolm. "The Revival of Conservative Thought." *Journal of Politics* 19 (February 1957): 66–80.

McClosky, Herbert. "Conservatism and Personality." *American Political Science Review* 52 (1958): 27–45.

McDonald, W. Wesley. "Reason, Natural Law, and Moral Imagination in the Thought of Russell Kirk." *Modern Age* 27 (Winter 1983): 15–24.

———. "Russell Kirk of Piety Hill." *The Alternative* (February 1971): 9–11.

Novak, Michael. "Father of Conservatives." *National Review* (May 11, 1992).

O'Brien, Christopher. "Liberal Studies through International College." *Journal of General Education* 32 (Summer 1980): 159–66.

Pontuso, James F. "Russell Kirk: The Conservatism of Tradition." In *American Conservative Opinion,* edited by Mark J. Rozell and James F. Pontuso (Boulder, Colo.: Westview Press, 1990).

Reagan, Ronald. "Advice and Dissent." *New Guard* 21 (Spring 1981): 2–4.

Regnery, Henry. "Russell Kirk and the Making of the Conservative Mind." *Modern Age* 21 (Fall 1977): 338–53.

Richert, Christine. "Russell Kirk Surveys Catholic Church." *Twin Circle* (January 31, 1975): 3ff.

Ross, Ralph Gilbert. "Campaign against Liberalism, Continued." *Partisan Review* 20 (September–October 1953): 568–75.

Russello, Gerald J. "The Jurisprudence of Russell Kirk." *Modern Age* 38 (Fall 1996): 354–63.

Ryn, Claes G. "Dimensions of Power: The Transformation of Liberalism and the Limits of 'Politics.'" *Humanitas* 13 (2000): 4–27.

———. "History and the Moral Order." In Francis Canavan, ed., *The Ethical Dimension of Political Life* (Durham, N.C.: Duke University Press, 1983), 92–106, 258–60.

———. "How Conservatives Have Failed 'The Culture.'" *Modern Age* 38 (Winter 1996): 117–27.

———. "The Humanism of Irving Babbitt Revisited." *Modern Age* 21 (Summer 1977): 251–62.

———. "Peter Viereck: Unadjusted Man of Ideas." *Political Science Reviewer* 7 (Fall 1977): 325–66.

———. "The Things of Caesar: Notes toward the Delimitation of Politics." *Thought* 55 (December 1980): 439–60.

Schlesinger, Arthur M. "The New Conservatism in America: A Liberal Comment." *Confluence: An International Forum* 2 (December 1953): 61–71.

Smith, Page. "Russell Kirk and the New Conservatism." *New Mexico Quarterly* 25 (Spring 1955): 93–105.

Strout, Cushing. "Liberalism, Conservatism and the Babel of Tongues." *Partisan Review* 25 (Winter 1958): 101–9.

Szamuely, Tibor. "Intellectuals and Conservatism." *National Review* (March 25, 1969): 273–77.

Vivas, Eliseo. "Animadversions upon the Doctrine of Natural Law." *Modern Age* 10 (Spring 1966): 150–66.

Ways, Max. Review of *The Conservative Mind,* by Russell Kirk. *Time,* July 1953, 88, 90–92.

Wheeler, Harvey. "Russell Kirk and the New Conservatism." *Shenandoah* 7 (1956): 20–34.

Wolfe, Alan. "The Revolution That Never Was." *New Republic,* June 7, 1999, 34–42.

Zoll, Donald Atwell. "Philosophical Foundations of the American Political Right." *Modern Age* 15 (Fall 1972): 114–29.

———. "The Social Thought of Russell Kirk." *Political Science Review* 2 (Fall 1972): 112–36.

Unpublished Materials

McDonald, W. Wesley. "The Political Thought of Russell Kirk: A Study in Contemporary Conservatism." Master's thesis, Bowling Green State University, 1969.

Pate, Ridgely Hill. "Russell Kirk, Friedrich Hayek and Peter Viereck: Three Positions in Contemporary Conservative Thought." Ph.D. diss., University of Texas at Austin, 1970.

Pournelle, Jerry Eugene. "The American Political Continuum: An Examination of the Validity of the Left-Right Model as an Instrument for Studying Contemporary Political 'Isms.'" Ph.D. diss., University of Washington, 1964.

Index

Hearnshaw, F. J. C., 38
Heidegger, Martin, 184
Hobbes, Thomas, 70, 104, 216
Hooker, Richard, 70, 73
Hubbel, Jay, 19
Hughes, H. Stuart, 35
Hume, David, 40, 94

Ideas Have Consequences (Weaver), 29–30
Ideologies, ideology, 34–38, 81–85, 89, 118, 129–32, 203–4
Illative Sense, xi, 58
Imagination, politics of, 204. *See also* Moral imagination
Individualism: false, 152–63; true, 163–67. *See also* Atomistic individualism
Industrialization, 146–48. *See also* Technology
Inge, Dean, 147
Inner check, control, 43, 45–47, 54, 64–65, 69, 119, 125, 126
Intelligent Woman's Guide to Conservatism, The (Kirk), 1, 170–71
Intemperate Professor, and Other Cultural Splenetics, The (Kirk), 170

Jefferson, Thomas, 196, 211
Joad, C. E. M., 179
Johnson, Amos, 15
Johnson, Samuel, 16, 88, 190
Judis, John B., Jr., 209
Justice, 119–25, 142, 146

Kemp, Jack, 206, 210
Kendall, Willmore, 65
King, Martin Luther, Jr., 210
Kirk, Annette, xi, xii, 214
Kirk, Marjorie Rachael, 16
Kirk, Russell: and America's traditions, 109–14; author's relations with, ix–xiii; and automobiles, his attitude toward, 18–19, 215; and Babbitt, 10–11, 62, 64–65; biography, early years, 14–21; Burke's influence on, 11, 16, 20–21, 31–32,

39, 62–64, 71, 74, 100, 105, 118, 169, 175, 204, 215; and Catholicism, 11, 62, 71–73; and Christianity, 42–43, 110, 218–19; and community, 139–69 passim; and conservatism, 1, 3–4, 9–13, 21–22, 31–54 passim, 89, 112, 201–19; and "conservatism," ix, 206; his critics, 3–7, 89–91, 139–40, 157–59, 198; and education, views on, 170–200 passim; and ethical dualism, 44, 69, 77, 103, 105, 131; and history, his appreciation of, 59; vs. ideology, 34–41, 81–85, 203–4; and justice, 119–25; vs. libertarianism, 8–10, 83, 139–41, 152–63; and moral imagination, 54, 55–85 passim, 186, 188–90, 194, 198–200; and moral order, objective, 36, 56; and natural aristocracy, 122–24; and natural law, 38, 70–80; vs. naturalism, 53, 84–85; and order as compatible with freedom, 125–32; and order, principle of, 116–19; and Providence (divine), 19–20, 59, 100, 169; as a reactionary radical regarding education, 170, 185–97; and reason, 65–70; and society, his understanding of, 104–9; and the South, American, 19–20, 135; and technology, 132–38, 215; vs. Thomistic reason, 75–78, 80; and tradition(s), 86–114 passim; vs. utilitarian assumptions, utilitarianism, 8, 53, 82–83, 111, 149, 177
Kirk, Russell Andrew, 15–16
Knight, Frank, 8
Kristol, Irving, 203, 206, 207
Kuehnelt-Leddihn, Erik von, 166, 197

Laissez-faire, 8, 27–31, 113, 141, 152, 164
Leadership, 173–76
Leander, Folke, 43–46, 57
Lecky, W. E. H., 32
Lewis, C. S., 130, 174, 185, 188, 201